BOLLINGEN SERIES XXII

ESSAYS

ON A

SCIENCE OF MYTHOLOGY

THE MYTH OF THE DIVINE CHILD
AND THE MYSTERIES OF ELEUSIS

BY C. G. JUNG AND C. KERÉNYI

TRANSLATED BY R. F. C. HULL

BOLLINGEN SERIES XXII

PRINCETON UNIVERSITY PRESS

TABLE OF CONTENTS

III

IV

EDITORIAL NOTE

This book was first published in Amsterdam, Leipzig, and Zurich in 1941 under the title *Einführung in das Wesen der Mythologie*. It was the second edition of two monographs, *Das göttliche Kind* and *Das göttliche Mädchen*, which were written in 1939–40 and first published separately in 1940 and 1941. The English translation, which is based on the second edition, was originally published in New York in 1949 and in London in 1950.

When the book was republished in Zurich in 1951, the two authors considered the possibility of revising the text and adding to it. Though this would have been feasible, they decided against any changes that would destroy the book's original form. They had written *essays* and preferred to maintain their character.

Now, some years later, Professor Jung is no longer living, but his part of the book was, during his lifetime, taken into Volume 9, part I, of his Collected Works, *The Archetypes and the Collective Unconscious* (1959; 2nd edn., 1968). In the meantime, Professor Kerényi has written a new work, *Eleusis: Archetypal Image of Mother and Daughter* (1967),* in which he deals with the reconstruction of the Mysteries. The 1967 publication modifies the details of his earlier essay printed here, adducing additional material concerning the experience of the initiates and bringing new evidence to bear. The perspective, however, and the whole mythological dimension which had been opened in the earlier volume are preserved. The book still remains—as its British edition was entitled—an "Introduction to a Science of Mythology."

In this revised edition, the Jung essays are given in the text of the Collected Works. The translation of the Kerényi

* Translated by Ralph Manheim. Archetypal Images in Greek Religion, 4. New York (Bollingen Series LXV:4) and London, 1967.

essays has been slightly revised, bringing it into accord with the 1951 German version. The reference apparatus has been brought up to date and a bibliography and new index have been supplied.

PROLEGOMENA

BY C. KERÉNYI

1

What is music? What is poetry? What is mythology? All questions on which no opinion is possible unless one already has a real feeling for these things. That is natural and obvious enough. Not so, however, our feeling in the case of the last named. Only the greatest creations of mythology proper could hope to make clear to modern man that here he is face to face with a phenomenon which "in profundity, permanence, and universality is comparable only with Nature herself." If we want to promote a real knowledge of mythology, we must not appeal at the outset to theoretical considerations and judgments (not even to Schelling's, from whom the quotation in praise of mythology comes). Neither should we talk overmuch of "sources." The water must be fetched and drunk fresh from the spring if it is to flow through us and quicken our hidden mythological talents.

But—here too there's many a slip between the cup and the lip. True mythology has become so completely alien to us that, before tasting of it, we would do well to pause and consider—not only the uses and dangers of mythology (the psychologist and physician of the mind will have something to say about this later on), but also our possible attitude towards it. We have lost our immediate feeling for the great realities of the spirit—and to this world all true mythology belongs—lost it precisely because of our all-too-willing, helpful, and efficient science. It explained the drink in the cup to us so well that we knew all about it beforehand, far better than the good old drinkers; and we were expected to rest content with our knowing better or even to rate it higher than unspoiled experience and enjoyment. We have to ask ourselves: is an immediate experience and enjoyment of mythology still in any sense possible?

At all events we can no longer dispense with the freedom from falsehood that true science confers upon us. What we demand besides this freedom, or rather demand *back* from science, is just this feeling of immediacy between ourselves and scientific subjects. Science herself must throw open the road to mythology that she blocked first with her interpretations and then with her explanations—science always understood in the broadest sense, in this case the historical and psychological as well as the cultural and anthropological study of myths. So, to define the attitude to mythology possible for us today, we shall begin by recapitulating what was said in some detail in the first chapter of *Die antike Religion*[1] and touched on in the Foreword to the first edition (1940) of *Das göttliche Kind* in this regard. The question as to the origins of mythology in the sense "Where and when did a great myth-creating culture arise that may have influenced all later mythologies with its products?" is not to be discussed here. We shall only concern ourselves with the question: what has mythology to do with origin or origins?—and here too only in order to broaden that immediate approach through which the reader has to find his own way to mythology.

2

The word "myth" is altogether too equivocal, blunted, and hazy for our purpose; it does not give us as much of a start as the expressions that combine the word μῦθος with the word λέγειν, meaning "to put together," "say." Plato, himself a great "teller of myths," teaches us from his own experience something of the vitality and motility of what the Greeks called μυθολογία. This is an art alongside and included within poetry (the two fields overlap), an art with a special assumption as regards its subject-matter. A particular kind of material determines the art of mythology, an immemorial and traditional body of material contained in tales about gods and god-like beings, heroic battles and journeys to the Underworld—"mythologem" is the best Greek word for them—tales already well known but not unamenable to further reshaping. Mythology is the *movement* of this material: it is something solid and yet mobile, substantial and yet not static, capable of transformation.

[1] Kerényi, *Die antike Religion: eine Grundlegung.*

The comparison with music—I shall often have to recur to it in order to bring out this aspect of mythology—lies nearest to hand. Mythology as art and mythology as material are fused in one and the same phenomenon, just as are the art of the composer and *his* material, the world of sound. The musical work or art shows us the artist as a shaper and at the same time the world of sound as shaped. In cases where the mind of the shaper is not in the foreground, as in the great mythologies of the Indians, the Finns, and the Oceanic peoples, we can speak with yet greater right of such a relationship, that is, of an art that reveals itself in the shaping and of a material peculiar to it that shapes itself in accordance with its own laws, together constituting the indivisible unity of one and the same phenomenon.

In mythology the shaping is pictorial. A torrent of mythological pictures streams out. But the streaming is at the same time an unfolding: held fast as the mythologems are in the form of sacred traditions, they are still in the nature of works of art. Various developments of the same ground-theme are possible side by side or in succession, just like the variations on a musical theme. For, although what "streams out" always remains pictorial in itself, the comparison with music is still applicable, certainly with definite *works* of music, i.e., something objective, that has become an object with a voice of its own, that one does justice to not by interpretation and explanation but above all by letting it alone and allowing it to utter its own meaning.

In a true mythologem this meaning is not something that could be expressed just as well and just as fully in a non-mythological way. Mythology is not simply a mode of expression in whose stead another simpler and more readily understandable form might have been chosen, only not just *then,* when it happened to be the only possible and appropriate one. Like music, mythology too can be more appropriate to the times or less. There are times when the greatest "thoughts" could only have been expressed in music. But in that case the "greatest" is precisely what can be expressed in music and in no other way. So with mythology. Just as music has a meaning that is satisfying in the sense that every meaningful whole is satisfying, so every true mythologem has its satisfying meaning. This meaning is so hard to translate into the language of science because it can be fully expressed only in mythological terms.

From this combined pictorial, meaningful, and musical aspect of mythology there follows the right attitude towards it: to let the mythologems speak for themselves and simply to listen. Any explanation has to be along the same lines as the explanation of a musical or poetic work of art. That a special "ear" is needed for it, just as for music or poetry, is obvious. Here as well "ear" means resonance, a sympathetic pouring out of oneself. "He who pours himself out as a spring shall find Recognition" (Rilke). But where is mythology's spring? In us? Only in us? Or outside and only outside? That is what we have to seek. We shall find our way to it more easily if we start from another aspect of mythology—an aspect which we shall now consider in more detail than was the case in my previous works.

3

Mythology, like the severed head of Orpheus, goes on singing even in death and from afar. In its lifetime, among the peoples where it was indigenous, it was not only sung like a kind of music, it was also lived. Material though it was, for those peoples, its carrier, it was a form of expression, thought, and life. Thomas Mann, in his essay on Freud, has spoken with good reason of the "quotation-like life" of the men of mythological times and has illustrated this with images that could not be bettered. Archaic man, he said, stepped back a pace before doing anything, like the toreador poising himself for the death-stroke. He sought an example in the past, and into this he slipped as into a diving-bell in order to plunge, at once protected and distorted, into the problems of the present. In this way his life achieved its own expression and meaning. For him the mythology of his people was not only convincing, that is, possessed of meaning, but explanatory, that is, an assigner of meaning.

This, then, is the other, the aetiological aspect of mythology, taken by and large an extremely paradoxical one. As historians of religion we could remain calm in the face of this paradox, which is that mythology is held to explain itself and everything else in the universe not because it was invented for the purpose of explanation but because it possesses among other things the property of being explanatory. Yet precisely those students who want to "explain" everything will be hard put to it to understand such a mysterious property save on the assumption that the mythologems were in fact *thought up* for the *purpose* of explanation. To point out that poetry and music often illuminate the world for us far more than any scientific explanation does not satisfy them and shall no longer satisfy us. Our aim is finally to come to real grips with the aetiological aspect of mythology, the "how" of it, and not to regard it as anything easy and self-evident.

The appearance of obviousness has already been shaken by the fact that the aetiological character of mythology is in one instance denied outright, moreover by a field-worker who has spent a long time in the presence of a living mythology—Bronislaw Malinowski. All that he learned in the Trobriand Islands about the nature of mythology he published in an exemplary empirical study entitled *Myth in Primitive Psychology*. His experiences confirm what we have just said about a "lived mythology." We repeat them here in his scientifically well-weighed words:

The myth in a primitive society, i.e., in its original living form, is not a mere tale told but a reality lived. It is not in the nature of an invention such as we read in our novels today, but living reality, believed to have occurred in primordial times and to be influencing ever afterwards the world and the destinies of men. . . . These stories are not kept alive by vain curiosity, neither as tales that have been invented nor again as tales that are true. For the natives on the contrary they are the assertion of an original, greater, and more important reality through which the present life, fate, and work of mankind are governed, and the knowledge of which provides men on the one hand with motives for ritual and moral acts, on the other with directions for their performance.

On the basis of his experience Malinowski denies two things: firstly, the symbolical, and secondly, the aetiological character of living myth. His denial of its symbolical character consists in the absolutely correct recognition that, for its carriers, the myth expresses in a primary and direct fashion precisely what it relates—something that happened in primordial times. That

5

this occurrence in its turn expresses something more universal, something of the world's content that finds its voice in mythological form, this possibility Malinowski does not even consider. His findings speak neither for nor against it. Hence he sets his face all the more against the aetiological view. The myth, he says, is not an explanation put forward to satisfy scientific curiosity; it is the re-arising of a primordial reality in narrative form. Myths never, in any sense, explain; they always set up some precedent as an ideal and as a guarantee of the continuance of that ideal. The "aetiological myth" is in his eyes a non-existent class of narrative corresponding to the non-existent "desire to explain."

Malinowski paraphrases in this way what he calls the "social function" of mythology, which is *not* scientific or pseudo-scientific "explanation." Evidently Malinowski lacks the proper word for what this function really is. He finds "explanation" in the sense of an "intellectual effort" inadequate. But in the other sense that mythology makes everything "clear" (*klar*) for its carriers without straining them, "explanation" (*Erklärung*) is applicable. For in this sense clarity streams out of every mythology—clarity as regards what is, what happens, and what is supposed to happen. The meaning of all *that* is contained in the mythologems. But what one *does* by means of mythology when one allows the "telling of myths" to function in the involuntary service of a human community, that is far from being the idle invention of explanations. It is something else. The German language has the right word for it: *begründen.*[2]

Mythology gives a ground, lays a foundation. It does not answer the question "why?" but "whence?" In Greek we can put this difference very nicely. Mythology does not actually indicate "causes," αἴτια. It does this (is "aetiological") only to the extent that, as taught by Aristotle (*Metaphysica*, Λ 2,

[2] [Since Malinowski "evidently lacked the proper word," although writing in English, it is highly unlikely that we shall be able to supply it. And in point of fact there is no single English equivalent that quite conveys the meaning, or various shades of meaning, intended by the author in his use of *begründen.* The root of the German word is *Grund,* which means both concrete "ground" and abstract "reason." It is generally translated by such words as to "found," "ground," "establish," "substantiate." It is hoped that the various periphrases to which we have been driven will not put too great a strain on the author's thought.—TRANS.]

6

1013a) the αἴτια are ἀρχαί, beginnings or first principles. For the earliest Greek philosophers, the ἀρχαί were, for instance, water, fire, or what they called ἄπειρον, the "Boundless." No mere "causes," therefore, but rather primary substances or primary states that never age, can never be surpassed, and produce everything always. It is the same with the happenings in mythology. They form the ground or foundation of the world, since everything rests on them. They are the ἀρχαί to which everything individual and particular goes back and out of which it is made, while they remain ageless, inexhaustible, invincible in timeless primordiality, in a past that proves imperishable because of its eternally repeated rebirths.

4

It is no groundless generalization to say that mythology tells of the origins or at least of what originally was. When it tells of a younger generation of gods, for instance the gods of Greek history, these too signify the beginning of a world—the world the Greeks lived in under the rule of Zeus. The gods are so "original" that a new world is always born with a new god—a new epoch or a new aspect of the world. They are "there," not only in the beginning when they themselves originated, and not only in the periodic repetitions of that first origination, i.e., cosmic reappearances and representations on festal occasions. Though they are present all the time, the mythologems which unfold in narrative form what is contained in the figures of the gods are always set in a *primordial* time. This return to the origins and to primordiality is a basic feature of every mythology.

We have found the exact expression for this: behind the "Why?" stands the "Whence?," behind the αἴτιον the ἀρχή. More strictly still, there is no initial question at all in mythology any more than there is in archaic Greek philosophy, nothing but the direct unquestioning return to the ἀρχαί, a spontaneous regression to the "ground." It is not only the man who experiences a living mythology that draws back a pace like the toreador, or slips as into a diving-bell; the true teller of myths does likewise, the creator or re-creator of mythologems. The philosopher tries to pierce through the world of appearances in order to say what "really is," but the teller of myths steps back into primordiality in order to tell us what "originally was." Primordiality is the same thing for him as authenticity. Without venturing to say whether this results in real authenticity, the true immediacy of subject and object, this procedure gives us some idea of mythological "fundamentalism" (*Begründung*).

Mythology provides a foundation insofar as the teller of myths, by living out his story, finds his way back to primordial times. Suddenly, without any digression or searching on his part, without any studious investigation or effort, he finds himself in the primordiality that is his concern, in the midst of the ἀρχαί of which he is speaking. What are the ἀρχαί in whose midst a man can really find himself? To which of them can he "dive down" straightaway? The ἀρχαί are as numerous as the elements composing man's world, including man himself. He has his own ἀρχαί, the ἀρχαί of his organic being from which he continually creates himself. As a developed organism he experiences his own origin thanks to a kind of identity, as though he were a reverberation of it multiplied a thousandfold and his origin were the first note struck. He experiences it as his own absolute ἀρχή, a beginning since when he was a unity fusing in itself all the contradictions of his nature and life to be. To this origin, understood as the beginning of a new world-unit, the mythologem of the *divine child* points. The mythologem of the *maiden goddess* points to yet another ἀρχή, also experienced as one's own origin but which is at the same time the ἀρχή of countless beings before and after oneself, and by virtue of which the individual is endowed with infinity already *in the germ*.

With the help of images taken from human and vegetable evolution, the two mythologems united in this book point, like signposts, to our mythological "fundamentalism" as a journey to the ἀρχαί, a journey which then results in the re-unfolding of those same images. Figuratively speaking, it is a kind of immersion in ourselves that leads to the living germ of our wholeness. The practice of this immersion is mythological fundamentalism and the result of such practice is that, our eyes having been opened to the images that stream out of the "ground," we find we have returned to the place where the two ἀρχαί—absolute and relative—coincide. The ἀρχή of the germ, or, as a modern writer puts it,[3] the "abyss of the nucleus," opens out there, and there, we must presume, is the mid-point about which and from which our whole being organizes itself. If we consider this purely internal aspect of our life in spatial terms, then the ideal spot where origination and our knowledge of the origins are identical can only be this central breach-point. Going back into ourselves in this way and rendering an account of it, we experience and proclaim the very foundations of our being; that is to say, we are "grounding" ourselves.

This mythological fundamentalism has its paradox, for the man who retires into himself at the same time lays himself open. Or, to put it the other way about, the fact that archaic man is open to all the world drives him back on his own foundations and enables him to discern in his own origins the ἀρχή κατ' ἐξοχήν, *the* origin. The mythologies speak in the image of a divine child, the first-born of primeval times, in whom the "origin" first was; they do not speak of the coming-to-be of some human being but of the coming-to-be of the divine cosmos or a universal God. Birth and sunrise merely endow that universal ἀρχή with physical features and a sort of golden haze. Keeping to the spatial concept of an ideal midpoint in man we can say: at that point where the abyss-like ἀρχή of the germ opens, the world itself breaks in. The world itself speaks in the images of origination that stream out from it. The mythological "fundamentalist" (*Begründer*) who, by immersion in the self, dives down to his own foundations, founds his world. He builds it up for himself on a foundation where everything is an out-flowing, a sprouting and springing up—"original" (*ursprüng-lich*) in the fullest sense of the word,[4] and consequently divine. The divinity of everything mythological is as obvious as the originality of everything divine. All the institutions of mythological times are founded on and illuminated, that is, hallowed, by a mythologem of origination, the common divine origin of life whose forms they are.

3 Stefan Andres.
4 [The etymology happens to be the same in English: "origin" comes from L. *oriri,* "to rise."—TRANS.]

5

To rebuild the world from that point *about* which and *from* which the "fundamentalist" himself is organized, *in* which he by his origin exists (absolutely as regards his unique and specific organization, relatively as regards his dependence on an infinite series of progenitors)—that is the great and paramount theme of mythology, that is foundation κατ' ἐξοχήν. With the construction of a new world in miniature, an image of the macrocosm, mythological fundamentalism is translated into action: it becomes a founding (*Gründung*). Cities built in periods that knew a living mythology, and claiming to be images of the cosmos, are *founded* just as the cosmogonic mythologems *give grounds for* the world. Their foundations are laid as if they grew out of the two ἀρχαί we have mentioned (the absolute ἀρχή where one begins and the relative ἀρχή where one becomes the continuation of one's ancestors). In this way they are based on the same divine ground as the world itself. They become what the world and the city equally were in antiquity—the dwelling-place of the gods.

The contradictions contained in the records as to the foundation ceremonies in ancient Rome are harmoniously resolved as soon as we understand the whole principle of archaic city-founding in this sense, namely that these little worlds of men were to be drawn to the same ideal plan in accordance with which man "knows," mythologically speaking, that his own totality is organized, and which he also sees in the world at large. At the same time we shall recognize some of the spatial concepts that most easily helped to visualize certain purely internal factors, when we now turn to this oft-treated problem of archaeology. Franz Altheim put forward a solution that was subsequently taken up by his pupils.[5] My own exposition which now follows refers exclusively to the apparent contradiction in the ceremony of city-founding, not to the topographical or various other difficulties to be met with in the records. Ceremonial is the translation of a mythological value into an act. If we keep strictly to the ceremony, we can speak of the execution

---

[5] W. Müller, *Kreis und Kreuz;* cf. A. Szabó, "Roma Quadrata," pp. 160–69.

of a mythological plan regardless of its realization in the historical city-plan of Rome.

The contradiction we allude to is that between two geometrical forms. According to the most detailed account of Roman city-founding, Plutarch's biography of Romulus, there is mention of a *circle* which, described from a centre, is then drawn with a plough. The centre takes the form of a circular pit called a *mundus*. Ovid, in his poetical account of a primitive city-founding (*Fasti*, IV, 819), speaks of a *fossa* that was filled in again after the sacrifice. An altar, equally simple, was built over it. Other sources describe the *mundus* of the historical Roman metropolis as a building whose lower part was consecrated to the *Di Manes*, the spirits of the ancestors and of the Underworld. Those admitted into it stated that seen from inside it was shaped like the vault of heaven. Whether in its primitive form as used in the founding-ceremony or as a solid bit of architecture, the *mundus* is the ἀρχή into which the older world of the ancestors, the subterranean storehouse of everything that will ever grow and come to birth, opens. The *mundus* is at once the relative ἀρχή and the absolute ἀρχή, and from it the new world of "Rome" radiates in all directions like a circle from its centre. There is no need even to look for confirmation in the meaning of the word *mundus;* it may also derive from the Etruscan, in which case it is probably not identical with *mundus,* "world."

The ceremony and mythology of the circle run counter to the traditions concerning the city of Romulus, which was called *Roma quadrata.* This description corresponds to the account furnished by Dionysius of Halicarnassus, who speaks of the rectangular form (τετράγωνον σχῆμα) of that "primal furrow," the *sulcus primigenius.* In line with this too is a building known as *Quadrata Roma,* where the instruments needed for the ritual city-founding were kept. "In the beginning it was square," so says one of the sources, and was built of stone. The place where it stood is not the same as that which Plutarch indicates for the *mundus.* If it marked the mid-point of the *Roma quadrata* as the *mundus* marked that of the circular *sulcus primigenius,* then the two mid-points cannot have been identical. Altheim thought he could solve the contradiction with an ideal mid-point. He reminds us—what seems to have been forgotten—that the verbal adjective *quadrata* also means "divided into four." Whether you took your stand at the *mundus* or at the *Quadrata Roma,* you could draw a circle round you and thus, according to the rules of Roman surveying, found a quadripartite city, a *Roma quadrata.* Such a division into four along two axes is described both in Roman surveying and in augury.

The proposed solution proves brilliantly that the ceremony of the circle and the founding of a *Roma quadrata* are not *in theory* irreconcilable. It is unsatisfactory, however, when we consider the records. Plutarch mentions the *Roma quadrata* of Romulus before giving his account of the ceremony of the circle; he takes it as being a rectangular city and still finds no contradiction there. The cities founded by Rome, the *coloniae,* were according to Varro called *urbes* in the old documents, from *orbis,* "round," or *urvo,* "plough up." Varro thus takes the ceremony of the circle for granted in the case of the founding of *coloniae.* Nevertheless, most of the *coloniae* show that in reality rectangular city-plans grew out of the ritual circular boundary. They are *quadrata* in both senses: divided into four by two main streets and provided accordingly with four gates, and at the same time more or less regularly "quadratic." Circle and city-plan fail to correspond. Even in difficult terrain an ideal geometrical form was adhered to. This form is theoretically conceivable only as a *square within a circle.*

According to Plutarch, the Romans learned the secrets of city-founding from Etruscan teachers "as in a Mystery." The figure that combines the circle with the square is in fact not unknown over a wide field of mystic usages and experiences. The historian of religion as well as the psychologist can confirm this. In ancient India such a figure was called a *mandala,* "circle" or "ring." A particularly instructive type is used in the Mahayana Buddhism of Tibet. There we have a square in a circle with a T-shaped appendix on each of its four sides. The square in its turn encloses concentric circles. In Buddhism it is a relic of Hindu mythology. I recapitulate here the interpretation given by Heinrich Zimmer in his book *Kunstform und Yoga im indischen Kultbild* based on the *Shrī-chakra-sambhara Tantra* (Tantrik Texts, 7).

The adept of Buddhist mystery in experiencing the *mandala*

develops out of and around himself an image of the world with the Mountain of the Gods, Sumeru, in the midst. This is for him the axis of the world-egg, "whose four-cornered and be-jewelled body sparkles with sides made of crystal, gold, ruby, and emerald, the colours of the world's four quarters. A faithful Hindu would see resting upon it the palace of the King of the Gods, Indra, and of his blessed companions—Amaravati, 'Seat of the Immortals.' The adept of the Buddhist *mandala* develops in its place a monastic temple as the one locality appropriate to Buddha: a square building made of precious stones with four entrances at the sides (these are the T-shaped appendices), girt by magic walls of diamond. The roof rises up to a point in the manner of those domed tombs on earth which, containing relics, bear witness to the attainment of Nirvana by the fully en-lightened. Inside, the floor takes the form of a circle with an open lotus blossom, the eight petals stretching to all points of the compass (the four cardinal points and the four points in between). In it the contemplative sees himself standing in the form of Mahasukha (one of the great god Shiva's manifesta-tions), holding a female figure in his embrace. He sees himself as the 'highest bliss of the circles' with four heads and eight arms, and becomes aware of his own essence through contem-plation. His four heads signify the four elements, Water, Fire, Earth, and Air, in their immaterial suprasensible state, and also the four infinite feelings, permeation by which through con-stant practice causes one to grow ripe for Nirvana."

Mandalas designed for such a mystic purpose, for a kind of inner "refounding" and reorganization, may be drawn in the sand or on the floor of the temple where initiation takes place. They could also be actual constructions, often on a gigantic scale, like Borobudur, the famous shrine and place of Buddhist pilgrimage in Java. In the Buddhist *mandala* there is a break-through of something older: a world-building mythology. Cir-cles and squares drawn from a common centre appear in ancient Italy as well as in the Buddhist East as the ground-plan *par excellence* on which everything is built.[6] Upon it all the little

6 An ideal city based on a *mandala*-plan is the Heavenly Jerusalem of the Apocalypse: its four corners being based on the circle of the zodiac. Cf. F. Boll, *Aus der Offenbarung Johannis: Hellenistische Studien zum Weltbild der Apokalypse*, pp. 39f.

worlds—cities and shrines—are constructed, since both macro-cosm and microcosm, Man, appear to be grounded on that.

So much can the historian of religion report of the facts as known to him. Further facts are added by the psychologist. Professor Jung long since made the discovery that modern man, who knows nothing of Oriental mysteries, draws or dreams *mandala*-like figures when he is on the road to wholeness, the fusion of opposites. We would only call this process the "re-founding" or reorganization of the individual; Professor Jung calls it "individuation." With all the caution of his empirical methods of investigation, he assures us that the *mandala* is an "autonomous psychic fact characterized by an ever-repeated phenomenology that is identical wherever it is met." The *mandala*-symbol is for him "a sort of atomic nucleus about whose innermost structure and ultimate meaning we know nothing."[7] But the most important thing about it he said in his commentary to the Chinese book *The Secret of the Golden Flower* (p. 105): "Such things cannot be thought out; they must grow again from the dark depths of oblivion if they are to express the supreme presentiments of consciousness and the loftiest intuitions of the spirit, and thus fuse the uniqueness of consciousness as it exists today with the immemorial past of life."

6

"Origin" means two things in mythology. As the content of a story or mythologem it is the "giving of grounds" (*Begründung*); as the content of an act it is the "founding" (*Gründung*) of a city or the world. In either case it means man's return to his own origins and consequently the emergence of something original, so far as accessible to him, in the form of primordial images, mythologems, ceremonies. All three manifestations may be manifestations of the same thing, the same mythological idea. Where, then, does a *definite* mythological idea spring from, such as the *mandala*, which is still drawn today in East and West alike with the same meaning and yet without any communication between them, and which was probably at the bottom of the Roman foundation-ceremonies? Is there any point

[7] *Psychology and Alchemy*, par. 249.

in looking for a particular historical origin at a particular place and time, now that *the* origin has shown itself as the origin in every case?

The question has particular relevance to one feature of the *mandala*-plans. This feature is the *exact* division into four. Quadripartition proves to be something cosmic even in Buddhist usage. The four elements to which it corresponds also correspond both in India and Greece to the fourfold division of the world. In Greece this may be a legacy from pre-Indo-European times, in India the legacy may be directly Indo-European. The obvious thing would be to connect quadripartition with the four cardinal points. And this is possible in the mystery of the Buddhist *mandala*. The adept, so Zimmer says, "causes rays coloured after the four quarters—blue, green, red and yellow—to proceed from the heads of Mahasukha, whose form he himself has taken in his mind's eye. The colours ensure that his feeling of universal compassion pervades the entire cosmos." Here an original process, the extension of axes *from* the four quarters, appears to be reversed. There is an emission of rays *to* the four quarters which are only "founded" by that fact. The fourfold division of the Roman city-plan would seem on the other hand to be the result of the first-named process, a natural north-south and east-west orientation, and the quadripartite *heaven* to be the common basis of all *mandala*-plans.

The question is acute. Is the origin of fourfold division to be sought not, after all, in man but in the world at large? And if so, in what part of the world? Werner Müller has rightly stressed in his aforementioned study of Roman and Germanic settlements that only the circle can be derived from the horizon, not the fourfold division. The natural boundary of our field of vision forms a closed ring that shows no articulation of any kind. Only in the far North can the horizon conveniently be used as a cosmic clock, whose hand is the sun. The sun's course and the horizon-sector actually coincide only when viewed from the Pole. The further south you go, the later the sun's arrival over the principal points. The Roman writers on the art of surveying warn against taking one's bearings by the rising sun and setting the axes of the quartering in this way. One should take one's bearings by the meridian and, for *exact* quartering, use a special instrument, the *gruma* (the Etruscan form of the

Greek *gnomon*). But whence the *compulsion* to construct such an instrument? From the need to keep up a tradition which according to Müller the Latins brought with them from the far North, or from the need whence arises *every* exact division, *the mental vision of regular forms?* The derivation of the *gruma* from Greece via the Etruscans would speak for the latter view or at least for a combination of both needs.

Professor Jung's theory of the collective unconscious admits in principle of both possibilities. The *mandalas* he has found in the dreams and drawings of modern man might as well be the reflection of age-old *observation of the heavens* as the reflection of a universal human *compulsion*. Certain elements in the series of visions and dreams which he discusses in *Psychology and Alchemy* actually seem to point to the cosmic origin of the *mandala*-symbol. In one dream the symbol appears as "a pendulum clock that goes without the weights ever running down" (p. 100), hence a world-clock such as the sky is for us. In the "Great Vision" (pp. 194ff.) there is explicit mention of the world-clock, *three-dimensional* and consisting of a vertical and a horizontal circle, with *three* rhythms in one. It made an impression of utmost harmony on the dreamer, we may well say the "harmony of the spheres."

Although it is absolutely possible in principle that in this vision the dreamer's collective unconscious was recalling ancestral experiences of the heavens, Professor Jung nevertheless does not believe in the direct cosmic origin of fourfoldness. He finds in fourfoldness a property of that "centre" of man's totality which he regards as the result of individuation and calls the "self." But besides the number four he not infrequently finds other numbers, for instance the number three, particularly in men. To his mind it seems "that there is normally a clear insistence on *four,* or as if there were a greater statistical probability of four."[8] On account of the possible variation of the numbers he rejects the idea of the four heavenly quarters but, with the necessary reservations, permits himself a suggestion as to quite another kind of cosmic origin: it is, he says, a strange *lusus naturae* that the main chemical constituent of the physical organism should be carbon, which is characterized by four va-

[8] *Psychology and Alchemy,* par. 327.

lencies. Moreover, he goes on, diamond—in Oriental texts the symbol of individuation accomplished (we call to mind the "diamond" walls of the Buddhist *mandala*)—is, we all know, crystallized carbon. If this is something more than a mere "sport of nature," then, as Jung emphasizes, since the phenomenon of fourfoldness is not just an invention of the conscious mind but "a spontaneous product of the objective psyche," a fundamental theme of mythology could be understood by referring it back to the inorganic in man.

But we have an example of fourfoldness rather nearer to the region of mind—in the origin of the organism itself. This is the third step in its evolution. The first was the union of the paternal spermatozoon with the maternal germ-cell to form the zygote. If these two together with the innumerable forebears comprised in them constitute the organism's *relative* ἀρχή, then the advent of a new entity, the zygote, constitutes its *absolute* ἀρχή. The second step was the subsequent division into two, the beginning of segmentation; and the third step an exact division into *four* and the *four*-cell stage, which is repeated over and over again in dichotomous progression. The life of the individual therefore has a period when it develops as it were on the basis of a geometrical plan, a sort of *mandala*.

The view that mythology tells us of the selfsame origin and "ground" which we once *were* and still in a sense *are* (as the elaboration and development of it) permits a general consideration of such possibilities. Only one of them—the possibility that mythology has an organic origin—shall be considered here and no more than that. It is outside the scope of a purely anthropological study, yet it implies the possibility of a psychic germ within the germ of life itself—a germ that would enable us to glimpse an ideal world-order. The answer to the question about the origin of the exact division into four can only be sought where fourfoldness and threefoldness appear as *psychic* activities and not just physical events. (The combination of both as the twelvefold division of the world-clock, whether read from the sky or not, is a remarkable mental achievement.) It is not only the psychologist that finds fourfoldness and threefoldness side by side. Ancient records speak of the part the number three played in the layout of cities both in Etruria and in Rome: three gates, three streets, three districts, three temples or temples divided into three. We have perforce to take account of plurality even when we are seeking one common thing, the original factor. And here we have an answer at least to the question as to whether there is any point in looking for a special origin in local and temporal differences.

7

Leo Frobenius describes a West African city-founding ceremony in his *Monumenta Africana*. He himself notices its correspondence with the Roman ceremony and connects this whole group of cultures (he calls it the "Syrtian culture") with the ancient world by way of the old Garamants of North Africa. This is not meant to imply any borrowing of culture, but a single cultural stream which, rising in the Mediterranean area or even further east, reached as far as western Sudan. We shall leave these and all the other historical explanations to one side and concern ourselves only with such facts in the African tradition as have immediate relevance here.

To these belongs among other things the city-plan. The longer of the accounts furnished by Frobenius only says that a place for the founding was marked out with "a circle or a square," and that four gates facing the four quarters were provided for. In what follows I repeat the shorter account: "With the appearance of the first quarter of the moon they began marking out the circumference and the four gates. A bull was led three times round the city. He was then brought into the place marked off, together with three cows. After covering three of them he was sacrificed. His member was buried in the middle of the new city, and a phallic altar erected alongside a sacrificial pit. (That is, in the middle of the city's layout there is a combined mother and father emblem!) Always three animals were sacrificed on the altar, four in the pit." On the one hand we have man, moon, and the number three, on the other woman, sun, and the number four, both closely connected here, according to Frobenius. Evidently the city is meant to be founded upon both—on the union of the Father and Mother principles.

Professor Jung's observation that *mandalas* divided into three occur particularly in men thus acquires a new significance. We do not of course know to which of the principles, male or female, his draughtsmen and dreamers are involuntarily paying homage. But if the triangle appears in the centre of an Indian *mandala,* it is always interpreted there as a female symbol. In the ancient world the triple-bodied Hecate ruled over the three realms. Constellations of three goddesses are to be found everywhere in Greece, becoming quaternities only by association with a male god. The great goddess to be described in our study of the Divine Maiden is threefold in relation to Zeus: mother (Rhea), wife (Demeter), daughter (Persephone). An exact counterpart to this is formed by the masculine Holy Trinity of Christianity, which, *mutatis mutandis,* stands in the same relation to the Virgin Mary. The number 3 was masculine also for the Pythagoreans, while 4, doubling the feminine 2, was to their way of thinking a basic number of feminine origin. The "balance," whose realization Varro sees in the Roman ceremony of city-founding, is struck in the number four—διά τὸ ἰσάκις ἴσον.

Even these examples, close as they are to our own culture, show remarkable discrepancies. Typical cultural elements such as the connection of the number three with man and four with woman are, to quote once more what Jung says about the *mandala*-symbol, "nuclear atoms of whose inmost structure and ultimate meaning we know nothing." Frobenius names such factors, which are not amenable to further explanation, "monads," and sees in them the "structural principles" of the various views of the world in various cultures. In West Africa he finds alongside the monad of "Syrtian" culture (man=three, woman=four) the presence of two others: the "Atlantic" monad (man=four, woman=three) and the "North Erythrean" monad (man=three, woman=two). Certain relations to certain heavenly bodies likewise belong to the ultimately unfathomable structure of the monad. If anywhere, the question of a cosmic origin finds answer here—and it is negative so far as concerns the derivability of these and similar relationships from the observation of the heavens.

The point is that these relationships are just as various as those to the two sexes. In Syrtian culture the moon pertains to man and the number three, the sun to woman and the number four. Frobenius even assures us that the Syrtian city-plan with its division into four is a replica of the sun or the sun's course. In German, in contrast to English, the idea of a masculine moon and a feminine sun still lives on. But in the ancient languages the moon is feminine and the sun masculine; the moon-goddess Hecate had three forms, while Apollo, who as Hecatos corresponded to her and was related to the sun, was, in the form of Agyieus (guardian of streets and public places), a conical pointed column with a four-sided base (i.e., a sort of square and circle combined). The secret tutelary goddess of the *Roma quadrata* was according to one source[9] *Luna,* and the secret name of the city was *Flora,* an appellative of the same great goddess who is no more lunar than terrestrial and sub-terranean.

Once more we have given only a few from a host of examples. They show us the same heavenly body, when seen in terms of the "monads" of different cultures, now as a woman, now as a man, now as three, now as four. If a monad means an *inability to see otherwise,* a "possession" in Frobenius' sense, then there are at least two grounds for this possession: the gripping world of *Nature* and something in the history of *culture* that is as manifold as it is variable, that fixes the characteristic "monadic" features of each and every view of the world. The first "ground" corresponds to archaic man's "openness" to the world of which we have spoken before, an openness that throws him back on his deepest foundations. The second can be described as follows: it is an exposure to certain aspects of the world which in their turn correspond to just those monadic features, themselves seeming to have grown up organically and to be comparable with the fundamental characteristics of plants and organisms in general. In order to define the *ultimate basis of the monads* we would have to say that it is the compulsion *in* man to produce something formed, formed in spirit just as only formed things are produced in the body. This compulsion is the origin —the first leap. But the next moment, in the leap itself, the monad, the spiritual plan is there. The plan is the first thing that is intelligible; here something original, experienced with all the immediacy of the origin, proves to be one with some

9 Macrobius, *Saturnalia,* III, 9, 4. I no longer believe, as I did in "Altitalische Götterverbindungen," p. 19, that Wilamowitz was right in his conjecture *Lua.*

aspect of the "open" world. If "cosmos" is understood in the Greek sense that everything spiritual and our compulsion towards the spiritual are an essential part of the cosmos, then here we have *the cosmos meeting with itself.*

Or, to put it in more scientific language, it seems as if there already were in the human plasm—the germ of life we have been speaking of—something spiritual, a compulsion towards the spiritual. What grows out of this compulsion is, like every growing thing, exposed to its environment—and woe to anything that wants to grow when there is nothing in the environment to correspond to it, when no meeting can take place there! The essence of anything that grows is as much an *exposure to* something as an *arising from* something. So with the essence of the plasm. We are not speaking, of course, of any physical thing that is so exposed in its growth, but of a spiritual thing. Not of "plasm" but, as Frobenius calls it, of "paideuma." If other organisms are plasmatic growths, cultures are "paideumatic." Yet "paideumatic" means little more than "exposed."[10] Spiritual origin is a sort of leap into the world—and woe to anything that wants to become actual when it corresponds to none of the possible aspects of the world, when it can unite with none of them! Cultural achievements—the various "foundings"—can only come into being and persist as actual *works* because, for the "plasm" as well as for the "paideuma," for the body-cell as well as for the monad, meeting and union are possible. So that it is possible to find, *in the world itself,* the basis of threefoldness as of fourfoldness, a sunlike quality in woman as in man, a female quality in the moon as well as fertilizing masculinity—all according to the monadic plan taken over by the mythological idea.

The "first step" is not really a step at all. It is the primary "ground" or beginning, "origin" understood as the primary source and issue from that source—the very thing that all mythologies speak of in the language of the *second* (the first intel-

---

10 "Paideuma," so I allowed myself to define it, as I thought, in Frobenius' sense (in the journal *Paideuma,* I, 1938-40, p. 158), is a reactive faculty and thus essentially passive despite the fact that the reaction works itself out in acts and creations, i.e., works of culture. Because of the paideuma, all those living in its particular time and place are so *exposed* that they can only have that particular life-style.

ligible) step, which is, in "monadic" language, the leap into the world and possession by it. At this stage everything is welling up, flowing, continually varying and changing shape, all variations within the same culture being determined by the same monad. Spiritual plans have now appeared in and bound up with the world, as ground-plans for unending development. Only with the *third* step is there a state of rest. The first two stages—compulsion and monadic structure—which could never have become actual without this third, are consummated in a rounded whole. Only here do things come to a standstill, achieve stability as a work. Yet for this stable existence a special power, a special talent is needed—that of the artist, creator, founder, of the philosopher too if, as a "giver of grounds," he may be counted among the "founders." The "leap," the possession, the monad already lodge us in time and place; with the artist and founder we find ourselves in the midst of a definite people—"people" being understood as a source of power and talent and also as a source of characteristics transcending the monadic.

Artists, even a whole nation of artists, city-builders and world-builders, are true creators, founders, and "fundamentalists" only to the extent that they draw their strength from and build on that source whence the mythologies have their ultimate ground and origin, namely, what was anterior to but revealed in the monadic. The "universally human" would be a fit term for the "pre-monadic" were it not too little and too feeble; for the important thing is not to become "universally human" but to encounter the divine in absolute immediacy. The mythologems that come closest to these naked encounters with Godhead we regard as the primary mythologems. Historically speaking, we possess only variations of the primary mythologems, not their timeless content, the mythological ideas. These in their pure state, e.g., the pure idea of the *mandala,* its "archetype," so to speak, are pre-monadic. What exists historically has the character not only of a monad, i.e., belonging locally and temporally to a definite culture, but also of a *work,* i.e., speaking in the manner typical of a certain people. On the other hand, every people displays its form most purely when it stands face to face with the Absolute, that is, on the frontiers of the pre-monadic. The deeper our insight into the pre-monadic, the more "archetypal" the vision. Examples would lead us out of the sphere of mythology into that of mystic experience.

When solidly constructed monads break down, as at the end of the antique era, or when their dissolution is already far advanced, as it is today, we find ourselves closer to various kinds of mysticisms than to mythology. That is why Plotinus can tell us about pure mystical experience, and why his contemporaries, the Gnostics, can tell us about what comes closest to mythology in mysticism. And that too is why the psychologist finds in modern man the same mystical or semi-mystical phenomena as in a handbook of Chinese mysticism or in the Gnosticism of late antiquity. What we meet in both cases has mostly the appearance of something midway between the archetype and a monadic fragment, a mythology at once germinating and disintegrating.[11] It is precisely these individual mythologies

[11] A particularly fine example of this, a purely psychic *mandala*-experience complete with monadic and mythological fragments (numbers and statues of gods) is to be found in Jung's *Two Essays on Analytical Psychology* (pars. 366–67). I quote it here together with Jung's commentary:

" 'I climbed the mountain and came to a place where I saw seven red stones in front of me, seven on either side, and seven behind me. I stood in the middle of this quadrangle. The stones were flat like steps. I tried to lift the four stones nearest me. In doing so I discovered that these stones were the pedestals of four statues of gods buried upside down in the earth. I dug them up and arranged them about me so that I was standing in the middle of them. Suddenly they leaned towards one another until their heads touched, forming something like a tent over me. I myself fell to the ground and said: "Fall upon me if you must! I am tired." Then I saw that beyond, encircling the four gods, a ring of flame had formed. After a time I got up from the ground and overthrew the statues of the gods. Where they fell, four trees shot up. At that blue flames leapt up from the ring of fire and began to burn the foliage of the trees. Seeing this I said: "This must stop. I must go into the fire myself so that the leaves shall not be burned." Then I stepped into the fire. The trees vanished and the fiery ring drew together to one immense blue flame that swept me up from the earth.'

"Here the vision ended. . . . At all events the unprejudiced reader will recognize at once the idea of a 'mid-point' that is reached by a kind of climb (mountaineering, effort, struggle, etc.). He will also recognize without difficulty the famous medieval conundrum of the squaring of the circle, which belongs to the field of alchemy. Here it takes its rightful place as a symbol of individuation. The total personality is indicated by the four cardinal points, the four gods, i.e., the four functions which give bearings in psychic space, and also by the circle enclosing the whole. Overcoming the four gods who threaten

of present-day men that do in fact largely correspond to the ideal *primary* mythology hovering as it were between the *one* origin and the fixed, monadic version of it. Living mythology, on the other hand, expands in infinite and yet shapely multiplicity, rather like the plant-world in comparison with Goethe's "primal plant." We must always keep our eyes on both: the historical Many and the unitive principle that is nearest to the origin.

---

to smother the individual signifies liberation from identification with the four functions, a fourfold *nirdvandva* ('free from opposites') followed by an approximation to the circle, to undivided wholeness. This in its turn leads to further exaltation."

Ancient parallels apart from the city-founding ceremony are not wanting. Even the "squaring of the circle" is ancient. I would only remark that ritual monuments that were buried or hidden in the earth (in Rome the so-called "Tarentum"; in Lykosura, cf. Pausanias, VIII, 37, 3) pertain to the same divinities as those to which the *mundus* pertains. Everywhere in the vision just quoted we can find elements that have a meaning both in individual mythology, i.e., psychology, and in the great mythologies of the cosmic religions.

I

THE PRIMORDIAL CHILD
IN PRIMORDIAL TIMES

BY C. KERÉNYI

1. *Child Gods*

Mythology is never the biography of the gods, as often appears to the observer. This is particularly true of "mythology properly so called": mythology in its purest, most pristine form.[1] It is both more and less. It is always less than a biography, even though it tells of the birth and childhood of the gods, the deeds of their youth, and sometimes of their early death. The remarkable thing about these childish or youthful feats is that they show the god in the full perfection of his power and outward form, and thus really preclude biographical thinking— thinking in periods of life as stages of development. At the same time mythology is more than any biography. For, although it may tell us nothing that relates organically to a particular period of life, it nevertheless comprehends the periods themselves as timeless realities: the figure of the child plays a part in mythology equal to that of the marriageable girl, or Kore, and the mother. In mythology these too, like every other possible form of being, are manifestations of the Divine.

The deeds of the child Apollo remain Apollonian, and the pranks of the child Hermes are not so much childish as Hermetic. Classical Greece was determined to view these two gods under an eternally youthful aspect, since, conceived as figures in all their purity and perfection, Apollo and Hermes are moulded most clearly, out of all possible earthly forms, in the timeless form of the youth. It is the same with the figure of Zeus as the regal-looking man in middle life, or Saturn in late antiquity as the grumpy old greybeard. Archaic Greece saw its Apollo, its Hermes and Dionysus as bearded figures, and this shows that divinity and humanity can touch at yet another point—at the summit of the only maturity we mortals can reach.

[1] See my paper "Was ist Mythologie?" pp. 557ff., and *Die antike Religion*, pp. 13ff., as well as the introduction to my *Gods of the Greeks*.

But to grasp the eternal, which is the essence of every one of these gods, in the perishable bloom of youth—that is by far the harder task. Until Greek art solved it, the bearded figures of men—figures that were almost ageless—were the most typical forms of expression.

In the figures of godlike men, youths, and ancients, Greek mythology never expresses any biographical element or phase of life, but always the nature or essence of the god. The bearded archaic type—Hermes, Apollo, Dionysus, depicted at the height of their powers, the acme of Greek manly perfection, as also Zeus and Poseidon—is the simplest visible expression of that timeless quality which Homer ascribes to the gods when he says: "They age not, they die not, they are eternal." Whether portrayed archaically in ageless maturity or classically in idealized form, the actual age of these divine youths or men has above all a symbolic value: in them, richness of life and richness of meaning are one. Their very nature removes them from every conceivable biographical relationship.

Many gods—almost all those we have mentioned—appear not only as men and youths but also in the likeness of child gods; and it might seem as if the *child* possessed that biographical significance which we have just denied. It may be asked whether Greek mythology introduces the child Hermes or the child Apollo merely because it happens to know his father and mother, and because the story of his birth naturally leads on to the story of his childhood. But this kind of biographical approach gets us no further than the inclusion of the age of childhood in the history of the gods. No sooner is the figure of the child there than it is cancelled and replaced by the figure of the god. Little Hermes at once becomes Hermes, little Heracles is at once in full possession of his strength and valour. But the richness of life and meaning in the wonder-working child is no whit smaller than in the bearded god. On the contrary, it seems to be even richer and more profoundly moving. With the appearance of the child god—whether in the Homeric hymn to Hermes, in the myth of Zeus or Dionysus, or in Virgil's Fourth Eclogue—we feel ourselves surrounded by that mythological atmosphere which modern man calls "fairy-tale-like." If anyone supposes that, in the child god, he has discovered the biographical element of mythology, he is heading

26

for surprises. For here, at this seemingly biographical point, he will find himself completely outside all biography and in the primordial realm of mythology where the most marvellous creations grow and flourish.

For which interpretation, then, have we to decide? For the assumption that the figure of the child god is the result of biographical thinking? Or for the idea that the biographical point of view is probably only of secondary importance, and that the primary thing, which directly concerns us, is the play of mythology itself? A play like the playing of an invisible great composer who varies the same theme—the primordial figure of the child—in the keys of the various gods? Is not the Primordial Child—the child god of so many mythologems—the one and only true *filius ante patrem,* whose life, seen in retrospect, first produced the checkered history of his origins? We must either put this idea in a clearer and more certain light or else refute it, if we wish to understand the mythological accounts of child gods. But the way to such an understanding is to let the mythologems speak for themselves. So we now present a series of them.

2. *The Orphan Child*

Ancient mythologems of child gods are surrounded by, and evoke, an aura of fairytale. Not for any unaccountable, essentially irrational reason, but rather because of their clearly visible and ever-recurring characteristics. The child god is usually an abandoned foundling. Often it is threatened by extraordinary dangers: it may be devoured, like Zeus, or torn to pieces, like Dionysus. On the other hand these dangers are not altogether surprising: they are features as natural to the vision of a Titanic world as discord and trickery are to the primitive mythologems. Sometimes the father is the child's enemy, as was Kronos, or he may be merely absent, as Zeus was when Dionysus was being torn to pieces by the Titans. We have a rarer case in the Homeric hymn to Pan. Little Pan was abandoned by his mother and nurse; terrified, they had let the new-born infant lie there. His father, Hermes, picked him up, wrapped him in a hare's skin, and bore him away to Olympus. Here again we have two contrasting fates: in the one the child god is an abandoned abortion, in the other he sits at Zeus' side among the gods.

The mother has a peculiar part to play: she *is* and *is not* at the same time. To take an ancient Italic example: the child Tages, from whom the Etruscans received their sacred science, sprang out of the earth before the eyes of a ploughman[2]—a child of Mother Earth and at the same time the purest type of fatherless and motherless foundling. Semele was already dead when Dionysus was born, and the mother of Asklepios did not survive her son's birth. We could also mention figures in heroic sagas who were likewise abandoned by their mothers as children, violently separated from them, or exposed to death; but we would rather confine ourselves to "mythology properly so called," and shall only tell of gods who occupy a central place in genuine mythologems and cults. Even to the greatest among them—Zeus—something very similar happened. When he was born his mother, in order to save him at all, exposed him. The nursing of the child by divinities or wild beasts in the myth of Zeus, and the imitation of it in the cult of the young Dionysus, show us two things: the *solitariness* of the child god, and the fact that he is nevertheless *at home* in the primeval world—an equivocal situation, at once that of the orphan child and a cherished son of the gods.

Another variation on the theme is when the mother shares the child's abandonment and solitude. She wanders about homeless and is persecuted, like Leto, whom her new-born son, the little Apollo, defends against the brutal Tityos. Or else she lives without honour, far from Olympus, like Maia the mother of Hermes. Her position—originally that of Mother Earth, one of whose names she bears—is no longer entirely simple in the Homeric hymn. The simple situation shows us the abandonment of the new-born god, in both variations. In the one, mother and child are abandoned as Leto was with Apollo on the barren island of Delos; in the other, the child is alone in the rough and primitive world. Here the fairytale atmosphere becomes concrete: we are reminded of the orphan child in

2 Cicero, *De divinatione*, II, 23; Ovid, *Metamorphoses*, XV, 553; Festus, s.v. Tages. The sources for the other references are to be found in the lexicons of mythology. On Hermes see my *Hermes der Seelenführer: das Mythologem vom männlichen Lebensursprung*.

European and Asiatic folklore, and how he was abandoned. "No matter where it was or was not—enough that there was a town and in the southern quarter of the town a tumble-down house inhabited by an orphan child, left all on its own after the death of its father and mother." So begins a Hungarian legend.[3] There are parallels both to the variation in which the child is wholly abandoned and to that in which it is left with mother or nurse.

A fairytale of the Black Forest Tatars in the Altai Mountains begins as follows:[4]

> Once upon a time, long ago,
> There lived an orphan boy,
> Created of God,
> Created of Pajana.
> Without food to eat,
> Without clothes to wear:
> So he lived.
> No woman to marry him.
> A fox came;
> The fox said to the youth:
> "How will you get to be a man?" he said.
> And the boy said:
> "I don't know myself
> How I shall get to be a man!"

One of the epic songs of another Altaic tribe, the Shor, comes closer to the mother-and-child variation:

> The woman called Altyn Sabak
> Lives in the wilderness,
> Without cattle, with nobody round her.
> She looks after a little boy.
> She casts her hook into the white sea;
> Every day she catches a young pike.
> In well water she cooks it,
> They eat the broth.
> So Altyn Sabak looks after
> This little orphan boy.

---

[3] *Ipolyi Arnold Népmesegyüjteménye*, No. 14.
[4] These verses are quoted from W. Radloff, *Proben der Volksliteratur der türkischen Stämme Süd-sibiriens*, I, pp. 271, 400.

Here the woman is the hero's elder sister—a peculiarity of these songs.

The appearance of this situation in folktale and saga—though it is a far cry from these examples to the world of antiquity—raises the question: Was not the orphan child the ancestor of the child god, and was not this child taken over into mythology from descriptions of a certain kind of human fate, such as is possible in the most diverse cultures, and there elevated to divine rank? Or was it the other way about? Is the child god earlier and the orphan child of folktale only a pale reflection of him? Which is primary: folktale or myth? Which came first: solitude in the primeval world, or the purely human picture of the orphan's fate? This question forces itself on us all the more urgently when we reflect that there are cases where the mythologem of the child god and the folktale of the orphan child are absolutely inseparable. A case of the kind now follows, although we stray even further for the nonce from the world of antiquity.

3. A Vogul God

The mythologem that allows us to see a little deeper into the original state of affairs is to be found among the Voguls. Their store of myths, collected by the Hungarian anthropologists A. Reguly and B. Munkácsi, is preserved for us in uncorrupt original texts, which the last-named has published with a literal Hungarian translation. In the following we attempt to reproduce this translation faithfully.

The Voguls worshipped—and perhaps still worship—one especially among their gods who bears the name of "The Man Who Looks at the World."[5] He is a god let down from heaven in two variations: with his mother and without her. With his mother he was "let down" in such a way that he was born as the son of a woman expelled from heaven. She fell upon the banks of the River Ob. "Under her right arm-pit two ribs broke out. A child with golden hands and feet was born."[6] This manner of birth, the emergence of the child from its mother's

[5] Cf. K. Meuli, "Scythia," pp. 16off., where, however, the Buddhist influence is not considered.
[6] B. Munkácsi, *Vogul népköltési gyüjtemény*, II, 1, p. 99.

right side, betrays Buddhist influence. The Bodhisattva who later became Gautama Buddha entered his mother's womb from the right side and at the end of ten months left the right side of his mother again in full consciousness and immaculate; thus it was according to the Buddha legend of the northern sect—Mahayana Buddhism, as it is called.[7] "The Man Who Looks at the World" is an exact translation of "Avalokiteshvara," the name of the world-ruling Bodhisattva in the above religion, whose missionaries are dispersed throughout Northern Asia. Avalokiteshvara is just such a divinity compassionately observing the world as the god of the Voguls became. From the latter's titles—which refer to him as a goose, swan, or crane—we get a glimpse of his original nature.[8] Golden limbs are as characteristic of him as of the new-born Buddha of the Avalokiteshvara world (our world),

> who gleamed, shining like gold
> Worked in the fire by the master's hand.[9]

The orphan's fate has nothing to do with all this and leads us into a world quite different from that of the Dalai Lama, the present-day embodiment of Avalokiteshvara.

The child god of the Voguls, however, before he became "The Man Who Looks at the World," i.e., while still a small boy, also came down to earth without his mother.[10] A council is held in heaven:

> Sometime the World of the Age of Man will come to be.
> His father's little son, his father's darling,
> His mother's little son, his mother's darling:
> How will man standing on his feet,
> How will man endure him?
> Let us give him into the hands of another,
> In another's hands he shall be taught tameness!
> To the uncle and aunt of his father,
> To the uncle and aunt of his mother
> He shall be given.

---

7 *Lalitavistara*, chs. 6–7.
8 Munkácsi, II, 2 (1910), pp. 058 and 067.
9 "Sutta Nipata," in Oldenberg, *Reden des Buddha*, p. 4.
10 The following from two "Songs of God-heroes," in Munkácsi, II, 1, pp. 100ff.

We hear of a cradle hanging between heaven and earth in which he is drawn up or let down according to the resolve of his father, the Upper Heaven:

> His father set him in a curved cradle with a silver edge,
> He let him down to the world of men, inhabitants of
>   the lower earth.
> On to the roof of his man-uncle, he of the eagle's feathers,
> He fell with the mighty voice of thunder.
> Instantly his uncle was outside, took him in.
> By day he teaches him, by night teaches him.
> So he grows, and his aunt beats him.
> So he grows, and his uncle beats him.
> So his bones grow hard, and hard his muscles.
> Yet a second time his aunt beats him,
> Yet a third time his uncle.

We hear of his sorry plight in the house of a Russian: how he is kept behind the door, how dish-water is emptied over him. Sorrier yet is his plight in the house of a Samoyed, who binds him to his sleigh with an iron cable thirty rods long. How hard he has to work for the Samoyed is less apparent from our text than from kindred accounts in fairytales of manhandled heroes and sons of gods. All the more moving, then, is the description of the child's sufferings, when, beaten almost to death with a "club of mammoth-bone," he is cast on the dunghill and intended as a sacrificial victim. Here the nadir is reached; now the turn sets in. The boy suddenly becomes possessed of snow-shoes, armour, quiver, bow, and sword. He shoots an arrow through seven stags, he shoots another through seven elks. He sacrifices the Samoyed's son, pulverizes seven Samoyed "cities," destroys the Russian and the Russian city "with the pressure of his back, the pressure of his breast," slays his uncle and aunt. It is an epiphany, no less terrible than that of Dionysus on the ship of the Etruscan pirates in the Homeric hymn. From the miserable plight of the orphan there emerges a god. The turning of the tide of fortune is not only impressive, it is also significant.

With the Vogul mythologem we approach very closely to a familiar type of fairytale, that of "Strong Hans."[11] But a com-

[11] Cf. A. A. Aarne, *The Types of the Folk-Tale* (trans. Thompson), No. 650, supplemented here on the basis of Hungarian legends.

parison with this particular tale shows how much less impressive and significant the fairytale is. What meaning it has comes solely from the grotesquely exaggerated feats of an exceptionally strong farmer's boy and the absurd situations that result. The difference lies not in the environment or in the social atmosphere (though the atmosphere of the Vogul myths is anything but regal), but in what we may call the dramatic structure of the mythologem. Such a structure is entirely lacking in this type of fairytale. The uncommon bodily strength of the youngster is explained in advance by references to his birth and mode of nourishment. He was suckled for several years or ate enough for nine people; his father was a bear, or—in one Hungarian tale— his mother a mare, a cow, a fairy; he was hatched out of an egg or forged of iron. All this, of course, points to the mythological origin of the tale, but reduces the action to a lower plane: from the world of high drama to the world of astonishing exceptions to which we are so accustomed in folktales. What is it, on the other hand, that affects us so powerfully in the mythologem? The very thing that constitutes its whole meaning, and that is the revelation of divinity in the paradoxical union of lowest and highest, weakest and strongest.

The question as to which is primary, orphan child or child god, is thus considerably simplified. The emergence of a god's son or a king's son from the orphan child, as a theme for myth or fairytale, presupposes the orphan situation: it is this situation that makes the emergence possible in the first place. But the plight of the orphan does not, insofar as it is purely human, furnish any *sufficient reason* for such an emergence. Considered apart from mythology, and from the standpoint of ordinary human life, that plight is not necessarily consummated in an epiphany. But if the epiphany is as it were the fruit and fulfilment of the orphan's fate, then the whole situation must be understood in mythological terms, and we have to inquire: Does mythology know of an orphan's fate that is compatible with divine form, or rather with the figure of a god in whom this fate is an *essential characteristic?*

4. *Kullervo*

We shall now be confronted with the picture of the orphan child of the folktales, a picture painted in full detail, so that we may decide on the ground of immediate evidence whether it points in the direction of mythology or merely to a realistic description of a certain type of human fate. Not individual themes, but the whole picture shall speak for itself. (The theme of the miraculous birth has already led us in the direction of mythology.) The picture stands in the *Kalevala* in heroic frame: a description of the servitude of Kullervo, Kalervo's son. He has been recognized afresh in the "Strong Hans" of the Finnish fairytale "Munapojka": "The Boy Born of an Egg."[12] Again, he has been compared wih the Hamlet of Danish saga; like him, Kullervo in the *Kalevala* remained alive to avenge his father.[13] But even this element is not the exclusive property of the saga: the orphaned child god of the Voguls, in their "Songs of God-heroes," was also the "deathless avenger."[14]

A hero of Finnish antiquity, Untamo by name—so we read in Book XXXI of the *Kalevala*[15]—exterminated the clan of his brother Kalervo.

Of all the tribe of Kalervo there was left only his young wife, and she was pregnant. Untamo's army led her away with them to their homeland to do the chores, the cleaning and sweeping.

Before long a little boy was born to this unhappy mother, and she cast about for a name. She called him Kullervo, the Battle Hero. The little boy was swaddled and laid fatherless in a cradle, and his mother sat rocking it. She rocked him till his hair tossed, rocked him all that day and the next, and on the third day the boy kicked out with his feet before and behind, tore off the swaddling-clothes, crawled out, and broke the lime-wood cradle to pieces.

"Already in the third month" thoughts of vengeance awoke in the "knee-high" boy: he wanted to avenge his father and mother. This came to Untamo's ears. They deliberated how best they might destroy the miraculous child. They tried first of all with water:

12 Cf. D. Comparetti, *Der Kalevala*, p. 197.
13 Cf. K. Krohn, *Kalevalastudien*, VI, p. 29.
14 Cf. Munkácsi, II, 2, pp. 0136ff., 0263f.
15 [In view of the length of the quotations and the discrepancies between the German version used by the author and the only English version of the *Kalevala* available to me—by W. F. Kirby in Everyman's Library, who reproduces the original metre, which Longfellow imitated in *Hiawatha*—I have compounded a prose version from this and from A. Schiefner's German text.—TRANS.]

They put him in a barrel, a little cask, and pushed it out upon the waves. After two nights they went to see whether the boy had sunk in the water or perished in his barrel. But he had not sunk in the water or perished in his barrel; he had crawled out of the barrel and was now sitting on the waves with a rod of copper in his hand. At the end of it there was a silken thread, and he was angling in the lake for fish as he floated through the water. There was enough water in the lake to fill two ladles, and possibly—if exactly measured —part of a third.

Untamo then sought to destroy the child with fire:

So they gathered and collected a large supply of dry birch-wood, the hundred-needled pine oozing with resin, a thousand sleighfuls of bark, and a hundred rods of dry ash. Having set fire to the wood-pile, they cast the boy into the middle of the blaze. The pyre burnt all that day and the next, and was still burning on the third day. Then they went to look. The boy was sitting up to his knees in ashes, up to his arms in embers, with a rake in his hand. He was stirring up the fire, raking the coals together. Not a hair was singed, not a lock displaced.

Finally a third attempt was made to destroy the child with what we may call in this connection the airy element: Untamo had the boy "strung up on an oak-tree." When after the usual time a lad was sent to look at him, he brought back this message:

"Kullervo is not yet perished, has not died upon the tree. He is carving pictures on it, holding a graver in his hand. The whole tree is covered with pictures, the oak is a mass of carving! There are men with swords, and spears at their sides."

Where should Untamo now seek aid against this most miserable boy! Whatever the death he prepared for him, whatever the destruction he planned, the wicked lad could never be brought to ruin.

Thus what we may call the first variation on the theme, in the musical sense of the word. Actually it consists of three variations. A more extensive analysis would only tend to break down certain units that are effective as *wholes,* e.g., the child *and* the element in which it subsists. Each of these variations has an instant effect on us, chiefly because of the poetic composition and the painter-like design. Later we shall see how the composition, the combination of child and water, is not only outwardly effective, but full of meaning too. For the present we shall only recall how child and fire go together in mythology:

> Heaven was in labour, earth was in labour,
> And the purple sea was in labour.
> The blood-red seaweed had birth-pangs.
> The hollow stem of the seaweed emitted smoke,
> The hollow stem of the seaweed emitted flame,
> And out of the flame sprang a little boy:
> Fire for hair, and fire for beard,
> And his eyes were suns.

Such was the birth of a divine child as reported in one of the ritual songs of the old heathen Armenians,[16] a mythologem to which reference has been made in my explanation of Virgil's Fourth Eclogue.[17] It is tempting to classify this mythologem under the "tube-birth myths," as Frobenius has called one of the groups in solar mythology.[18] But the faint echo of it in the variation "Kullervo in the fire" is enough to make us realize what sort of elemental material it is out of which are moulded the images of the orphan's fate, for example these three ways of compassing Kullervo's doom. This material is undoubtedly the primal stuff of mythology, and not that of biography; a stuff from which the life of the gods, and not the life of men, is formed. What, from the purely human point of view, is an unusually tragic situation—the orphan's exposure and persecution—appears in mythology in quite another light. It simply shows up the loneliness and solitude of elemental beings—a loneliness peculiar to the primordial element. If anything, the fate of the orphaned Kullervo, delivered up to every force of destruction and exposed to all the elements, must be the *true orphan's fate* in the fullest sense of the word: exposure and persecution. But at the same time this fate is the triumph of the elemental nature of the wonder-child. The *human* fate of the orphan does not truly express the fate of

[16] Quoted in Vetter's translation by H. Gelzer, "Zur armenischen Götterlehre," p. 107, from Moses of Chorene, *History of Armenia,* I, 31.
[17] Kerényi, "Das persische Millennium im 'Mahābhārata,' bei der Sibylle und Vergil," p. 31.
[18] *Das Zeitalter des Sonnengottes,* pp. 271ff.

such miraculous beings, is only secondary. Yet it is just their symbolical orphanhood which gives them their significance: it expresses the *primal solitude* which alone is appropriate to such beings in such a situation, namely in mythology.

The first, three-part variation on the Kullervo theme occurs on this original, mythological level. But it is very instructive to find that everything in the *Kalevala* that reminds us of the feats of Strong Hans in the fairytale can be fitted into this mythlike episode as a further variation of it. Kullervo solves all the tasks set him in such a way that the solution exceeds all expectations and redounds to the injury of the taskmaster. Elias Lönnrot acted in full accord with the stylistic feelings of the *Kalevala* singers when he compiled these songs.[19] Finnish folklore refers the variations of the Kullervo-cycle to one and the same person, although it is familiar with the picture of the child floating on the water in other connections as well. The "fairytale" element stands beside the mythological element like another variation on the same "musical" theme.

The savage consummation of the first task does not so much conjure up the fairytale atmosphere as echo the savagery of primitive mythology. Kullervo, the "knee-high" boy, having now grown "about a span in height," is charged with the care of a small baby.

So he watched all one day and the next, broke the baby's hands, gouged out his eyes; and on the third day let him die altogether of sickness, threw the napkins in the river, and burned the baby's cradle.

Untamo, in the true manner of primitive mythology, is not in the least indignant but merely reflects:

> Such a one is quite unfitted
> To attend to little children
> Or to touch them with his fingers.
> Now I know not where to send him,
> Nor what work I ought to give him.
> Maybe he could clear the forest?
> So he told him: "Clear the forest!"

[19] Cf. K. Krohn, pp. 3ff.

There follows the story of how Kullervo gets an axe made and how he himself sets to work. A clearing of enormous proportions is effected by means of this axe, and then—better in keeping with the spirit of the Finnish epic—by means of magic song. The next task is crowned with similar immoderate success: that of building a fence. The final task set by Untamo—threshing—is particularly reminiscent of the Strong Hans fairy-tale of other European nations.

Kullervo, the son of Kalervo, now began threshing the corn. He threshed the corn to a fine dust and pounded the ears to chaff.

The climax of his lethal exertions is reached when Kullervo is employed as a cowherd by the wife of the blacksmith Ilmarinen in Book XXXIII of the *Kalevala*. The jocular lady, "toothless old hag" that she was,

baked a loaf for him, gave him two great slabs of bread with oats below, corn on top, and a stone in the middle,

and with this provision sent Kullervo out with her cows. In revenge he slaughtered the whole herd, summoned a pack of wolves and bears, magically caused the wild beasts to appear in the form of cattle, and constructed various musical instruments from the bones of the slaughtered:

Then he made a pipe out of a cow-bone, and a whistle out of an ox-horn, and a cow-horn out of Tuomikki's leg, and a flute out of Kiryo's shin-bone; and he played on his pipe and tooted on his horn, three times on his native hills and six times at the opening of the pathway. But Ilmarinen's wife, the old woman of the blacksmith, had long been waiting for the milk and was looking forward to the summer butter. When she heard the tramping in the marshes and the uproar on the heath, she exclaimed:
"Praise be to Yumala! The horn sounds and the herd is coming! But where on earth has the wretch got a cow's horn and made himself a horn to blow on? Why does he come with such a noise, blowing with lungs fit to burst, splitting my ear-drums, and making my poor old head ache?"
Then Kullervo, son of Kalervo, answered and said: "The wretch found the horn in the marshes and picked the pipe out of the bog! Your herd is in the run, the cows are in the hurdle field. Go and smoke the cattle and milk the cows."

So Ilmarinen's wife told an old crone to do the milking:
"Go, old one, and milk the cattle and look after the beasts, for I can't leave my kneading."
Then Kullervo, son of Kalervo, answered and said:
"A good housewife, a clever housewife always milks the cows herself."
So Ilmarinen's wife went herself to smoke the cattle and look after the beasts, and herself milk the cows. She surveyed the herd and gazed on the horned cattle, saying:
"What a fine sight is the herd! The cattle are all sleek and glossy as though rubbed with lynx-skin, with wild sheep's wool! Their udders are full to bursting, the teats all hard."
She stooped down to milk them, bent down to coax the milk out, pulled once, pulled twice, pulled yet a third time, when a wolf sprang at her fiercely and a bear rushed to the attack. The wolf tore at her mouth, the bear tore at her leg, bit through the flesh of her calf and crushed the shin-bone.
Thus Kullervo, son of Kalervo, repaid the old woman's jest and had his revenge for the wicked old woman's mockery.

It is impossible to try to derive Finnish mythology from Greek mythology or vice versa; but it is equally impossible not to notice that Kullervo, the wonder-child and mighty youngster in one, ultimately reveals himself as Hermes and Dionysus. He reveals himself as Hermes because of the making of musical instruments in connection with the destruction of cattle (compare in particular that version of the mythologem of the Hermes child where the stealing and slaying of cattle precede the invention of the lyre);[20] he reveals himself as Dionysus because of what he does with the wild beasts and with his enemy. It is purely Dionysian—we can call it no less if we regard it in terms of Greek mythology—when the wolves and the bears are magicked by him into docile cows; and Dionysian that it is they who punish his enemy. With something of a shudder we recognize the tragic and ironic atmosphere of Euripides' *Bacchantes* as we read the dramatic scene of the milking of the wild beasts. The fate of the Etruscan pirates, Dionysus' enemies, who were punished by the onset of the beasts of prey, forms a still closer analogy to the vengeful epiphany of the child god of the Voguls.

20 Apollodorus, III, 10, 2.

5. *Narayana*

The child god, prototype of the wonderful orphan child, feeling quite at home in the primal element, reveals his full significance when the scene of his epiphany is water.

When we recall the epiphany of Kullervo, "sitting on the waves with a *rod of copper* in his hand," when we further recall his skill in clearing forests, we see at once his affinity with the little copper man in Book II of the *Kalevala*. But apart from that Kullervo was quite obviously neither "knee-high" nor "a span in height," but a giant for whom there was only "enough water in the lake to fill two ladles, and possibly—if exactly measured—part of a third." In Book II much the same thing happens, and moreover there is a striking parallel to this giantism, which seems incompatible with the hero's *childhood*, in another great mythology. The Hindu Markandeya, the eternally youthful hermit, encountered such a wonder-child at the termination of the last, and beginning of the present, cosmic year. The story is to be found in the Markandeyasamasya-parvan of the *Mahabharata*.

The wise hermit was wandering about over the face of the world-ocean and came to a nyagrodha tree (*Ficus indica*), in whose branches a "little boy" lay. The boy bade the hermit rest in him. Markandeya tells what then happened:[21]

The god offers me resting-place within him. I become weary of my long life and mortal existence. He opens his mouth, and I am drawn into it with irresistible force. There in his belly I see the whole world with its lands and cities, with the Ganges and the other rivers and the sea; the four castes, each at its work; lions, tigers, and wild pigs; Indra and all the heavenly host, the Rudras, the Adityas and the Fathers, snakes and elephants—in short, everything that I have seen in the world I see in his belly as I wander about in it. For more than a hundred years I wander about in it without coming to the end of his body; then I call upon the god and am instantly expelled from his mouth with the force of the wind. Once more I see him sitting in the branches of the nyagrodha tree with the signs of divinity upon him, clothed in yellow garments.

This child god, who is the god of the universe, is Narayana,

21 Reitzenstein and Schäder, *Studien zum antiken Synkretismus*, p. 83.

and according to the Indian etymology "he who has water as his dwelling-place."

However much in this story is in the style of the Indian world, e.g., the detailed description and the philosophical complexion of the whole, it cannot obscure the outlines of the mythologem. The picture of a divine being adrift in the solitude of the world-ocean, at once child and giant, is clear enough. In the less philosophical world of Finnish woodsmen the pictorial style is different, though the outline is the same. We have already met it in the Kullervo variation, but have still to make its acquaintance in the variation of the "little copper man."

Väinamöinen, the proto-shaman, rose from the ocean at the beginning of the world and met a wonder-child, we might almost say the Finnish counterpart to the Etruscan Tages. The name of the child, Sampsa ('Samson"), probably alludes to his gigantic strength.

Pellervoinen, son of the earth, Sampsa the slender-limbed boy, came to sow the land and scatter the seed.

He sows the land with trees, among them an oak which later rises to heaven and covers the sun and moon with its branches. The giant tree had to be felled, and Väinamöinen turns to the *power of water*. Here we see the Finnish counterpart to the Indian Narayana:

A man rose out of the sea, a hero from the waves. He was not the hugest of the huge nor yet the smallest of the small: he was as big as a man's thumb, the span of a woman. His helmet was of copper, copper the boots on his feet, copper the gauntlets on his hands, copper their lacings, copper the belt at his body, copper the axe in the belt, and the haft was a thumb's length and the blade a nail's length.

Väinamöinen, old and wily, pondered as follows:

"He looks like a man and has the mien of a hero, but he's no bigger than a thumb and is no higher than an ox-hoof." Then he said:

"You seem more like a man to me and the most contemptible of heroes. You're no better than a dead man and a face on you like a corpse!"

Whereat the little man from the sea, the hero of the waves, made answer:

"I am a man as you see—small, but a mighty water-hero. I have come to fell the oak-tree and splinter it to fragments!"

Väinamöinen, old and wily, scoffed:

"Why, you haven't the strength, you'll never be able to fell the magic oak-tree and splinter it to fragments!"

Scarcely had he said these words when, before his eyes, the little man was transformed into a giant. He stamped with his feet on the earth and his head reached up to the clouds; his beard flowed to his knees and his hair to his heels. His eyes were fathoms wide and his legs fathoms long; his knees were one and a half fathoms in girth and his hips two fathoms. He whetted his axe-blade and swiftly brought it to a fine edge, using six hard grindstones and seven polishing-stones.

Then he strode off, his wide trousers fluttering round his legs in the wind, and with one stride reached the sandy seashore. The next stride took him far into the dark land, and the third to the roots of the oak-tree. He struck the tree with his axe and smote it with the polished blade, once, twice, and a third time. Sparks flew from the axe and flame from the oak as he tried to bend the magic tree to his will. At the third stroke the oak-tree was shattered; the hundred boughs had fallen. The trunk stretched to the east, the top to the west, the leaves were scattered to the south and the branches to the north. . . .

Now that the oak-tree was felled and the proud trunk levelled, the sun shone again and the dear moon glimmered pleasantly, the clouds sailed far and wide and a rainbow spanned the heavens.

Book II of the *Kalevala,* from which these lines are taken, was undoubtedly written later than the passage just quoted from the *Mahabharata;* but, judging by its sense as a story about the liberation of light, it may be ranged alongside the earliest of primitive mythologems. It is true that similar features relating to a miraculous childhood are to be found among the near neighbours of the Finns, that is to say in the Russian folk-epics, the *byliny,* which a Russian scholar of the last century attempted to derive from Indian sources, namely the story of Krishna's childhood.[22] But the correspondence between the childhood adventures of Russian heroes and those of the Hindu gods is at best nothing but the borrowing of a sumptuous foreign garment—a borrowing mediated through many

22 V. Stasov in 1868; cf. W. Wollner, *Untersuchungen über die Volksepik der Grossrussen,* pp. 22ff.

hands. It is not only Russian or Indian saints and heroes that literature and legend adorn with, for instance, a birth which causes the world to shake and all the elements to tremble. Markandeya's and Väinamöinen's encounters with the giant child who is quite at home in the primal water show a correspondence at a much deeper level. The question, therefore, is not: Which of the two mythologems is the variant of the other? but: What is the common primary theme of which *both* are variants?

To this we have an answer of fundamental importance in both Hindu and Finnish mythology, and it leaves us in no doubt as to the nature of the divine figure whose essential characteristic is some kind of orphan's fate. Narayana is the same child god, i.e., the divine principle of the universe at the moment of its first manifestation, who is called Prajapati in the most ancient Indian sacrificial books, the *Brahmanas,* and even in the *Rig-Veda*.[23] He was hatched out of an egg which came into being in the waters of the beginning—hatched, that is to say, out of the void. He reclines on the back of sea-monsters, floats in the cup of water-flowers. He is the primordial child in the primordial solitude of the primordial element; the primordial child that is the unfolding of the primordial egg, just as the whole world is *his* unfolding. Thus far Indian mythology. Finnish mythology also has this primal element: the waters of the beginning. It is likewise familiar with the creation of the world from an egg, i.e., Munapojka, son of the egg, who also bears the name of Kullervo, the child for whom the sea contains not quite three ladlefuls of water and who may be recognized in the light-bringing "little copper man," the Finnish brother of the egg-born Prajapati and the yellow-garbed Narayana.

The ethnological investigation of myths, especially Frobenius' unfinished *Zeitalter des Sonnengottes,* points in two directions once a common basic theme has been ascertained. The first direction goes deep into the undermost layers of culture. For the mythologem under discussion is not confined to Indian or Finnish territory but evidently belongs to a very ancient period

[23] Cf. Hymn to Hiranyagarbha, the "Golden Germ" (*Rig-Veda,* X, 121), and the cosmogonic texts in K. F. Geldner, *Vedismus und Brahmanismus,* pp. 89ff. Also *Puranatexten* in H. Zimmer, *Maya.*

of mankind, an epoch compared with which not only Indian and Finnish sources but the whole character of Greek civilization as well are considerably younger. We shall not, however, begin with this hypothesis but, conversely, with mythologems whose provenance is known; and we shall utilize this hypothesis only when the mythologems themselves point to it and to nothing else. We shall content ourselves with the reflection that the basic theme may possibly be looming in the background wherever its variations—however faint and hard to recognize— are heard. In these cases we shall be sounding the primary note "offstage" and making audible again the melody that was on the point of fading away.

The other direction indicated, over and above this, in Frobenius' book points to solar mythology. Our basic theme, the image of a child hatched from an egg, a golden egg risen from the sea, includes all kinds of origination and birth, rising and coming into being, hence also *sunrise;* and in this way could be reduced to a "solar myth," the simple allegory of a natural phenomenon. But we should then be going beyond mythology and destroying the very world in which we are now trying to find our bearings. A situation would arise as in the well-known case of play.[24] Like mythology, play too can only be understood from the inside. Once we become conscious while playing that it is only an expression of vitality *and nothing more,* then the game is up. People who stand outside the game and regard it only in this light may be right in one point, but all their knowledge tells us nothing: they reduce play to non-play without understanding its essence. Similarly, our basic theme can be regarded as the human experience of sunrise, or a form of this experience; as a manifestation of it in dreams, visions, poetry —all human material. But this says nothing about the theme itself, nothing about the mythologem *qua* mythologem, which on the contrary is banished and dissolved like a dream. Can we say that this is the whole aim of understanding the art of poetry—to take an example analogous to mythology—mere banishment and dissolution?

If we stay within the bounds of mythology it is immediately evident why this reduction to a natural phenomenon—to "non-myth," as Frobenius calls it—is unjust and unsatisfactory and

[24] Cf. J. Huizinga, *Homo Ludens.*

44

therefore false. In mythology the allegorical value of a mythological image, such as the primordial image of all the child gods, and the allegorical value of the natural phenomena themselves, the rising sun and the arising of a new-born child, are reciprocal and *equal:* the rising sun and the new-born child are just as much an allegory of the Primordial Child as the Primordial Child is an allegory of the rising sun and of all the new-born children in the world. "Allegory" means "the description of one thing under the image of another." In both modes, the mode of the rising sun and the new-born human being, and the mode of the mythological child, the *world itself* tells of its origin, birth, and childhood. It speaks a symbolic language: one symbol is the sun, another the human child (in Goethe's words: "Alles Vergängliche ist nur ein Gleichnis"), and yet another the Primordial Child. The world tells us what *is* in the world and what *is true* in the world. A "symbol"[25] is not an "allegory," not just another way of speaking: it is an image presented by the world itself. In the image of the Primordial Child the world tells of its own childhood, and of everything that sunrise and the birth of a child mean for, and say about, the world.

The childhood and orphan's fate of the child gods have not evolved from the stuff of human life, but from the stuff of cosmic life. What appears to be biographical in mythology is, as it were, an anecdote that the world relates from its own biography, in dreams, visions, and—far more vividly and graphically than in these, more vividly and graphically than is ever possible for the "profane" arts—in mythology. To take mythological images as "allegories" of natural phenomena would be tantamount to robbing mythology of that nucleus which alone gives it life and meaning; it would be to rob it of its timelessly valid human and more than human, i.e., cosmic, content which, mythologically, is expressed in the images of gods just as, in music, mathematics, or philosophy, it is expressed in musical, mathematical, or philosophical ideas. Hence the relations of mythology to science, hence its spiritual character, by virtue of

---

25 I use the word in the same sense as I did in "Die Geburt der Helena," p. 173, and in my *Antike Religion,* carrying a stage further Goethe's distinction between symbol and allegory (*Farbenlehre* §916). Jung's theory of "natural symbols" and of dreams as products of nature is in agreement with this.

which it, like science, transcends the individual phenomenon. A mythologem speaks for itself, acts for itself, and is true of itself just like any other lofty scientific theory or musical creation, or indeed any true work of art.

6. *Apollo*

The primal water conceived as the womb, the breast of the mother, and the cradle, is a genuinely mythological image, a pictorial unit packed with meaning and brooking no further analysis. It crops up in Christianity as well, with especial clarity in the so-called theological discussion at the Court of the Sassanides.[26] There it was said of the mother who was pregnant with the child god, of Hera-Pege-Myria, that she carried in her womb, as in a *sea*, a ship freighted a thousandfold. "She has but *one* fish," it is added—the same that is also called her ship. The Christian allegory of the fish is a secondary phenomenon in the history of the mythological fish-symbol;[27] light will be thrown on this by mythologems still to be discussed. On the other hand the primal water as the womb is, in combination with fishes or fishlike creatures, a scientific idea—not merely a mythologem but a "philosophem" as well. As such it appears in both India and Greece.

Thales, the earliest Greek philosopher, asserted that everything came of water. In this he was only saying what Homer did, who speaks of Oceanus now as the "source of the gods," now as the "source of all things."[28] The same doctrine was held by Anaximander, the second Greek philosopher, but he applied it to living creatures and, according to a quotation from Censorinus, to mankind too:[29] "Fish or fishlike beings were born of warm water and earth. In these beings men were formed. The embryos remained in them till puberty. Then the fishlike beings opened. Men and women came out, already capable of sustaining themselves." From a Greek compilation we also

26 Cf. H. Usener, *Das Weihnachtsfest*, pp. 33ff.
27 Cf. idem, *Die Sintflutsagen*, pp. 223ff., also the collection of texts and monuments in F. J. Dölger's IXΘΥΣ (2nd edn.), which, however, places not mythology but cults and their monuments in the foreground.
28 *Iliad*, XIV, 201, 246, 302.
29 *De die natali*, 4, 7; Anaximander, A 30 (Diels and Kranz).

learn that these beings which arose "in the damp" were plant-like as well as fishlike, and that they were protected by a sheath of acanthus leaves.[30]

What are we to think of this account which transforms, as it were, the image of the Primordial Child born of a water-plant into scientific theory? At the beginning of the last century Oken, the romantic natural philosopher and scientist of Jena, propounded the same teaching.[31] He based himself neither on Anaximander nor on Censorinus, but on the scientific and philosophical knowledge of his time. According to him, the first man "must have developed in a uterus much larger than the human one. This uterus is the sea. That all living things have come from the sea is a truth nobody will dispute who has occupied himself with natural history and philosophy. Contemporary science disregards every other doctrine. The sea has nourishment for the foetus; slime to be absorbed through its membranes, oxygen for these membranes to breathe; the foetus is not confined, so that it can move its membranes at will even though it should remain swimming about for more than two years. Such foetuses arise in the sea by the thousand if they arise at all. Some are cast up immature on the shore and perish; others are crushed against rocks, others devoured by carnivorous fishes. What does that matter? There are still thousands left to be washed, soft and mature, on to the beaches, where they tear off their membranes, scratch for worms, and pull mussels and snails out of their shells."

Is this mythologem of Primordial Children intended seriously as science? In Oken's view unquestionably. And yet the closest parallel to it, outside Anaximander, is the story which Maui, a child god of the Polynesians, tells of his own birth. Apart from the sea, he had a divine mother who bore him on the seashore, and prematurely at that.[32] "I was born at the side of the sea, and was thrown by you"—so he tells his mother—"into the foam of the surf, after you had wrapped me up in a tuft of your hair, which you cut off for the purpose; then the seaweed formed and fashioned me, as caught in its long tangles

---

[30] Aetius, V, 19, 4; Anaximander, loc. cit.
[31] "Entstehung des ersten Menschen," in his "encyclopaedic journal" *Isis*, IV (1819), cols. 1117ff.
[32] Cf. Sir George Grey, *Polynesian Mythology*, p. 18.

the ever-heaving surges of the sea rolled me, folded as I was in them, from side to side; at length the breezes and squalls which blew from the ocean drifted me onto shore again, and the soft jelly-fish of the long sandy beaches rolled themselves round me to protect me." His divine ancestor, Tama-nui-ki-te Rangi, unwound the jelly-fishes and perceived a human being—Maui.

Oken himself betrays how fond he is of mythological images and above all those of the Primordial Child. In his essay on the origin of the first man he speaks also of the evolution of animals from plants, and remarks: "The animal, not merely poetically speaking but in actual fact, is the final flowering or true fruit of the plant, a genius rocked on the flower."[33] So that not only is his scientific thinking inadvertently mythological—the Maui parallel reveals as much—but he was also acquainted with the image of Prajapati, probably through the mythological studies of the Romantics. There is no need to describe precisely how this happened.[34] It is enough to observe that an image like "This world was water, a single flood: only Prajapati could be seen, sitting on a lotus-leaf"[35] is resuscitated in Oken's science. Besides the original god of the Hindus we could also mention Harpocrates, the Egyptian sun-child, who is often shown sitting on a lotus-blossom.[36]

These ancient mythologems do not undergo a *revival* in Anaximander, they simply go on living. In his age, the epoch of the great Ionian thinkers, the cosmic content that forms the nucleus of mythology passes over into Greek philosophy. What had hitherto been a highly convincing and effective set of divine figures now begins to turn into a rational teaching. In order to find such images in the process of transforming themselves into more and more rational mythologems, it was not necessary for Anaximander to turn to Oriental or even Egyptian sacred legends. His doctrines on the origin of man are an echo

[33] Loc. cit., 1119.

[34] Edward Moor, *The Hindu Pantheon*, had given many mythological images of the Hindus to the West. Creuzer refers to him in his *Symbolik und Mythologie* (2nd edn.; 1819). Cf. his illustrations, Pls. XXI (Narayana) and XXIV (Vishnu and Brahma).

[35] *Taittiriya-Aranyaka*, I, 23.

[36] Cf. Erman, *Die Religion der Ägypter*, p. 62; Creuzer, Pls. I, 6 and XVII, 2.

of the basic mythological theme with which we are concerned here. And, since we have a Greek "philosophem" before us, we must seek that theme first of all in Greek mythology.

Among the Greek gods we find Proteus, the ever-changing god of the sea, whose name means "the first being." The world of Oceanus and the world of Proteus, respectively primal water and sea, relate to one another as Primordial Child and new-born children; both are symbols—or *Gleichnisse* in the Goethean sense—of timeless birth and transformation. In Greek mythology, however, Oceanus and the sea are the abode of an immense number of peculiar divinities, but the Primordial Child, who might well be the prototype of the childhood of the great Olympians, is not immediately noticeable among them. Also the distance that separates the timeless inhabitants of Olympus —the mighty gods of Homer and Hesiod—from the world of being and becoming is far too great. How could we expect the Olympians to feel at home in the liquid element? All the more significant, then, is the fact that one of the Olympian children, Apollo, nevertheless has an affinity with the sea. This affinity is not merely that his birth-place, Delos, was originally a floating island,[37] although this merits attention from a mythological point of view. There is a deeper-lying affinity between Apollo and the sea, and this leads us to the classic Greek image of the connections between sea and child.

Like the womb of the mother, boundless water is an organic part of the image of the Primordial Child. The Hindus gave emphatic expression to this relationship. In the sacred legend Matsya-purana (named after the fish: *matsya*), Manu, the first man, says to the fish-bodied Vishnu: "How did this world, shaped like a lotus, spring from your navel in the lotus epoch when you lay in the world-ocean? You lay sleeping in the world-ocean with your lotus-navel; how did the gods and the host of seers arise in your lotus in those distant times, called forth by your power?"[38] The Primordial Child, here called Vishnu, is accordingly fish, embryo, and womb at once, something like Anaximander's primal being. Precisely such a "fish," which is simultaneously the bearer of children and youths and the changeling shape of a child god, is known to Greek mythol-

37 Pindar, fragments, 78–9 (ed. Bowra).
38 Zimmer, *Maya*, p. 49.

49

ogy. The Greeks called it the "uterine beast" and revered it above all the denizens of the deep, as though recognizing in it the ocean's power to bear children. This creature is the dolphin (δελφ means "uterus"),[39] an animal sacred to Apollo, who, in view of this relationship, is himself named Apollo Delphinios.

There is a whole series of Greek coins showing a dolphin carrying a boy or youth on its back.[40] Eros is another such boyish figure, the winged child whom we shall be discussing soon. Then we have Phalanthos and Taras, the last-named being the legendary founder and name-giver of the city of Tarentum. The boy riding on a dolphin often wears a flower in his hair,[41] and this seems to indicate a creature midway between fish and bud. Another numismatic figure approximates very closely in type—though without being dependent on it—to the Indian picture of a child asleep on a sea-monster, and this is Palaimon, *alias* Melikertes, lying dead or asleep on a dolphin, a child god who deserves special study from our point of view. There are Greek legends, translations of the mythological theme into purely human language, which tell how dolphins rescued their mortal favourites or carried the dead safely to shore.[42] But the names of those favoured of the dolphins are often unmistakably mythological, such as Koiranos ("Master"), or Enhalos ("he in the sea"). The story of Arion the Singer, who was rescued from the clutches of pirates by a dolphin, is the best-known example of these legends, proving at the same time that we are in the sphere of influence of Apollo, the lord-protector of poets. The second part of the Homeric hymn to Apollo, held by many to be a second hymn on its own, relates the epiphany of Apollo Delphinios. In the form of a dolphin the god conducts his first priests to Krisa, the bay on which his shrine has just been founded. His epiphany is an epiphany on a ship: the delphiform Apollo makes a place for himself on the ship of his future priests—a proof that here as in the Oriental Christian text mentioned at the beginning of this section (p. 46) "fish" and

39 Cf. δελφύς, "the womb," ἀ-δελφός, "the brother" (from the same mother): an old and reliable etymology in Athenaeus, IX, 375.
40 Cf. the plates of coins in Usener's *Sintflutsagen.*
41 Ibid., p. 157.
42 Evidence collected and interpreted by Usener, ibid., pp. 140ff.

"ship" are equivalent mythical images.[43] As variants of the same theme they mean the same when combined in one.

Apollo founds his Delphic shrine while yet a child.[44] Apart from Delos itself, the spot chosen forms a significant background for his childhood—the sea between Crete and the Greek mainland. It was there that the dolphin-epiphany occurred. No less significant is the seat of the celebrated oracle at Delphi. And the meaning remains the same. Just as the dolphin is the "womb" among animals, so Delphi is the womb among places: the name means that. For the Greeks the rocky landscape symbolized what was itself symbolized by the dolphin, the sea, the womb; it was a symbol of the uttermost beginning of things, of the non-being that came before being and the life that came afterwards; of the original condition of which every symbol says something different and new, a primal source of mythologems. To these mythologems also belongs the "mighty feat," so typical of child gods, that Apollo performed at Delphi, namely the destruction of the primeval monster. But this would carry us too far afield, as would a mythological appreciation of the island of Delos. It is enough to know what Ge and Themis, the first two Mistresses of Delphi who were worshipped along with Apollo, prove, or rather what the Earth Mother revered under these two names proves: that even a rocky landscape can appear in the mythology of the Primordial Child as the world of the Mother—the maternal world.

7. Hermes

The Homeric hymn to Hermes is a poem which, while paying homage to a Greek god as a divine child, describes him in such a way that the description became for us the classic Greek picture of divine childhood. Hermes' childhood is the special theme of the hymn, and, from this source alone, it casts its shadow on everything that is here under discussion. It is different with the hymn to Apollo. There Apollo shed his childhood almost immediately and we had to sketch in the childish features of the original mythologem more vividly, on the basis of

[43] Ibid., pp. 138f.
[44] Cf. Euripides, *Iphigenia in Tauris*, 1271.

other sources.[45] In the Hermetic hymn we cannot forget for a moment that the god who is being honoured is a child.

In archaic vase-paintings, Apollo and his sister Artemis are shown in the arms of their mother Leto, just as Hermes is shown lying in a cradle. But where Hermes also appears with Leto, then this indicates other relations between him and Leto's children than those mentioned in the Hermetic hymn.[46] In the latter, Apollo is the full-grown god contrasted with the child Hermes, while in the vase-paintings the situation is reversed. Mythology admits both: the presence of a full-grown Hermes beside a child Apollo as well as the other way round. In such cases the fact that a god is shown as a child does not mean that he is of lesser power or significance. On the contrary, where one divinity appears among the others as a child it means that its epiphany occupies the central place, or, to be more accurate, the epiphany is there always the epiphany of a child god. The question is: For what reason does the divine *child* in the god concerned suddenly come to the fore?

What has Hermes in him that he should thus become the hero of the Greek classic of divine childhood? The story of the Hermetic hymn is separated from the fluid state of primeval mythology by two layers, both of which helped to clarify and define it. The first layer is the Greek pantheon itself. It is as though that cosmic substance which, in the godlike figures of the original mythologems, now concentrates its whole radiance on one point, now scatters in all directions, now mingles with darkness, were broken up and refracted in the world of Greek gods like a spectrum. The place each divinity occupies in this spectrum, the colour it has, is determined for all time, the various possibilities being limited by the characteristics of each individual figure, who is one aspect of the world. The other clarifying and formative layer is the Olympian hierarchy of Homeric poetry, which immutably fixes each god's relations to all the rest. The state of genuinely mythological fluidity, such as the swopping of Apollo's and Hermes' childhood and adult-

45 Cf., besides Euripides, *Iphigenia in Tauris,* Apollonius Rhodius, *Argonautica,* I, 760.
46 Cf. L. Radermacher, *Der homerische Hermeshymnus,* pp. 201f; also Kerényi, *Hermes der Seelenführer.*

hood, is only possible outside the Olympian hierarchy. The childhood of the gods is outside the hierarchy altogether. In a more primitive state, which was prior to this hierarchy, the Olympians were child gods. So too was Hermes. The unknown poet of the so-called "Homeric" hymn to Hermes solved the problem of bringing the more primitive elements into line with the Olympian hierarchy and expressing them in those terms.

The figure of Hermes never lost that more primitive character; it persisted alongside the Olympian hierarchy and the Homeric hymn, and it determined Hermes' "colour-band" in the cosmic spectrum from the very beginning. Hermes is the only, or almost the only, one among the great Olympians (Apollo alone in his capacity as Agyieus shares this primitive feature with him) whose presence is marked by an upright piece of wood or stone, the "herm."[47] Sacred emblems of this kind, in which it is easy to recognize the naked phallus, were said in ancient times to be "in the Kyllenic manner,"[48] no doubt because Hermes possessed these emblems not only in the Elian port of Kyllene[49] but also on the Arcadian Mount Kyllene,[50] his birth-place. The latter was the more celebrated and is connected with the story of his childhood. The Kyllenic emblem was a gigantic phallus of wood. In the Boeotian village of Thespiae a bare stone was the sacred emblem of another divine child—Eros,[51] whom we must mention along with Hermes not merely on this account.

Eros is a divinity very closely related by nature to Hermes.[52] Greek mythology always preserved him in child-form, and the mythologem of the birth of the Primordial Child was also referred to him. His nature, explicit in his name—Eros: "demanding love"—is more uniform in tone than that of Hermes. Nevertheless, the same ground-tone is unmistakable in Hermes too. The universe knows a melody—so we could describe these

---

[47] The ἕρμανες, heaps of stone in honour of Hermes, presupposes on etymological grounds the ἕρμα, or pillar, just as λίθαξ presupposes λίθος.

[48] Philostratus, *Vita Apollonii Tyanae*, VI, 20.

[49] Pausanias, VI, 26, 5.

[50] Ibid., VIII, 17, 2.

[51] Ibid., IX, 27, 1.

[52] Cf. Kerényi, *Hermes der Seelenführer*, p. 64.

somewhat complex phenomena—whose theme is the eternal relationship of love, thievery, and "affairs."[53] In the masculine key this melody is Hermes; in the feminine key the same melody—and yet not the same, since man and woman are different—is Aphrodite. The essential affinity between Eros and Hermes is best shown in their relations with the goddess of love. Aphrodite and Eros go together as essentially concomitant forces or principles. Eros, the divine child, is Aphrodite's natural companion and consort. But if the masculine and feminine aspects of the nature common to both Aphrodite and Eros be comprised in *one* figure, this figure immediately becomes Hermes and Aphrodite rolled into one: Hermaphroditos. This bisexual being has its genealogical place in the Olympian hierarchy as the child of Aphrodite and Hermes.[54] Hellenistic and still later representations of it are well known. Yet the "hermaphrodite" is not in any sense the invention of a late and decadent art; by the time art had become decadent the hermaphrodite had lost its original meaning and evolved into a mere decoration—a very charming one. No; the hermaphrodite is a primitive type of divine image.[55] In ethnology there is a whole literature on this subject.[56] The primitive character of this type in the ancient world is attested by the common cult of Hermes and Aphrodite in Argos in ancient times,[57] and by the Cyprian cult of Aphroditos, the male Aphrodite,[58] which was in accord with Argive customs.[59] The Etruscans knew both divinities from the remotest times under the same Greek, or

---

53 Cf. the erotic meaning of the Latin word for theft (*furtum:* W. F. Otto, *The Homeric Gods,* p. 111, n. 34), and the German word *Liebeshandel.* For the Homeric Hermes-world, see Otto's classic account of Hermes, ibid., pp. 104ff.

54 Ovid, *Metamorphoses,* IV, 288.

55 Cf. J. P. B. Josselin de Jong, "De Oorsprong van den goddelijken bedrieger," pp. 5ff.

56 J. Winthuis, *Das Zweigeschlechterwesen* (1928); *Die Wahrheit über das Zweigeschlechterwesen* (1930); *Einführung in die Vorstellungswelt primitiver Völker* (1931); *Mythos und Kult der Steinzeit* (1935).

57 Pausanias, II, 19, 6.

58 Nilsson, *Griechische Feste,* pp. 373f.

59 The feast of Aphrodite called "Hybristika" in the month of Hermes. Cf. Nilsson, pp. 371f., and Jessen in Pauly and Wissowa, *Realencyclopädie der classischen Altertumswissenschaft,* s.v. Hermaphroditos.

rather, pre-Greek, name: Hermes as *turms*, Aphrodite as *turan*.[60] The one is the "master" (ὁ τύραννος), the other the "mistress" (ἡ τύραννος): an age-old pair,[61] or, to delve more deeply, two aspects of the same primal being.

The mythologem of the emergence of the child god out of the original condition of things is, in Greece, connected with two divinities, Eros and Aphrodite, and it occurs accordingly in two variations: as the birth of a bisexual "primal being" and as the birth of Aphrodite. The first variation is Orphic, so called because contained in a cosmogony ascribed to Orpheus. In the beginning, so we read in this variation,[62] a bisexual being was born of an egg. Orpheus called it Phanes, while in Aristophanes, in the famous Chorus of the Birds, the primal being that came out of the egg bears the name of Eros. We have no reason to suspect in the bisexual nature of this being a secret doctrine of later date, which always remained alien to Greek thought and was invented for a special sect. The Aphrodite cults alluded to, which, because of the exchange of clothing between the men and women participating in them, caused sexual differences to appear only as possible variations of one and the same being, are in harmony with the meaning of the Orphic mythologem. The winged figure of the egg-born Eros can likewise hardly be separated from the winged goddesses of archaic times, and the meaning of this figure lies where ritual and cosmogonic hermaphroditism lies. The two things, wingedness and bisexuality, hark back to the same pre-human, indeed pre-childish, still completely undifferentiated state—one of whose forms of expression is the primal water. Eros is the first among the dolphin-riding children. We can now put this significant fact in another way, and say that the winged boy bestriding a dolphin and holding in his hand a strange beast like a cuttle-fish[63] is none other than the Primordial Child whose home is the primal water, and the best-known of whose many names is "Eros."

---

[60] Cf. C. Clemen, *Die Religion der Etrusker*, p. 35.

[61] Cf. Plutarch, *Conjugalia praecepta*, 138d.

[62] *Orphicorum fragmenta* (ed. Kern), No. 56.

[63] Cf. the medallion in relief on a Tarentine vase, reproduced in Usener's *Sintflutsagen* as frontispiece.

In one respect the other variation expresses something even more profound, and is itself more comprehensive. It is a well-known mythologem; in his *Theogony*, Hesiod relates the birth of Aphrodite as follows. In vain was the race of the Titans born of the marriage of Heaven and Earth—Uranos and Gaia. Uranos tried to prevent his children from emerging out of the womb of the earth, but in the end the youngest of them, Kronos, with his mother's help, did a terrible thing. With a sickle he cut off his father's procreative organ as his father was approaching his mother, and threw it into the sea. *From it* there arose Aphrodite out of the foaming waves.[64] In this version, as in a melody that utters the unutterable, the beginning and end of an ontogeny coincide: begetting and birth are identical, as also the begetter and the begotten. The phallus is the child, and the child —Aphrodite—an eternal stimulus to further procreation. The image of the foam-born goddess puts the idea of genesis and timeless beginning as succinctly, as perfectly as only the language of mythology can. The birth of Aphrodite is a variation on the mythologem of the Primordial Child which makes intelligible for us—intelligible in the only way possible to Greek religion, the mythological way—how it is that the stone in Thespiae is identical with Eros, and the Kyllenic emblem with the Hermes child. We also understand why procreation and birth, herms and mythological images—all variations on the Primordial Child —are equivalent symbols expressing the same unutterable thought.

The original herm stood on the mountain where the child Hermes was born in a cave. This cave was a place of primeval chaos, the nature of which is indicated in the name "Delphi." At another very ancient spot sacred to Hermes,[65] the god possessed not only a herm but also a spring with fishes in it, which belonged to him and were not allowed to be caught. In the Homeric hymn there is no trace of these archaic characteristics; there the cave appears as a habitation worthy of a goddess, the mother of Zeus' son. The Hermes child takes his place at once in the Olympian hierarchy and, as he leaves the cave, the sun and moon shine down on him. In the hymn only such

64 Hesiod, *Theogony*, 168–206.
65 Pharai in Achaia; Pausanias, VII, 22, 4.

unusual things occur as are possible in moonlight, the sort of thing characteristic of the Hermetic world Homer knows and acknowledges. The Homeric poet is restrained. He achieves great art because he manages to portray, in the figure of a child, an aspect of the world which is at the same time a whole cosmos on its own. Hermes, in relation to the other grown-up gods, keeps within the bounds of his childishness, whereas the footprints of an Indian child god are always the footprints of a giant even when the child is a mere midget.[66] The Greek poet has to resort to considerable cunning in order to make such giant footprints plausible in Hermes' case. This only shows Hermes the better as the father of all cunning.

His first encounter in the Homeric world brings something very primitive, mythologically speaking, to light. The fortuitous nature of this encounter is typical of Hermes, and it is primitive only insofar as chance and accident are an intrinsic part of primeval chaos. In fact, Hermes carries over this peculiarity of primeval chaos—accident—into the Olympian order. Hermes meets a tortoise, a primeval-looking creature, for even the youngest tortoise could, by the looks of it, be described as the most ancient creature in the world. It is one of the oldest animals known to mythology. The Chinese see in it the mother, the veritable mother of all animals.[67] The Hindus hold Kaśyapa in honour, the "tortoise-man," father of their eldest gods,[68] and say that the world rests on the back of a tortoise, a manifestation of Vishnu: dwelling in the nethermost regions, it supports the whole body of the world.[69] The Italian name *tartaruga* keeps alive a designation dating from late antiquity, according to which the tortoise holds up the lowest layer of the universe, namely Tartarus (Ταρταροῦχος).[70] Further, although in less striking a manner, the tortoise like the dolphin is one of the shapes of Apollo.[71] In the Homeric hymn it appears only as a most innocuous beast, the plaything and sacrificial victim of an ingenious child, albeit divine. The tortoise seems to be no more

[66] Cf. Zimmer, *Maya,* p. 202.
[67] Ibid., p. 7.
[68] Ibid., p. 206.
[69] Ibid., pp. 124f.
[70] Etymology from R. Egger.
[71] Antoninus Liberalis, 32, 2.

"cosmic" than the playthings of gods generally are, when the gods happen to be Greek gods and do not trespass beyond the natural order of things. The tortoise merely undergoes a Homeric miracle. Something divine glimmers through, the chance for a divine game: Hermes makes it into a lyre.

But can we not say that the invention of the first lyre, which the Hermes child gave to Apollo as a gift, is in a certain sense "cosmic"? We are speaking here of a *cosmic content* that can express itself in a mythological, philosophical, mathematical, musical, or any other way. This is only possible because of the nature of the cosmic content as such. As an idea, that is to say intellectually, it can be expressed in purely philosophical and mathematical terms. But it is at the same time pictorial and musical. Of the pictorial wealth of mythology we can best speak in terms of music. C. de Tolnay was the first to see the musical nature of this cosmic content in the most pictorial of all material—classical painting. And another Hungarian scholar, D. Kövendi, showed how for the Greeks the birth of the divine child, in his capacity as Eros Proteurhythmos, signified the rhythmic-musical creation of the universe.[72] The lyre in the hand of the Primordial Child expresses the musical quality of the world quite apart from the poet's intention. It is first and foremost characteristic of Hermes himself. The Homeric poet sensed the musical nature of the universe as essentially Hermetic and located it in the Hermes colour-band of the world spectrum. In all probability the poet was not seeking this primeval music, but its higher, Apollonian form. If, however, the boy riding a dolphin (who sometimes bears the name of Phalanthos) has a lyre in his hand,[73] we are driven to think not merely of his relations with Apollo Delphinios but of a more general, primary connection that existed before all specific names: the connection of water, child, and music.

8. *Zeus*

Zeus, the protector and mainstay, ruler and representative of the Olympic order—which is *his* order and is in absolute con-

---

[72] *Sziget*, III, pp. 35ff. (Hungarian). Cf. Tolnay, "The Music of the Universe," 1943, pp. 83ff.
[73] Cf. Usener, *Stintflutsagen*, p. 159, 3.

trast to the original "fluid" condition of things—is the "biggest boy" among the child gods. He too was a divine child before he became the "father of gods and men." We must therefore ask a sort of historical question: What does this "before" mean in the history of religion?

We know that the biographical sequence "child god: adult god" has only an incidental significance in mythology. It serves to group different mythologems together, or it acquires a special significance only when actual *cosmic growth* is symbolized in the growing god, as in the divine child of Virgil's Fourth Eclogue. It is the same with the death of certain divinities: it is never a biographical death, always a cosmic one. Zeus has no "life history," but, since his rule is an essential part of his nature, there is a mythologem of how this rulership came to be attained, a story of struggle and victory and new world-order, a story which reveals the *meaning* of the new world founded by Zeus. In mythology the child god can exist side by side with the "ageless god," and independent of him. Consequently it is quite possible for the earlier life-phase of a divinity to appear considerably later in the history of religion. This was the case with the classical, youthful figures of gods whom the Greeks knew in the archaic period as bearded men.

We cannot deny the priority of the Primordial Child, whose various reflections are the individual child gods, when compared with the Olympian world-picture. Wherever we meet him in Greek mythology he seems to have broken through the barrier of the Olympian hierarchy or—in the case of the dolphin-riding boy—to be something of a survival. Such is the general impression we have gained from our study of ancient material, without giving specific proofs. We have not used the terms "primitive," "primordial," "primeval," etc., in a chronological sense any more than we did in our study of the birth of Helen;[74] what we meant was a timeless quality which can crop up as much in later times as in earlier ones. We can call psychological research—above all Jung's—to witness in this respect, since it has demonstrated exactly, step by step, the existence of "archaic" elements in the psychic life of modern man. Here as there the terms "archaic" and "primitive" have

---

[74] Kerényi, "Die Geburt der Helena," p. 16.

no chronological significance, though they have a strictly scientific meaning. This meaning lies in the fact that the phenomena so described have an actual correspondence with certain earlier phenomena in the history of mankind, which can be determined chronologically. Mixed forms, or, to put it in another way, undifferentiated forms can be shown to exist in an early period of Greek art.

The relative earliness of the Primordial Child becomes very probable in the light of such considerations, but it is not proved. We have not yet inquired into the origins of the mythological image under discussion. It cannot be emphasized too much that the question of its origins can only be solved on a planetary scale, or, to express it in more human terms, in a way that takes account of man's whole existence from every conceivable scientific angle. We must content ourselves here with the likelihood that a common basic theme is present in the background wherever we hear the harmony of its variations. As to *when* this basic theme came into being, all we have said is that it may perhaps be relegated to a period compared with which not only the Indian and Finnish sources are considerably younger, but the whole character of Greek culture as well. We have drawn no conclusions from the Indian, Finnish, or other parallels as to the time or place of origin. We leave undecided in principle the question of whether the place of origin was an "ideal" place, that is to say, the possible result of the human mind's seeing the same aspect of the "cosmic content" everywhere in the same image, or whether it was a definite geographical focus of culture where the great mythological archetypes were created for all time. For the present it is not a question of the place of origin so much as of the most accessible layer underlying the Olympian order. In the case of the child Zeus the primacy of the Primordial Child, which we have conceived only in a very general way, can be proved in the history of religion.

In a sacred hymn probably composed *c*. 300 B.C. and graved upon stone much later in Crete,[75] Zeus is apostrophized as the "biggest boy"—μέγιστος κοῦρος. This hymn is typical of Cretan religion in historical times. It hails the youthful Zeus in his sanctuary situated on, or rather, as the sanctuary was probably

[75] *Anthologia Lyrica Graeca* (ed. Diehl), II (1925), pp. 279f.; trans. into English by J. E. Harrison, *Themis*, p. 7.

a cave, *in* Mount Dikte. The god was depicted "beardless," in the form of a youth,[76] and thus, like the dolphin-riding boy of the coins, appeared as a young Apollonian figure. This was in keeping with classical and post-classical taste. Originally the nature of this spot, which is named among the birth-places of Zeus, was exemplified by the figure of a child. All this is characteristically Cretan, as can be shown from a very carefully conducted investigation that takes all the monuments into account.[77] Two indisputable points have been ascertained which enable us to form an opinion on Cretan religion. The first[78] is that the child god must be regarded as a given fact in Crete, something to which all the other local mythological variants subsequently became attached. Besides the one already mentioned, two other mountains are indicated as the birth-place of Zeus. And Zeus is far from being the only child god in Crete to be exposed and nourished by animals. For secondly,[79] not only is the child god itself a proven fact in Crete, but its orphan's fate as well. For the Cretans, Zeus, like the other child gods of more modest rank, was a child abandoned by its mother.

The island of Crete was the centre of a very rich and important civilization that preceded the Greek in the Eastern Mediterranean. It is almost impossible to think of the peculiar features of the Creto-Grecian religion as altogether independent of that more ancient period of culture. Evidently we have to do with a peculiarity of this kind here. Some investigators have believed that they could see two originally completely independent divinities in the Zeus child of the Cretans and Zeus the Thunderer and Ruler of the World on the Hellenic mainland.[80] But how such totally different figures, if they are not an ideal unity, could possibly be designated with the same name is a question to which no satisfactory answer has of course been forthcoming.[81] Neither can any proof be adduced that Zeus' birthplaces on the mainland are really later and secondary, the

[76] *Etymologicon magnum*, s.v. Δίκτη; Nilsson, *The Minoan-Mycenaean Religion and its Survivals in Greek Religion*, p. 476.
[77] Ibid., pp. 471ff.
[78] Ibid., p. 469.
[79] Ibid., p. 471.
[80] Welcker, *Griechische Götterlehre*, II, pp. 218ff.; Nilsson, p. 462.
[81] As attempted in Nilsson, pp. 469f.

result of competition with the Cretans.[82] On the other hand, it is a striking fact that certain extremely ancient features are associated with the birth-places on the mainland, which in Crete have receded into the background or disappeared altogether.

A peculiar antiquity attaches to everything that has been handed down about Zeus' Arcadian birth-place, Mount Lykaion.[83] Here the birth-place is not confined to a cave; no cave is even mentioned. That in itself seems to be a contrast with the Cretan story. But when we examine the Cretan localities more closely,[84] we find that there too the mountain itself is every bit as important as the cave: the cave is a part of the mountain which forms the sacred spot, just as Mount Kyllene is the sanctuary of Hermes. An "unmentionable sacrifice" that took place at the Dikte shrine is marked by a spring.[85] On the other hand, we know what it was that was sacrificed to Zeus on Mount Lykaion. It is expressed very inaccurately when the scholars speak of a "human sacrifice": an infant was sacrificed, obviously to the divine infant.[86] The place was a true place of the dead, where the phantoms cast no shadow; whoever trod its precincts was bound to die within a year.[87] Another tradition speaks of a birth-place of Zeus in Thebes, where the Islands of the Blest were supposed to be.[88] Both traditions explain why nobody could die in Zeus' Cretan cave, and why even the thieves that broke in were transformed into birds—among others into a bird with the name of "Kerberos."[89] In all these places we find ourselves beyond life as we know it: either we cease to exist, or are eternal, outside time. Water, too, is associated with the birth-place of Zeus in Arcady.[90] Water nymphs —in particular Nede, the goddess of the river that bears her name—became the first nurses of the new-born child. In Zeus' birth-place in Messenia, Mount Ithome, water was brought

82 Ibid., p. 463.
83 Pausanias, VIII, 2 and 38, 6f.
84 Nilsson, p. 462, 2.
85 Athenaeus, 375 F.
86 Pausanias, VIII, 2, 3; the child god Palaimon also received child-sacrifices on Tenedos, cf. Lycophron, 229, with scholium.
87 Pausanias, VIII, 38, 6; cf. Kerényi, *Niobe*, p. 200.
88 Tzetzes, scholium in Lycophron, 1194.
89 Antoninus Liberalis, 19.
90 According to Callimachus' *Hymn to Zeus*, 15–41.

daily to the shrine of Zeus Ithomatas from the spring in which he was first bathed.[91] Water probably played a part in the Cretan cult of Zeus besides milk and honey, the ritual aliment of infants; but the traditions of the mainland are most eloquent in this respect and point as a whole more clearly to the basic theme than do the Cretan.

The basic theme is the same both in Crete and on the mainland: the appearance of the Primordial Child in a primitive spot connected with the maternal elements—rock and water. In both cases the antiquity, the extreme age, of its variants is unquestionable. And yet we have no adequate grounds for concluding that the mythologem and cult of the Primordial Child came out of Crete to Arcady, Messenia, and Thebes. Compared with the traditions concerning the cult on Mount Lykaion, all modern reconstructions of the Cretan cult are so many insubstantial shades. An older layer underlying the more recent Homeric-Greek layer seems unmistakable; but two things are still out of place. We cannot with any certainty ascribe the older layer geographically to Crete as a place of origin of the cult, and the newer layer to Hellas as its receiver; nor can we make a clean division between Cretan or Minoan-Mycenaean religion on the one hand, and Greek on the other. We get a working basis for the division only when we take into account another portion of the Mediterranean world, the area of the ancient Italic and the Roman religion.

"Ancient Italic" and "Roman" cannot be distinguished as purely chronological or geographical layers, nor can these terms be linked up exclusively with new migrations of racial groups. Nonetheless, the ancient Italic layer is older and more saturated with old Mediterranean elements than the Roman.[92] Older, but contemporary too. Taking up our stand in early Rome we find characteristically Roman elements already present in the religion, while at the same time the ancient Italic style of religion still persists in sacred localities outside Rome. There are in fact two styles which can be distinguished from one another exactly. Characteristic of the Roman style of religion, compared with the ancient Italic, is something negative, namely the absence of

[91] Pausanias, IV, 33, 1.
[92] Cf. F. Altheim, *A History of Roman Religion*, pp. 46ff.

mythologems. That is the result of a process fully in keeping with the Roman mentality, for which the word "de-mythification" (*Entmythisierung*) has recently been coined.[93] If it was intended to say that the true religion of the Romans was wholly devoid of myths, with a purely political idea at its centre, then such a term would be mistaken and misleading. The Roman religion was neither empty of myth[94] nor, in its mature form, did it show itself incompatible with the myths of the Homeric order. Against what, then, was the process of "de-mythification" directed?

One certain example of the kind of thing that was debarred from Roman religion by de-mythification is the figure of *Juppiter puer,* the child Jupiter. The divinity corresponding to the Greek Zeus was known in Rome only as *pater,* or *Ju-piter.* Another of his manifestations, the subterranean Vediovis, was also worshipped in Rome, but they tried to separate him as far as possible from Jupiter's heavenly-father aspect. The Vediovis who was portrayed as an Apollonian youth can only be thought of as the beardless, youthful Zeus of the Cretans. Originally he was a *Juppiter puer* like the one who had his cult in the immediate neighbourhood of Rome, in Praeneste;[95] an underground cult in the grottoes of the mountain on which the town was built, beside a sacred spring connected with the goddess Fortuna. Grottoes, water, rocks, even Fortuna herself recall the undifferentiated state in which we are accustomed to meet the Primordial Child.[96]

He appears still more clearly in the cult of Jupiter Anxurus in Tarracina, south of Rome. His shrine, set on a rocky prominence of the foothills, juts into the oceanic world of the Tyrrhenian. An ancient Italic form of Jupiter, he belongs to the same group as the Roman Vediovis and the *Juppiter puer* of Praeneste.[97] How much his cult concentrated on his childhood is shown by a discovery made during the excavations on his temple.[98] This is a collection of leaden votive offerings that we

93 C. Koch, *Der römische Juppiter,* pp. 9ff.
94 Kerényi, *Die antike Religion,* ch. vi.
95 Koch, pp. 47ff.
96 Further details in a long-awaited work of A. Brelich, *Fortuna.*
97 Koch, pp. 82ff.
98 L. Borsari, "XII.—Del Tempio di Giove Anxure," pp. 96ff.

can only call children's playthings—a toy kitchen.[99] Among the sacrificial kitchen utensils there are fifteen dishes, most of them empty, but three with fishes on them; of the two gridirons in the collection the larger contains no food, but two fishes are lying on the smaller. The divinity probably received fish-offerings, which is not without precedent in the old Italic style of Jupiter cult.[100]

Thus the mythologem of the Primordial Child existed in ancient Italy as in Crete and in the older strata of Greek religion on the mainland. It was as alien to the Homeric hierarchy of the gods as it was to the genuinely Roman pantheon, or rather, it became alienated from them. We cannot with any certainty derive it from Crete, nor ascribe it exclusively to the sphere of old Mediterranean culture. We can, however, assert that in Crete there existed an older sphere of culture that embraced pre-Homeric Greece and ancient Italy, the spirit of which was more fundamentally mythological than the spirit of Homer or Rome. The mythologem of the Primordial Child is characteristic not of this more recent but of an older mentality. That the spirit of this older sphere was fundamentally mythological is certain, though its temporal and spatial boundaries are not so certain. For an age of primitive mythology still projects into the historical epochs of Greece and Italy.

We have now won a vantage-point from which the classic youthfulness of the Greek gods can be understood and judged correctly, not merely ontologically, as in our first chapter, but historically. Central to the Olympian order which replaced the primitive mythological state of things is Zeus the Father. In spite of that, he is represented in his Diktean birth-place as a beardless youth and worshipped in this form elsewhere in Crete.[101] Thus far those scholars are right who interpreted the μέγιστος κοῦρος of the hymn as the "biggest boy." Greek religion in its classical form is the religion of the world-order established by Zeus, as related in Hesiod. The images of divine childhood are relegated to the margin of the new Zeus world, and the Primordial Child of mythology remains outside its borders. In

99 Reproduced and interpreted by Dölger, ΙΧΘΥΣ, Pl. 47, and V (1932), pp. 1ff. Dölger's reference to Venus is superfluous.
100 Ibid., II, pp. 297ff.
101 Nilsson, p. 479.

this religion the youth is a more acceptable manifestation of divinity than the child.

The youthfulness of Greek divinities is the result of a transformation, albeit a different one from that which can be deduced from the artistic remains by themselves. In the monuments, the reign of the bearded gods precedes the age of the youths. We see now that the reign of the child is still older. The image of the Primordial Child breaks through, transfigured into the ideal figure of the youth. That such a transformation is possible is implicit in the meaning of the Greek word for "boy," and is therefore attested by etymology as well. The (supposedly) male child while yet in its mother's womb is called κοῦρος;[102] the ephebe and the youth capable of bearing arms is still a κοῦρος. Eros himself appears in well-known vase-paintings as a winged ephebe.[103] The divine youths of classical Greek art —the classic ideal of Apollo, Hermes, and the young Dionysus— are not to be taken as indicating a general rejuvenescence of the Hellenic world. It is not that the bearded divinities have gone back on their development (even in the Iliad Hermes appears as a youth), but that the idealized ephebe of the "agonal" age gave validity to the divine *child* in a somewhat maturer form more in keeping with the essence of those divinities than that of the full-grown man. Also, the hermaphroditic character of the Primordial Child gained acceptance when the ideal of the *nymph-like* boy appeared in Greek culture. It is as though this were only the recrudescence of the bisexual Primordial Child in secularized form.

9. *Dionysus*

Not all the child gods of the older and younger Mediterranean world can be mentioned here. Yet besides Zeus, Apollo, and Hermes we must also recall one of the greatest—Dionysus.

W. F. Otto, in his book on this divinity,[104] devotes a beautiful chapter to the latter's profound connections with the "humid element." Suffice it here only to recapitulate what is most im-

---

102 *Iliad*, VI, 59.
103 Cf. Figs. 169 and 171 in J. E. Harrison's *Prolegomena to the Study of Greek Religion*.
104 *Dionysus*, pp. 148ff., where the evidence for what follows is to be found.

portant. The Iliad speaks of the sea as Dionysus' refuge, where Thetis acts as a nurse to the young god. According to a Laconian variant of the mythologem, the Dionysus child was washed ashore in a chest with his dead mother. Another of Dionysus' nurses, Ino, the mother of the child god Palaimon, also appears as a sea-goddess. In his cult at Lerna, Dionysus is summoned to rise from the deep. He is also known as Πελάγιος ("he of the sea"), Λιμναῖος ("he of the lake"), and Λιμναγένης ("the lake-born"). His epiphany on a ship, in the shape, according to a Homeric hymn, of a boy, distinguishes him in the same sense that Apollo Delphinios was distinguished. Only about one thing are we not altogether clear: How could anybody, even a god, come out of the depths of the sea on a ship, which *floats* on the water?

We now know that the prime element whose symbol—and nothing more than a symbol—is the sea has the peculiarity that floating in it and rising out of it mean the same thing. Both imply a state of being not yet separated from non-being, yet still being. The dolphin-riding boy of the coins—the classic Greek representation of the Primordial Child-god—is sometimes shown winged, sometimes holding a lyre, sometimes holding the club of Heracles.[105] Accordingly he is to be viewed now as Eros, now as an Apollonian, now as a Hermetic or Herculean figure; we must take him, in fact, as these divinities while they were in the womb of the universe, floating, in their embryonic state, on the primal waters. It is not for nothing that the cupids of late antiquity have the attributes of the great gods; not for nothing that their activities embrace (as in the frescoes of the Pompeian Casa dei Vetti) the whole gamut of existence. They are the ground-tone which the world of late antiquity, deaf to all subtler melodies, could still perceive. The Primordial Child—to continue the metaphor—is the *monotone* that consists of all notes at once, the *Leitmotiv* that develops into all the other divine "figures." It develops first and foremost into its polar opposite—Zeus. For the "biggest boy" of the Cretan hymn is the summation and epitome of all the *undifferentiated* possibilities as well as of all those that are realized in the pure forms of the gods.

105 Usener, *Sintflutsagen*, p. 159, 3.

In this way, then, as his polar opposite, Zeus stands closest to the Primordial Child—for the one pole always implies the possibility of the other and, together with it, forms a higher unity, as is here the case with the child Zeus and Zeus the Father. Dionysus stands in a different relationship to the Primordial Child. He is *so close* to it that—to stick to our metaphor and express the gods acoustically—he is the overtone to the groundtone. The dolphin-riding boy is more often shown with the attributes of Dionysus than with those of any other god.[106] And in no Greek cult, save that of Zeus, is the childhood state so important as in the cult of Dionysus. Here we have the same sort of identity we met with in the Hermetic sphere. There the god and the herm were the same; here something is hidden in the winnowing-basket and is called Λικνίτης—"the slumberer in the winnowing-basket."[107] It is the child Dionysus, and in exactly the same way that the Kyllenic emblem was the child Hermes. In some incomprehensible, or perhaps only mythological, manner Dionysus is identical on the one hand with the emblem that was carried round in his cult and with the symbol concealed in the winnowing-basket, namely the phallus;[108] and on the other hand with the "bearded god" who, in one of his appellations, is "man and woman" in *one person*.[109] Dionysus was bisexual in the first place, not merely in the "effeminate" later portrayals. The rounded figures of his archaic companions, the daemonic dancers whom he has possessed, are only reflections of his hermaphroditic nature.[110] Dionysus is a low note in the divine scale, but we have still not plumbed his deepest vibrations. We shall let them ring out for a moment in conclusion.

"Väinämöinen, old and wily" greeted the little copper man who emerged from the waves with the strange words: "Most contemptible of heroes, no better than a dead man and a face on you like a corpse!" He is evidently alluding to the new-

[106] Ibid., pp. 155ff.
[107] Otto, pp. 76ff.
[108] Cf. Otto, pp. 152f. On the evidence of numerous representations of the phallus in the winnowing-basket, I differ from him in his interpretation.
[109] Ibid., p. 163.
[110] This would explain the phenomenon discussed by me in "Satire und Satura," pp. 144ff.

comer's kinship with the souls of the dead, which dwell in the water.[111] The psychic aspect of Hermes Psychopompos, shepherd of souls, is equally obvious: as a divinity he is no less ghost-like than childish. Apollo in his ancient Italic form exhibits the same dark aspects as Vediovis, the Jupiter of the Underworld.[112] The Zeus child of the Cretans, fed by a swarm of little creatures who were souls—the bees—had something of a god of the dead about him; his Cretan cave had the property of a place of the dead just as his other sanctuary had on Mount Lykaion. In Crete they even showed his grave.[113] The state which, glimpsed through the image of the Child, we described as "being not yet separated from non-being, yet still being," can also be put like this: "not yet separated from being, yet still non-being." Such is the condition of the departed as expressed by the figures of divine youths on antique gravestones: a boy in cloak and hood, the *genius cucullatus*,[114] as well as numberless cupids. The sea-gods and dolphins on tombs and sarcophagi point in the same direction. And here, in this sepulchral world, we come to the deepest shadow in all the darkness of Dionysus. All his symbols appear on sepulchres too. What the men of antiquity were representing by this was not merely the tense equilibrium of the two aspects of that state, the hovering of the new-born and the departed between being and non-being, but the certainty that the downward-trending path takes an *upward* turn leading to the Divine, and that the strongest will be born of the weakest.

Are we speaking of the orphan child of folklore, or were we speaking at the outset of the dismembered Dionysus child? Are we concerned with a primitive dream, a vision, something in a bygone religion, or with an ancient philosophem? Are we evoking an immemorial melody, an immemorial picture? We shall let the issue remain vague and undecided in its essence. For that was our subject: the undecided, the undifferentiated of old, the Primordial Child.

111 Cf. Weisweiler, "Seele und See," pp. 31ff.
112 Kerényi, *Apollon* (2nd edn., 1941), pp. 44f.
113 Callimachus, *Hymn to Zeus*, 8f., with scholium.
114 R. Egger, "Genius Cucullatus," pp. 311ff.; Kerényi, "Telesphoros," pp. 156ff.;
F. M. Heichelheim, "Genii Cucullati," pp. 187ff.

II

THE PSYCHOLOGY OF THE CHILD ARCHETYPE

BY C. G. JUNG

I.   INTRODUCTION

The author of the companion essay [1] on the mythology of the "child" or the child god has asked me for a psychological commentary on the subject of his investigations. I am glad to accede to his request, although the undertaking seems to me no small venture in view of the great significance of the child motif in mythology. Kerényi himself has enlarged upon the occurrence of this motif in Greece and Rome, with parallels drawn from Indian, Finnish, and other sources, thus indicating that the presentation of the theme would allow of yet further extensions. Though a comprehensive description would contribute nothing decisive in principle, it would nevertheless produce an overwhelming impression of the world-wide incidence and frequency of the motif. The customary treatment of mythological motifs so far in separate departments of science, such as philology, ethnology, the history of civilization, and comparative religion, was not exactly a help to us in recognizing their universality; and the psychological problems raised by this universality could easily be shelved by hypotheses of migration. Consequently Adolf Bastian's [2] ideas met with little success in their day. Even then there was sufficient empirical material available to permit far-reaching psychological conclusions, but the necessary premises were lacking. Although the psychological knowledge of that time included myth-formation in its province—witness Wundt's *Völkerpsychologie*—it was not in a position to demonstrate this same process as a living function actually present in the psyche of civilized man, any more than it could understand mythological motifs as structural elements of the psyche. True to its history, when psychology was metaphysics first of

---

[1] Kerényi, "The Primordial Child in Primordial Times."
[2] *Der Mensch in der Geschichte* (1860).

all, then the study of the senses and their functions, and then of the conscious mind and *its* functions, psychology identified its proper subject with the conscious psyche and its contents and thus completely overlooked the existence of a nonconscious psyche. Although various philosophers, among them Leibniz, Kant, and Schelling, had already pointed very clearly to the problem of the dark side of the psyche, it was a physician who felt impelled, from his scientific and medical experience, to point to the *unconscious* as the essential basis of the psyche. This was C. G. Carus,[3] the authority whom Eduard von Hartmann followed. In recent times it was, once again, medical psychology that approached the problem of the unconscious without philosophical preconceptions. It became clear from many separate investigations that the psychopathology of the neuroses and of many psychoses cannot dispense with the hypothesis of a dark side of the psyche, i.e., the unconscious. It is the same with the psychology of dreams, which is really the *terra intermedia* between normal and pathological psychology. In the dream, as in the products of psychoses, there are numberless interconnections to which one can find parallels only in mythological associations of ideas (or perhaps in certain poetic creations which are often characterized by a borrowing, not always conscious, from myths). Had thorough investigation shown that in the majority of such cases it was simply a matter of forgotten knowledge, the physician would not have gone to the trouble of making extensive researches into individual and collective parallels. But, in point of fact, typical mythologems were observed among individuals to whom all knowledge of this kind was absolutely out of the question, and where indirect derivation from religious ideas that might have been known to them, or from popular figures of speech, was impossible.[4] Such conclusions forced us to assume that we must be dealing with "autochthonous" revivals independent of all tradition, and, consequently, that "myth-forming" structural elements must be present in the unconscious psyche.[5]

3 *Psyche* (1846).

4 A working example in "The Concept of the Collective Unconscious," pars. 105ff., Coll. Works, 9, i.

5 Freud, in his *Interpretation of Dreams* (p. 261), paralleled certain aspects of infantile psychology with the Oedipus legend and observed that its "universal

These products are never (or at least very seldom) myths with a definite form, but rather mythological components which, because of their typical nature, we can call "motifs," "primordial images," types or—as I have named them—*archetypes*. The child archetype is an excellent example. Today we can hazard the formula that the archetypes appear in myths and fairytales just as they do in dreams and in the products of psychotic fantasy. The medium in which they are embedded is, in the former case, an ordered and for the most part immediately understandable context, but in the latter case a generally unintelligible, irrational, not to say delirious sequence of images which nonetheless does not lack a certain hidden coherence. In the individual, the archetypes appear as involuntary manifestations of unconscious processes whose existence and meaning can only be inferred, whereas the myth deals with traditional forms of incalculable age. They hark back to a prehistoric world whose spiritual preconceptions and general conditions we can still observe today among existing primitives. Myths on this level are as a rule tribal history handed down from generation to generation by word of mouth. Primitive mentality differs from the civilized chiefly in that the conscious mind is far less developed in scope and intensity. Functions such as thinking, willing, etc. are not yet differentiated; they are pre-conscious, and in the case of thinking, for instance, this shows itself in the circumstance that the primitive does not think *consciously*, but that thoughts *appear*. The primitive cannot assert that he thinks; it is rather that "something thinks in him." The spontaneity of the act of thinking does not lie, causally, in his conscious mind, but in his unconscious. Moreover, he is incapable of any conscious effort of will; he must put himself beforehand

---

validity" was to be explained in terms of the same infantile premise. The real working out of mythological material was then taken up by my pupils (A. Maeder, "Essai d'interprétation de quelques rêves," 1907, and "Die Symbolik in den Legenden, Märchen, Gebräuchen, und Träumen," 1908; F. Riklin, "Über Gefängnispsychosen," 1907, and *Wishfulfilment and Symbolism in Fairy Tales*, orig. 1908); and by K. Abraham, *Dreams and Myths*, orig. 1909. They were succeeded by Otto Rank of the Viennese school (*The Myth of the Birth of the Hero*, orig. 1922). In the *Psychology of the Unconscious* (orig. 1911; revised and expanded as *Symbols of Transformation*), I presented a somewhat more comprehensive examination of psychic and mythological parallels. Cf. also my essay, "Concerning the Archetypes, with special reference to the Anima Concept."

into the "mood of willing," or let himself be put—hence his *rites d'entrée et de sortie*. His consciousness is menaced by an almighty unconscious: hence his fear of magical influences which may cross his path at any moment; and for this reason, too, he is surrounded by unknown forces and must adjust himself to them as best he can. Owing to the chronic twilight state of his consciousness, it is often next to impossible to find out whether he merely dreamed something or whether he really experienced it. The spontaneous manifestation of the unconscious and its archetypes intrudes everywhere into his conscious mind, and the mythical world of his ancestors—for instance, the *alchera* or *bugari* of the Australian aborigines—is a reality equal if not superior to the material world.[6] It is not the world as we know it that speaks out of his unconscious, but the unknown world of the psyche, of which we know that it mirrors our empirical world only in part, and that, for the other part, it moulds this empirical world in accordance with its own psychic assumptions. The archetype does not proceed from physical facts, but describes how the psyche experiences the physical fact, and in so doing the psyche often behaves so autocratically that it denies tangible reality or makes statements that fly in the face of it.

The primitive mentality does not *invent* myths, it *experiences* them. Myths are original revelations of the preconscious psyche, involuntary statements about unconscious psychic happenings, and anything but allegories of physical processes.[7] Such allegories would be an idle amusement for an unscientific intellect. Myths, on the contrary, have a vital meaning. Not merely do they represent, they *are* the psychic life of the primitive tribe, which immediately falls to pieces and decays when it loses its mythological heritage, like a man who has lost his soul. A tribe's mythology is its living religion, whose loss is always and everywhere, even among the civilized, a moral catastrophe. But religion is a vital link with psychic processes independent of and beyond consciousness, in the dark hinterland of the psyche. Many of these unconscious processes may be indirectly occasioned by consciousness, but never by conscious choice. Others appear to arise spontaneously, that is to say, from no discernible or demonstrable conscious cause.

[6] This fact is well known, and the relevant ethnological literature is too extensive to be mentioned here.   [7] Cf. "The Structure of the Psyche," pars. 330ff.

Modern psychology treats the products of unconscious fantasy-activity as self-portraits of what is going on in the unconscious, or as statements of the unconscious psyche about itself. They fall into two categories. First, fantasies (including dreams) of a personal character, which go back unquestionably to personal experiences, things forgotten or repressed, and can thus be completely explained by individual anamnesis. Second, fantasies (including dreams) of an impersonal character, which cannot be reduced to experiences in the individual's past, and thus cannot be explained as something individually acquired. These fantasy-images undoubtedly have their closest analogues in mythological types. We must therefore assume that they correspond to certain *collective* (and not personal) structural elements of the human psyche in general, and, like the morphological elements of the human body, are *inherited*. Although tradition and transmission by migration certainly play a part, there are, as we have said, very many cases that cannot be accounted for in this way and drive us to the hypothesis of "autochthonous revival." These cases are so numerous that we are obliged to assume the existence of a collective psychic substratum. I have called this the *collective unconscious*.

The products of this second category resemble the types of structures to be met with in myth and fairytale so much that we must regard them as related. It is therefore wholly within the realm of possibility that both, the mythological types as well as the individual types, arise under quite similar conditions. As already mentioned, the fantasy-products of the second category (as also those of the first) arise in a state of reduced intensity of consciousness (in dreams, delirium, reveries, visions, etc.). In all these states the check put upon unconscious contents by the concentration of the conscious mind ceases, so that the hitherto unconscious material streams, as though from opened side-sluices, into the field of consciousness. This mode of origination is the general rule.[8]

Reduced intensity of consciousness and absence of concentration and attention, Janet's *abaissement du niveau mental,* correspond pretty exactly to the primitive state of consciousness

---

[8] Except for certain cases of spontaneous vision, *automatismes téléologiques* (Flournoy), and the processes in the method of "active imagination" which I have described [e.g., in "The Transcendent Function" and *Mysterium Coniunctionis,* pars. 706, 753f.—EDITORS].

in which, we must suppose, myths were originally formed. It is therefore exceedingly probable that the mythological archetypes, too, made their appearance in much the same manner as the manifestations of archetypal structures among individuals today.

The methodological principle in accordance with which psychology treats the products of the unconscious is this: Contents of an archetypal character are manifestations of processes in the collective unconscious. Hence they do not refer to anything that is or has been conscious, but to something essentially unconscious. In the last analysis, therefore, it is impossible to say what they refer to. Every interpretation necessarily remains an "as-if." The ultimate core of meaning may be circumscribed, but not described. Even so, the bare circumscription denotes an essential step forward in our knowledge of the pre-conscious structure of the psyche, which was already in existence when there was as yet no unity of personality (even today the primitive is not securely possessed of it) and no consciousness at all. We can also observe this pre-conscious state in early childhood, and as a matter of fact it is the dreams of this early period that not infrequently bring extremely remarkable archetypal contents to light.[9]

If, then, we proceed in accordance with the above principle, there is no longer any question whether a myth refers to the sun or the moon, the father or the mother, sexuality or fire or water; all it does is to circumscribe and give an approximate description of an *unconscious core of meaning*. The ultimate meaning of this nucleus was never conscious and never will be. It was, and still is, only interpreted, and every interpretation that comes anywhere near the hidden sense (or, from the point of view of scientific intellect, nonsense, which comes to the same thing) has always, right from the beginning, laid claim not only to absolute truth and validity but to instant reverence and religious devotion. Archetypes were, and still are, living psychic forces that demand to be taken seriously, and they have a strange way of making sure of their effect. Always they were the bringers

[9] The relevant material can be found in the unpublished reports of the seminars I gave at the Federal Polytechnic Institute (ETH) in Zurich in 1936–39, and in Michael Fordham's book *The Life of Childhood*.

of protection and salvation, and their violation has as its consequence the "perils of the soul" known to us from the psychology of primitives. Moreover, they are the unfailing causes of neurotic and even psychotic disorders, behaving exactly like neglected or maltreated physical organs or organic functional systems.

An archetypal content expresses itself, first and foremost, in metaphors. If such a content should speak of the sun and identify with it the lion, the king, the hoard of gold guarded by the dragon, or the power that makes for the life and health of man, it is neither the one thing nor the other, but the unknown third thing that finds more or less adequate expression in all these similes, yet—to the perpetual vexation of the intellect—remains unknown and not to be fitted into a formula. For this reason the scientific intellect is always inclined to put on airs of enlightenment in the hope of banishing the spectre once and for all. Whether its endeavours were called euhemerism, or Christian apologetics, or Enlightenment in the narrow sense, or Positivism, there was always a myth hiding behind it, in new and disconcerting garb, which then, following the ancient and venerable pattern, gave itself out as ultimate truth. In reality we can never legitimately cut loose from our archetypal foundations unless we are prepared to pay the price of a neurosis, any more than we can rid ourselves of our body and its organs without committing suicide. If we cannot deny the archetypes or otherwise neutralize them, we are confronted, at every new stage in the differentiation of consciousness to which civilization attains, with the task of finding a new *interpretation* appropriate to this stage, in order to connect the life of the past that still exists in us with the life of the present, which threatens to slip away from it. If this link-up does not take place, a kind of rootless consciousness comes into being no longer oriented to the past, a consciousness which succumbs helplessly to all manner of suggestions and, in practice, is susceptible to psychic epidemics. With the loss of the past, now become "insignificant," devalued, and incapable of revaluation, the saviour is lost too, for the saviour is either the insignificant thing itself or else arises out of it. Over and over again in the "metamorphosis of the gods" he rises up as the prophet or first-born of a new

76

generation and appears unexpectedly in the unlikeliest places (sprung from a stone, tree, furrow, water, etc.) and in ambiguous form (Tom Thumb, dwarf, child, animal, and so on).

This archetype of the "child god" is extremely widespread and intimately bound up with all the other mythological aspects of the child motif. It is hardly necessary to allude to the still living "Christ-child," who, in the legend of Saint Christopher, also has the typical feature of being "smaller than small and bigger than big." In folklore the child motif appears in the guise of the *dwarf* or the *elf* as personifications of the hidden forces of nature. To this sphere also belongs the little metal man of late antiquity, the ἀνθρωπάριον,[10] who, till far into the Middle Ages, on the one hand inhabited the mine-shafts,[11] and on the other represented the alchemical metals,[12] above all Mercurius reborn in perfect form (as the hermaphrodite, *filius sapientiae*, or *infans noster*).[13] Thanks to the religious interpretation of the "child," a fair amount of evidence has come down to us from the Middle Ages showing that the "child" was not merely a traditional figure, but a vision spontaneously experienced (as a so-called "irruption of the unconscious"). I would mention Meister Eckhart's vision of the "naked boy" and the dream of Brother Eustachius.[14] Interesting accounts of these spontaneous experiences are also to be found in English ghost-stories, where we read of the vision of a "Radiant Boy" said to have been seen in a place where there are Roman remains.[15] This apparition was supposed to be of evil omen. It almost looks as though we were dealing with the figure of a *puer aeternus* who had become inauspicious through "metamorphosis," or in other words had shared the fate of the classical and the Germanic gods, who have all become bugbears. The mystical character of the experience is also confirmed in Part II of Goethe's *Faust*, where Faust him-

10 Berthelot, *Alchimistes grecs*, III, xxv.

11 Agricola, *De animantibus subterraneis* (1549); Kircher, *Mundus subterraneus* (1678), VIII, 4.

12 Mylius, *Philosophia reformata* (1622).

13 "Allegoria super librum Turbae" in *Artis auriferae*, I (1572).

14 *Texte aus der deutschen Mystik des 14. und 15. Jahrhunderts*, ed. Spamer, pp. 143, 150.

15 Ingram, *The Haunted Homes and Family Traditions of Great Britain*, pp. 43ff.

self is transformed into a boy and admitted into the "choir of blessed youths," this being the "larval stage" of Doctor Marianus.[16]

In the strange tale called *Das Reich ohne Raum*, by Bruno Goetz, a *puer aeternus* named Fo (= Buddha) appears with whole troops of "unholy" boys of evil significance. (Contemporary parallels are better let alone.) I mention this instance only to demonstrate the enduring vitality of the child archetype.

The child motif not infrequently occurs in the field of psychopathology. The "imaginary" child is common among women with mental disorders and is usually interpreted in a Christian sense. Homunculi also appear, as in the famous Schreber case,[17] where they come in swarms and plague the sufferer. But the clearest and most significant manifestation of the child motif in the therapy of neuroses is in the maturation process of personality induced by the analysis of the unconscious, which I have termed the process of *individuation*.[18] Here we are confronted with preconscious processes which, in the form of more or less well-formed fantasies, gradually pass over into the conscious mind, or become conscious as dreams, or, lastly, are made conscious through the method of active imagination.[19] This material is rich in archetypal motifs, among them frequently that of the child. Often the child is formed after the Christian model; more often, though, it develops from earlier, altogether non-Christian levels—that is to say, out of chthonic animals such as crocodiles, dragons, serpents, or monkeys. Sometimes the child appears in the cup of a flower, or out of a golden egg, or as the centre of a mandala. In dreams it often appears as the dreamer's son or daughter or as a boy, youth, or young girl; occasionally it seems to be of exotic origin, Indian or Chinese, with a dusky skin, or, appearing more cosmically, surrounded by stars or with a starry

16 An old alchemical authority variously named Morienes, Morienus, Marianus ("De compositione alchemiae," Manget, *Bibliotheca chemica curiosa*, I, pp. 509ff.). In view of the explicitly alchemical character of *Faust*, Part II, such a connection would not be surprising.

17 Schreber, *Memoirs of My Nervous Illness*.

18 For a general presentation see my "Conscious, Unconscious, and Individuation." Special phenomena in the following text, also in *Psychology and Alchemy*, Part II.

19 "The Relations between the Ego and the Unconscious," Part II, ch. 3 [also "The Transcendent Function"—EDITORS].

coronet; or as the king's son or the witch's child with daemonic attributes. Seen as a special instance of "the treasure hard to attain" motif,[20] the child motif is extremely variable and assumes all manner of shapes, such as the jewel, the pearl, the flower, the chalice, the golden egg, the quaternity, the golden ball, and so on. It can be interchanged with these and similar images almost without limit.

II. THE PSYCHOLOGY OF THE CHILD ARCHETYPE

1. *The Archetype as a Link with the Past*

As to the *psychology* of our theme I must point out that every statement going beyond the purely phenomenal aspects of an archetype lays itself open to the criticism we have expressed above. Not for a moment dare we succumb to the illusion that an archetype can be finally explained and disposed of. Even the best attempts at explanation are only more or less successful translations into another metaphorical language. (Indeed, language itself is only an image.) The most we can do is to *dream the myth onwards* and give it a modern dress. And whatever explanation or interpretation does to it, we do to our own souls as well, with corresponding results for our own well-being. The archetype—let us never forget this—is a psychic organ present in all of us. A bad explanation means a correspondingly bad attitude to this organ, which may thus be injured. But the ultimate sufferer is the bad interpreter himself. Hence the "explanation" should always be such that the functional significance of the archetype remains unimpaired, so that an adequate and meaningful connection between the conscious mind and the archetypes is assured. For the archetype is an element of our psychic structure and thus a vital and necessary component in our psychic economy. It represents or personifies certain instinctive data of the dark, primitive psyche, the real but invisible roots of consciousness. Of what elementary importance the connection with these roots is, we see from the preoccupation of the primitive mentality with certain "magic" factors, which are nothing less than what we would call archetypes. This original form of

[20] *Symbols of Transformation*, index, s.v.

religio ("linking back") is the essence, the working basis of all religious life even today, and always will be, whatever future form this life may take.

There is no "rational" substitute for the archetype any more than there is for the cerebellum or the kidneys. We can examine the physical organs anatomically, histologically, and embryologically. This would correspond to an outline of archetypal phenomenology and its presentation in terms of comparative history. But we only arrive at the *meaning* of a physical organ when we begin to ask teleological questions. Hence the query arises: What is the biological purpose of the archetype? Just as physiology answers such a question for the body, so it is the business of psychology to answer it for the archetype.

Statements like "The child motif is a vestigial memory of one's own childhood" and similar explanations merely beg the question. But if, giving this proposition a slight twist, we were to say, "The child motif is a picture of certain *forgotten* things in our childhood," we are getting closer to the truth. Since, however, the archetype is always an image belonging to the whole human race and not merely to the individual, we might put it better this way: "The child motif represents the preconscious, childhood aspect of the collective psyche." [21]

We shall not go wrong if we take this statement for the time being *historically,* on the analogy of certain psychological experiences which show that certain phases in an individual's life can become autonomous, can personify themselves to the extent

[21] It may not be superfluous to point out that lay prejudice is always inclined to identify the child motif with the concrete experience "child," as though the real child were the cause and pre-condition of the existence of the child motif. In psychological reality, however, the empirical idea "child" is only the means (and not the only one) by which to express a psychic fact that cannot be formulated more exactly. Hence by the same token the mythological idea of the child is emphatically not a copy of the empirical child but a *symbol* clearly recognizable as such: it is a wonder-child, a divine child, begotten, born, and brought up in quite extraordinary circumstances, and not—this is the point—a human child. Its deeds are as miraculous or monstrous as its nature and physical constitution. Only on account of these highly unempirical properties is it necessary to speak of a "child motif" at all. Moreover, the mythological "child" has various forms: now a god, giant, Tom Thumb, animal, etc., and this points to a causality that is anything but rational or concretely human. The same is true of the "father" and "mother" archetypes which, mythologically speaking, are equally irrational symbols.

that they result in a *vision of oneself*—for instance, one sees oneself as a child. Visionary experiences of this kind, whether they occur in dreams or in the waking state, are, as we know, conditional on a dissociation having previously taken place between past and present. Such dissociations come about because of various incompatibilities; for instance, a man's present state may have come into conflict with his childhood state, or he may have violently sundered himself from his original character in the interests of some arbitrary persona more in keeping with his ambitions.[22] He has thus become unchildlike and artificial, and has lost his roots. All this presents a favourable opportunity for an equally vehement confrontation with the primary truth.

In view of the fact that men have not yet ceased to make statements about the child god, we may perhaps extend the individual analogy to the life of mankind and say in conclusion that humanity, too, probably always comes into conflict with its childhood conditions, that is, with its original, unconscious, and instinctive state, and that the danger of the kind of conflict which induces the vision of the "child" actually exists. Religious observances, i.e., the retelling and ritual repetition of the mythical event, consequently serve the purpose of bringing the image of childhood, and everything connected with it, again and again before the eyes of the conscious mind so that the link with the original condition may not be broken.

2. *The Function of the Archetype*

The child motif represents not only something that existed in the distant past but also something that exists *now*; that is to say, it is not just a vestige but a system functioning in the present whose purpose is to compensate or correct, in a meaningful manner, the inevitable one-sidednesses and extravagances of the conscious mind. It is in the nature of the conscious mind to concentrate on relatively few contents and to raise them to the highest pitch of clarity. A necessary result and precondition is the exclusion of other potential contents of consciousness. The exclusion is bound to bring about a certain one-sidedness of the conscious contents. Since the differentiated consciousness of

[22] *Psychological Types*, Def. 48; and *Two Essays on Analytical Psychology*, index, s.v. "persona."

civilized man has been granted an effective instrument for the practical realization of its contents through the dynamics of his will, there is all the more danger, the more he trains his will, of his getting lost in one-sidedness and deviating further and further from the laws and roots of his being. This means, on the one hand, the possibility of human freedom, but on the other it is a source of endless transgressions against one's instincts. Accordingly, primitive man, being closer to his instincts, like the animal, is characterized by fear of novelty and adherence to tradition. To our way of thinking he is painfully backward, whereas we exalt progress. But our progressiveness, though it may result in a great many delightful wish-fulfilments, piles up an equally gigantic Promethean debt which has to be paid off from time to time in the form of hideous catastrophes. For ages man has dreamed of flying, and all we have got for it is saturation bombing! We smile today at the Christian hope of a life beyond the grave, and yet we often fall into chiliasms a hundred times more ridiculous than the notion of a happy Hereafter. Our differentiated consciousness is in continual danger of being uprooted; hence it needs compensation through the still existing state of childhood.

The symptoms of compensation are described, from the progressive point of view, in scarcely flattering terms. Since, to the superficial eye, it looks like a retarding operation, people speak of inertia, backwardness, scepticism, fault-finding, conservatism, timidity, pettiness, and so on. But inasmuch as man has, in high degree, the capacity for cutting himself off from his own roots, he may also be swept uncritically to catastrophe by his dangerous one-sidedness. The retarding ideal is always more primitive, more natural (in the good sense as in the bad), and more "moral" in that it keeps faith with law and tradition. The progressive ideal is always more abstract, more unnatural, and less "moral" in that it demands disloyalty to tradition. Progress enforced by will is always *convulsive*. Backwardness may be closer to naturalness, but in its turn it is always menaced by painful awakenings. The older view of things realized that progress is only possible *Deo concedente,* thus proving itself conscious of the opposites and repeating the age-old *rites d'entrée et de sortie* on a higher plane. The more differentiated consciousness becomes, the greater the danger of severance from the root-condition. Complete severance comes when the *Deo concedente* is forgotten. Now it is an axiom of psychology that when a part of the psyche is split off from consciousness it is only *apparently* inactivated; in actual fact it brings about a possession of the personality, with the result that the individual's aims are falsified in the interests of the split-off part. If, then, the childhood state of the collective psyche is repressed to the point of total exclusion, the unconscious content overwhelms the conscious aim and inhibits, falsifies, even destroys its realization. Viable progress only comes from the co-operation of both.

3. *The Futurity of the Archetype*

One of the essential features of the child motif is its futurity. The child is potential future. Hence the occurrence of the child motif in the psychology of the individual signifies as a rule an anticipation of future developments, even though at first sight it may seem like a retrospective configuration. Life is a flux, a flowing into the future, and not a stoppage or a backwash. It is therefore not surprising that so many of the mythological saviours are child gods. This agrees exactly with our experience of the psychology of the individual, which shows that the "child" paves the way for a future change of personality. In the individuation process, it anticipates the figure that comes from the synthesis of conscious and unconscious elements in the personality. It is therefore a symbol which unites the opposites; [23] a mediator, bringer of healing, that is, one who makes whole. Because it has this meaning, the child motif is capable of the numerous transformations mentioned above: it can be expressed by roundness, the circle or sphere, or else by the quaternity as another form of wholeness.[24] I have called this wholeness that transcends consciousness the "self." [25] The goal of the individuation process is the synthesis of the self. From another point of view the term "entelechy" might be preferable to "synthesis." There is an empirical reason why "entelechy" is, in certain conditions, more fitting: the symbols

[23] *Psychological Types*, ch. V, 3: "The Significance of the Unifying Symbol."
[24] *Psychology and Alchemy*, pars. 327ff.; and "Psychology and Religion," pars. 108ff.
[25] *Two Essays on Analytical Psychology*, pars. 399ff. [Cf. also *Aion: Researches into the Phenomenology of the Self*, ch. 4.—EDITORS.]

of wholeness frequently occur at the beginning of the individuation process, indeed they can often be observed in the first dreams of early infancy. This observation says much for the *a priori* existence of potential wholeness,[26] and on this account the idea of *entelechy* instantly recommends itself. But in so far as the individuation process occurs, empirically speaking, as a synthesis, it looks, paradoxically enough, as if something already existent were being put together. From this point of view, the term "synthesis" is also applicable.

4. *Unity and Plurality of the Child Motif*

In the manifold phenomenology of the "child" we have to distinguish between the *unity* and *plurality* of its respective manifestations. Where, for instance, numerous homunculi, dwarfs, boys, etc., appear, having no individual characteristics at all, there is the probability of a *dissociation*. Such forms are therefore found especially in schizophrenia, which is essentially a fragmentation of personality. The many children then represent the products of its dissolution. But if the plurality occurs in normal people, then it is the representation of an as yet incomplete synthesis of personality. The personality (viz., the "self") is still in the *plural stage,* i.e., an ego may be present, but it cannot experience its wholeness within the framework of its own personality, only within the community of the family, tribe, or nation; it is still in the stage of unconscious identification with the plurality of the group. The Church takes due account of this widespread condition in her doctrine of the *corpus mysticum,* of which the individual is by nature a member.

If, however, the child motif appears in the form of a unity, we are dealing with an unconscious and provisionally complete synthesis of the personality, which in practice, like everything unconscious, signifies no more than a possibility.

5. *Child God and Child Hero*

Sometimes the "child" looks more like a *child god,* sometimes more like a young *hero.* Common to both types is the

26 *Psychology and Alchemy,* pars. 328ff.

84

miraculous birth and the adversities of early childhood—abandonment and danger through persecution. The god is by nature wholly supernatural; the hero's nature is human but raised to the limit of the supernatural—he is "semi-divine." While the god, especially in his close affinity with the symbolic animal, personifies the collective unconscious which is not yet integrated into a human being, the hero's supernaturalness includes human nature and thus represents a synthesis of the ("divine," i.e., not yet humanized) unconscious and human consciousness. Consequently he signifies the potential anticipation of an individuation process which is approaching wholeness.

For this reason the various "child"-fates may be regarded as illustrating the kind of psychic events that occur in the entelechy or genesis of the "self." The "miraculous birth" tries to depict the way in which this genesis is experienced. Since it is a psychic genesis, everything must happen non-empirically, e.g., by means of a virgin birth, or by miraculous conception, or by birth from unnatural organs. The motifs of "insignificance," exposure, abandonment, danger, etc. try to show how precarious is the psychic possibility of wholeness, that is, the enormous difficulties to be met with in attaining this "highest good." They also signify the powerlessness and helplessness of the life-urge which subjects every growing thing to the law of maximum self-fulfilment, while at the same time the environmental influences place all sorts of insuperable obstacles in the way of individuation. More especially the threat to one's inmost self from dragons and serpents points to the danger of the newly acquired consciousness being swallowed up again by the instinctive psyche, the unconscious. The lower vertebrates have from earliest times been favourite symbols of the collective psychic substratum,[27] which is localized anatomically in the subcortical centres, the cerebellum and the spinal cord. These organs constitute the snake.[28] Snake-dreams usually occur, therefore, when the conscious mind is deviating from its instinctual basis.

The motif of "smaller than small yet bigger than big" complements the impotence of the child by means of its equally

[27] Higher vertebrates symbolize mainly affects.
[28] This interpretation of the snake is found as early as Hippolytus, *Elenchos*, IV, 49–51 (Legge trans., I, p. 117). Cf. also Leisegang, *Die Gnosis*, p. 146.

miraculous deeds. This paradox is the essence of the hero and runs through his whole destiny like a red thread. He can cope with the greatest perils, yet, in the end, something quite insignificant is his undoing: Baldur perishes because of the mistletoe, Maui because of the laughter of a little bird, Siegfried because of his one vulnerable spot, Heracles because of his wife's gift, others because of common treachery, and so on.

The hero's main feat is to overcome the monster of darkness: it is the long-hoped-for and expected triumph of consciousness over the unconscious. Day and light are synonyms for consciousness, night and dark for the unconscious. The coming of consciousness was probably the most tremendous experience of primeval times, for with it a world came into being whose existence no one had suspected before. "And God said: 'Let there be light!' " is the projection of that immemorial experience of the separation of the conscious from the unconscious. Even among primitives today the possession of a soul is a precarious thing, and the "loss of soul" a typical psychic malady which drives primitive medicine to all sorts of psychotherapeutic measures. Hence the "child" distinguishes itself by deeds which point to the conquest of the dark.

III. THE SPECIAL PHENOMENOLOGY OF THE CHILD ARCHETYPE

1. *The Abandonment of the Child*

Abandonment, exposure, danger, etc. are all elaborations of the "child's" insignificant beginnings and of its mysterious and miraculous birth. This statement describes a certain psychic experience of a creative nature, whose object is the emergence of a new and as yet unknown content. In the psychology of the individual there is always, at such moments, an agonizing situation of conflict from which there seems to be no way out—at least for the conscious mind, since as far as this is concerned, *tertium non datur*.[29] But out of this collision of opposites the unconscious psyche always creates a third thing of an irrational nature, which the conscious mind neither expects nor understands. It presents itself in a form that is neither a straight "yes"

29 *Psychological Types*, Def. 51.

nor a straight "no," and is consequently rejected by both. For the conscious mind knows nothing beyond the opposites and, as a result, has no knowledge of the thing that unites them. Since, however, the solution of the conflict through the union of opposites is of vital importance, and is moreover the very thing that the conscious mind is longing for, some inkling of the creative act, and of the significance of it, nevertheless gets through. From this comes the numinous character of the "child." A meaningful but unknown content always has a secret fascination for the conscious mind. The new configuration is a nascent whole; it is on the way to wholeness, at least in so far as it excels in "wholeness" the conscious mind when torn by opposites and surpasses it in completeness. For this reason all uniting symbols have a redemptive significance.

Out of this situation the "child" emerges as a symbolic content, manifestly separated or even isolated from its background (the mother), but sometimes including the mother in its perilous situation, threatened on the one hand by the negative attitude of the conscious mind and on the other by the *horror vacui* of the unconscious, which is quite ready to swallow up all its progeny, since it produces them only in play, and destruction is an inescapable part of its play. Nothing in all the world welcomes this new birth, although it is the most precious fruit of Mother Nature herself, the most pregnant with the future, signifying a higher stage of self-realization. That is why Nature, the world of the instincts, takes the "child" under its wing: it is nourished or protected by animals.

"Child" means something evolving towards independence. This it cannot do without detaching itself from its origins: abandonment is therefore a necessary condition, not just a concomitant symptom. The conflict is not to be overcome by the conscious mind remaining caught between the opposites, and for this very reason it needs a symbol to point out the necessity of detaching itself from its origins. Because the symbol of the "child" fascinates and grips the conscious mind, its redemptive effect passes over into consciousness and brings about that separation from the conflict-situation which the conscious mind by itself was unable to achieve. The symbol anticipates a nascent state of consciousness. So long as this is not actually in being, the "child" remains a mythological projection which requires religious repetition and renewal by ritual. The Christ Child, for instance, is a religious necessity only so long as the majority of men are incapable of giving psychological reality to the saying: "Except ye become as little children. . . ." Since all such developments and transitions are extraordinarily difficult and dangerous, it is no wonder that figures of this kind persist for hundreds or even thousands of years. Everything that man should, and yet cannot, be or do—be it in a positive or negative sense—lives on as a mythological figure and anticipation alongside his consciousness, either as a religious projection or—what is still more dangerous—as unconscious contents which then project themselves spontaneously into incongruous objects, e.g., hygienic and other "salvationist" doctrines or practices. All these are so many rationalized substitutes for mythology, and their unnaturalness does more harm than good.

The conflict-situation that offers no way out, the sort of situation that produces the "child" as the irrational third, is of course a formula appropriate only to a psychological, that is, modern stage of development. It is not strictly applicable to the psychic life of primitives, if only because primitive man's child-like range of consciousness still excludes a whole world of possible psychic experiences. Seen on the nature-level of the primitive, our modern *moral* conflict is still an *objective* calamity that threatens life itself. Hence not a few child-figures are culture-heroes and thus identified with things that promote culture, e.g., fire,[30] metal, corn, maize, etc. As bringers of light, that is, enlargers of consciousness, they overcome darkness, which is to say that they overcome the earlier unconscious state. Higher consciousness, or knowledge going beyond our present-day consciousness, is equivalent to being *all alone in the world*. This loneliness expresses the conflict between the bearer or symbol of higher consciousness and his surroundings. The conquerors of darkness go far back into primeval times, and, together with many other legends, prove that there once existed a state of *original psychic distress,* namely *unconsciousness.* Hence in all probability the "irrational" fear which primitive man has of the dark even today. I found a form of religion among a tribe living on Mount Elgon that corresponded to

30 Even Christ is of a fiery nature ("he that is near to me is near to the fire"—Origen, *In Jeremiam Homiliae,* XX, 3); likewise the Holy Ghost.

pantheistic optimism. Their optimistic mood was, however, always in abeyance between six o'clock in the evening and six o'clock in the morning, during which time it was replaced by fear, for in the night the dark being Ayik has his dominion—the "Maker of Fear." During the daytime there were no monster snakes anywhere in the vicinity, but at night they were lurking on every path. At night the whole of mythology was let loose.

2. *The Invincibility of the Child*

It is a striking paradox in all child myths that the "child" is on the one hand delivered helpless into the power of terrible enemies and in continual danger of extinction, while on the other he possesses powers far exceeding those of ordinary humanity. This is closely related to the psychological fact that though the child may be "insignificant," unknown, "a mere child," he is also divine. From the conscious standpoint we seem to be dealing with an insignificant content that has no releasing, let alone redeeming, character. The conscious mind is caught in its conflict-situation, and the combatant forces seem so overwhelming that the "child" as an isolated content bears no relation to the conscious factors. It is therefore easily overlooked and falls back into the unconscious. At least, this is what we should have to fear if things turned out according to our conscious expectations. Myth, however, emphasizes that it is not so, but that the "child" is endowed with superior powers and, despite all dangers, will unexpectedly pull through. The "child" is born out of the womb of the unconscious, begotten out of the depths of human nature, or rather out of living Nature herself. It is a personification of vital forces quite outside the limited range of our conscious mind; of ways and possibilities of which our one-sided conscious mind knows nothing; a wholeness which embraces the very depths of Nature. It represents the strongest, the most ineluctable urge in every being, namely the urge to realize itself. It is, as it were, an incarnation of *the inability to do otherwise,* equipped with all the powers of nature and instinct, whereas the conscious mind is always getting caught up in its supposed ability to do otherwise. The urge and compulsion to self-realization is a law of nature and thus of invincible power, even though its effect, at the start, is insignificant and improbable. Its power is revealed in the miraculous deeds of the child hero, and later in the *athla* ('works') of the bondsman or thrall (of the Heracles type), where, although the hero has outgrown the impotence of the "child," he is still in a menial position. The figure of the thrall generally leads up to the real epiphany of the semi-divine hero. Oddly enough, we have a similar modulation of themes in alchemy—in the synonyms for the *lapis*. As the *materia prima,* it is the *lapis exilis et vilis.* As a substance in process of transmutation, it is *servus rubeus* or *fugitivus;* and finally, in its true apotheosis, it attains the dignity of a *filius sapientiae* or *deus terrenus,* a "light above all lights," a power that contains in itself all the powers of the upper and nether regions. It becomes a *corpus glorificatum* which enjoys everlasting incorruptibility and is therefore a panacea ("bringer of healing").[31] The size and invincibility of the "child" are bound up in Hindu speculation with the nature of the atman, which corresponds to the "smaller than small yet bigger than big" motif. As an individual phenomenon, the self is "smaller than small"; as the equivalent of the cosmos, it is "bigger than big." The self, regarded as the counter-pole of the world, its "absolutely other," is the *sine qua non* of all empirical knowledge and consciousness of subject and object. Only because of this psychic "otherness" is consciousness possible at all. Identity does not make consciousness possible; it is only separation, detachment, and agonizing confrontation through opposition that produce consciousness and insight. Hindu introspection recognized this psychological fact very early and consequently equated the subject of cognition with the subject of ontology in general. In accordance with the predominantly introverted attitude of Indian thinking, the object lost the attribute of absolute reality and, in some systems, became a mere illusion. The Greek-Occidental type of mind could not free itself from the conviction of the world's absolute existence—at the cost, however, of the cosmic significance of the self. Even today Western man finds it hard to see the psychological necessity for a transcendental subject of cognition as the counter-pole of the empirical universe, although the postulate of a world-

31 The material is collected in *Psychology and Alchemy,* Parts II and III. For Mercurius as a servant, see the parable of Eirenaeus Philalethes, *Ripley Reviv'd: or, An Exposition upon Sir George Ripley's Hermetico-Poetical Works* (1678).

confronting self, at least as a *point of reflection,* is a logical necessity. Regardless of philosophy's perpetual attitude of dissent or only half-hearted assent, there is always a compensating tendency in our unconscious psyche to produce a symbol of the self in its cosmic significance. These efforts take on the archetypal forms of the hero myth such as can be observed in almost any individuation process.

The phenomenology of the "child's" birth always points back to an original psychological state of non-recognition, i.e., of darkness or twilight, of non-differentiation between subject and object, of unconscious identity of man and the universe. This phase of non-differentiation produces the *golden egg,* which is both man and universe and yet neither, but an irrational third. To the twilight consciousness of primitive man it seems as if the egg came out of the womb of the wide world and were, accordingly, a cosmic, objective, external occurrence. To a differentiated consciousness, on the other hand, it seems evident that this egg is nothing but a symbol thrown up by the psyche or—what is even worse—a fanciful speculation and therefore "nothing but" a primitive phantasm to which no "reality" of any kind attaches. Present-day medical psychology, however, thinks somewhat differently about these "phantasms." It knows only too well what dire disturbances of the bodily functions and what devastating psychic consequences can flow from "mere" fantasies. "Fantasies" are the natural expressions of the life of the unconscious. But since the unconscious is the psyche of all the body's autonomous functional complexes, its "fantasies" have an aetiological significance that is not to be despised. From the psychopathology of the individuation process we know that the formation of symbols is frequently associated with physical disorders of a psychic origin, which in some cases are felt as decidedly "real." In medicine, fantasies are *real things* with which the psychotherapist has to reckon very seriously indeed. He cannot therefore deprive of all justification those primitive phantasms whose content is so real that it is projected upon the external world. In the last analysis the human body, too, is built of the stuff of the world, the very stuff wherein fantasies become visible; indeed, without it they could not be experienced at all. Without this stuff they would be like a sort of abstract crystalline lattice in a solution where the crystallization process had not yet started.

The symbols of the self arise in the depths of the body and they express its materiality every bit as much as the structure of the perceiving consciousness. The symbol is thus a living body, *corpus et anima;* hence the "child" is such an apt formula for the symbol. The uniqueness of the psyche can never enter wholly into reality, it can only be realized approximately, though it still remains the absolute basis of all consciousness. The deeper "layers" of the psyche lose their individual uniqueness as they retreat farther and farther into darkness. "Lower down," that is to say as they approach the autonomous functional systems, they become increasingly collective until they are universalized and extinguished in the body's materiality, i.e., in chemical substances. The body's carbon is simply carbon. Hence "at bottom" the psyche is simply "world." In this sense I hold Kerényi to be absolutely right when he says that in the symbol the *world itself* is speaking. The more archaic and "deeper," that is the more *physiological,* the symbol is, the more collective and universal, the more "material" it is. The more abstract, differentiated, and specific it is, and the more its nature approximates to conscious uniqueness and individuality, the more it sloughs off its universal character. Having finally attained full consciousness, it runs the risk of becoming a mere allegory which nowhere oversteps the bounds of conscious comprehension, and is then exposed to all sorts of attempts at rationalistic and therefore inadequate explanation.

3. *The Hermaphroditism of the Child*

It is a remarkable fact that perhaps the majority of cosmogonic gods are of a bisexual nature. The hermaphrodite means nothing less than a union of the strongest and most striking opposites. In the first place this union refers back to a primitive state of mind, a twilight where differences and contrasts were either barely separated or completely merged. With increasing clarity of consciousness, however, the opposites draw more and more distinctly and irreconcilably apart. If, therefore, the hermaphrodite were only a product of primitive non-differentiation, we would have to expect that it would soon be eliminated with increasing civilization. This is by no means the case; on the contrary, man's imagination has been preoccupied with this idea over and over again on the high and even the highest levels of culture, as we can see from the late Greek and syncretic philosophy of Gnosticism. The hermaphroditic *rebis* has an important part to play in the natural philosophy of the Middle Ages. And in our own day we hear of Christ's androgyny in Catholic mysticism.[32]

We can no longer be dealing, then, with the continued existence of a primitive phantasm, or with an original contamination of opposites. Rather, as we can see from medieval writings,[33] the primordial idea has become a *symbol of the creative union of opposites,* a "uniting symbol" in the literal sense. In its functional significance the symbol no longer points back, but forward to a goal not yet reached. Notwithstanding its monstrosity, the hermaphrodite has gradually turned into a subduer of conflicts and a bringer of healing, and it acquired this meaning in relatively early phases of civilization. This vital meaning explains why the image of the hermaphrodite did not fade out in primeval times but, on the contrary, was able to assert itself with increasing profundity of symbolic content for thousands of years. The fact that an idea so utterly archaic could rise to such exalted heights of meaning not only points to the vitality of archetypal ideas, it also demonstrates the rightness of the principle that the archetype, because of its power to unite opposites, mediates between the unconscious substratum and the conscious mind. It throws a bridge between present-day consciousness, always in danger of losing its roots, and the natural, unconscious, instinctive wholeness of primeval times. Through this mediation the uniqueness, peculiarity, and one-sidedness of our present individual consciousness are linked up again with its natural, racial roots. Progress and development are ideals not lightly to be rejected, but they lose all meaning if man only arrives at his new state as a fragment of himself, having left his essential hinterland behind him in the shadow of the unconscious, in a state of primitivity or, indeed, barbarism. The conscious mind, split off from its origins, incapable of

[32] Koepgen, *Die Gnosis des Christentums,* pp. 315ff.
[33] For the *lapis* as mediator and medium, cf. *Tractatus aureus,* in Manget, *Bibliotheca chemica curiosa,* I, p. 408b, and *Artis auriferae* (1572), p. 641.

realizing the meaning of the new state, then relapses all too easily into a situation far worse than the one from which the innovation was intended to free it—*exempla sunt odiosa!* It was Friedrich Schiller who first had an inkling of this problem; but neither his contemporaries nor his successors were capable of drawing any conclusions. Instead, people incline more than ever to educate *children* and nothing more. I therefore suspect that the *furor paedogogicus* is a god-sent method of by-passing the central problem touched on by Schiller, namely the *education of the educator.* Children are educated by what the grown-up *is* and not by what he *says.* The popular faith in words is a veritable disease of the mind, for a superstition of this sort always leads farther and farther away from man's foundations and seduces people into a disastrous identification of the personality with whatever slogan may be in vogue. Meanwhile everything that has been overcome and left behind by so-called "progress" sinks deeper and deeper into the unconscious, from which there re-emerges in the end the primitive condition of *identity with the mass.* Instead of the expected progress, this condition now becomes reality.

As civilization develops, the bisexual primordial being turns into a symbol of the unity of personality, a symbol of the self, where the war of opposites finds peace. In this way the primordial being becomes the distant goal of man's self-development, having been from the very beginning a projection of his unconscious wholeness. Wholeness consists in the union of the conscious and the unconscious personality. Just as every individual derives from masculine and feminine genes, and the sex is determined by the predominance of the corresponding genes, so in the psyche it is only the conscious mind, in a man, that has the masculine sign, while the unconscious is by nature feminine. The reverse is true in the case of a woman. All I have done in my anima theory is to rediscover and reformulate this fact.[34] It had long been known.

The idea of the *coniunctio* of male and female, which became almost a technical term in Hermetic philosophy, appears in Gnosticism as the *mysterium iniquitatis*, probably not uninfluenced by the Old Testament "divine marriage" as

[34] *Psychological Types,* Def. 48; and "Relations between the Ego and the Unconscious," pars. 296ff.

performed, for instance, by Hosea.[35] Such things are hinted at not only by certain traditional customs,[36] but by the quotation from the Gospel according to the Egyptians in the second epistle of Clement: "When the two shall be one, the outside as the inside, and the male with the female neither male nor female." [37] Clement of Alexandria introduces this logion with the words: "When ye have trampled on the garment of shame (with thy feet) . . . ," [38] which probably refers to the body; for Clement as well as Cassian (from whom the quotation was taken over), and the pseudo-Clement, too, interpreted the words in a spiritual sense, in contrast to the Gnostics, who would seem to have taken the *coniunctio* all too literally. They took care, however, through the practice of abortion and other restrictions, that the biological meaning of their acts did not swamp the religious significance of the rite. While, in Church mysticism, the primordial image of the *hieros gamos* was sublimated on a lofty plane and only occasionally—as for instance with Mechthild of Magdeburg [39]—approached the physical sphere in emotional intensity, for the rest of the world it remained very much alive and continued to be the object of especial psychic preoccupation. In this respect the symbolical drawings of Opicinus de Canistris [40] afford us an interesting glimpse of the way in which this primordial image was instrumental in uniting opposites, even in a pathological state. On the other hand, in the Hermetic philosophy that throve in the Middle Ages the *coniunctio* was performed wholly in the physical realm in the admittedly abstract theory of the *coniugium solis et lunae,* which despite this drawback gave the creative imagination much occasion for anthropomorphic flights.

Such being the state of affairs, it is readily understandable that the primordial image of the hermaphrodite should reappear in modern psychology in the guise of the male-female antithesis, in other words as *male* consciousness and personified *female* unconscious. But the psychological process of bringing things to consciousness has complicated the picture considerably. Whereas the old science was almost exclusively a field in

---

35 Hosea 1 : 2ff.   36 Cf. Fendt, *Gnostische Mysterien.*

37 James, *The Apocryphal New Testament,* p. 11.

38 Clement, *Stromata,* III, 13, 92, 2.   39 *The Flowing Light of the Godhead.*

40 Salomon, *Opicinus de Canistris.*

which only the man's unconscious could project itself, the new psychology had to acknowledge the existence of an autonomous female psyche as well. Here the case is reversed, and a feminine consciousness confronts a masculine personification of the unconscious, which can no longer be called *anima* but *animus*. This discovery also complicates the problem of the *coniunctio*.

Originally this archetype played its part entirely in the field of fertility magic and thus remained for a very long time a purely biological phenomenon with no other purpose than that of fecundation. But even in early antiquity the symbolical meaning of the act seems to have increased. Thus, for example, the physical performance of the *hieros gamos* as a sacred rite not only became a mystery—it faded to a mere conjecture.[41] As we have seen, Gnosticism, too, endeavoured in all seriousness to subordinate the physiological to the metaphysical. Finally, the Church severed the *coniunctio* from the physical realm altogether, and natural philosophy turned it into an abstract *theoria*. These developments meant the gradual transformation of the archetype into a psychological process which, in theory, we can call a combination of conscious and unconscious processes. In practice, however, it is not so simple, because as a rule the feminine unconscious of a man is projected upon a feminine partner, and the masculine unconscious of a woman is projected upon a man. The elucidation of these problems is a special branch of psychology and has no part in a discussion of the mythological hermaphrodite.

4. *The Child as Beginning and End*

Faust, after his death, is received as a boy into the "choir of blessed youths." I do not know whether Goethe was referring, with this peculiar idea, to the *cupids* on antique grave-stones. It is not unthinkable. The figure of the *cucullatus* points to the hooded, that is, the *invisible* one, the genius of the departed, who reappears in the child-like frolics of a new life, surrounded by the sea-forms of dolphins and tritons. The sea is the favourite

---

41 Cf. the diatribe by Bishop Asterius (Foucart, *Mystères d'Eleusis,* pp. 477ff.) According to Hippolytus' account the hierophant actually made himself impotent by a draught of hemlock. The self-castration of priests in the worship of the Mother Goddess is of similar import.

symbol for the unconscious, the mother of all that lives. Just as the "child" is, in certain circumstances (e.g., in the case of Hermes and the Dactyls), closely related to the phallus, symbol of the begetter, so it comes up again in the sepulchral phallus, symbol of a renewed begetting.

The "child" is therefore *renatus in novam infantiam*. It is thus both beginning and end, an initial and a terminal creature. The initial creature existed before man was, and the terminal creature will be when man is not. Psychologically speaking, this means that the "child" symbolizes the pre-conscious and the post-conscious essence of man. His pre-conscious essence is the unconscious state of earliest childhood; his post-conscious essence is an anticipation by analogy of life after death. In this idea the all-embracing nature of psychic wholeness is expressed. Wholeness is never comprised within the compass of the conscious mind—it includes the indefinite and indefinable extent of the unconscious as well. Wholeness, empirically speaking, is therefore of immeasurable extent, older and younger than consciousness and enfolding it in time and space. This is no speculation, but an immediate psychic experience. Not only is the conscious process continually accompanied, it is often guided, helped, or interrupted, by unconscious happenings. The child had a psychic life before it had consciousness. Even the adult still says and does things whose significance he realizes only later, if ever. And yet he said them and did them as if he knew what they meant. Our dreams are continually saying things beyond our conscious comprehension (which is why they are so useful in the therapy of neuroses). We have intimations and intuitions from unknown sources. Fears, moods, plans, and hopes come to us with no visible causation. These concrete experiences are at the bottom of our feeling that we know ourselves very little; at the bottom, too, of the painful conjecture that we might have surprises in store for ourselves.

Primitive man is no puzzle to himself. The question "What is man?" is the question that man has always kept until last. Primitive man has so much psyche outside his conscious mind that the experience of something psychic outside him is far more familiar to him than to us. Consciousness hedged about by psychic powers, sustained or threatened or deluded by them, is the age-old experience of mankind. This experience has pro-

jected itself into the archetype of the child, which expresses
man's wholeness. The "child" is all that is abandoned and
exposed and at the same time divinely powerful; the insignificant, dubious beginning, and the triumphal end. The "eternal
child" in man is an indescribable experience, an incongruity,
a handicap, and a divine prerogative; an imponderable that determines the ultimate worth or worthlessness of a personality.

IV. CONCLUSION

I am aware that a psychological commentary on the child
archetype without detailed documentation must remain a mere
sketch. But since this is virgin territory for the psychologist, my
main endeavour has been to stake out the possible extent of the
problems raised by our archetype and to describe, at least cur-
sorily, its different aspects. Clear-cut distinctions and strict for-
mulations are quite impossible in this field, seeing that a kind
of fluid interpenetration belongs to the very nature of all archetypes. They can only be roughly circumscribed at best. Their
living meaning comes out more from their presentation as a
whole than from a single formulation. Every attempt to focus
them more sharply is immediately punished by the intangible
core of meaning losing its luminosity. No archetype can be reduced to a simple formula. It is a vessel which we can never
empty, and never fill. It has a potential existence only, and
when it takes shape in matter it is no longer what it was. It
persists throughout the ages and requires interpreting ever
anew. The archetypes are the imperishable elements of the unconscious, but they change their shape continually.

It is a well-nigh hopeless undertaking to tear a single archetype out of the living tissue of the psyche; but despite their
interwovenness they do form units of meaning that can be apprehended intuitively. Psychology, as one of the many expressions of psychic life, operates with ideas which in their turn are
derived from archetypal structures and thus generate a somewhat more abstract kind of myth. Psychology therefore trans-
lates the archaic speech of myth into a modern mythologem—not
yet, of course, recognized as such—which constitutes one element of the myth "science." This seemingly hopeless undertaking

is a *living and lived myth,* satisfying to persons of a corresponding temperament, indeed beneficial in so far as they have been cut off from their psychic origins by neurotic dissociation.

As a matter of experience, we meet the child archetype in spontaneous and in therapeutically induced individuation processes. The first manifestation of the "child" is as a rule a totally unconscious phenomenon. Here the patient identifies himself with his personal infantilism. Then, under the influence of therapy, we get a more or less gradual separation from and objectification of the "child," that is, the identity breaks down and is accompanied by an intensification (sometimes technically induced) of fantasy, with the result that archaic or mythological features become increasingly apparent. Further transformations run true to the hero myth. The theme of "mighty feats" is generally absent, but on the other hand the mythical dangers play all the greater part. At this stage there is usually another identification, this time with the hero, whose role is attractive for a variety of reasons. The identification is often extremely stubborn and dangerous to the psychic equilibrium. If it can be broken down and if consciousness can be reduced to human proportions, the figure of the hero can gradually be differentiated into a symbol of the self.

In practical reality, however, it is of course not enough for the patient merely to *know about* such developments; what counts is his experience of the various transformations. The initial stage of personal infantilism presents the picture of an "abandoned" or "misunderstood" and unjustly treated child with overweening pretensions. The epiphany of the hero (the second identification) shows itself in a corresponding inflation: the colossal pretension grows into a conviction that one is something extraordinary, or else the impossibility of the pretension ever being fulfilled only proves one's own inferiority, which is favourable to the role of the heroic sufferer (a negative inflation). In spite of their contradictoriness, both forms are identical, because conscious megalomania is balanced by unconscious compensatory inferiority and conscious inferiority by unconscious megalomania (you never get one without the other). Once the reef of the second identification has been successfully circumnavigated, conscious processes can be cleanly separated from the unconscious, and the latter observed objectively. This leads to the possibility of an accommodation with the unconscious, and thus to a possible synthesis of the conscious and unconscious elements of knowledge and action. This in turn leads to a shifting of the centre of personality from the ego to the self.[42]

In this psychological framework the motifs of abandonment, invincibility, hermaphroditism, and beginning and end take their place as distinct categories of experience and understanding.

[42] A more detailed account of these developments is to be found in "The Relations between the Ego and the Unconscious."

III

KORE

BY C. KERÉNYI

How can a man know what a woman's life is? A woman's life is quite different from a man's. God has ordered it so. A man is the same from the time of his circumcision to the time of his withering. He is the same before he has sought out a woman for the first time, and afterwards. But the day when a woman enjoys her first love cuts her in two. She becomes another woman on that day. The man is the same after his first love as he was before. The woman is from the day of her first love another. That continues so all through life. The man spends a night by a woman and goes away. His life and body are always the same. The woman conceives. As a mother she is another person than the woman without child. She carries the fruit of the night for nine months in her body. Something grows. Something grows into her life that never again departs from it. She is a mother. She is and remains a mother even though her child die, though all her children die. For at one time she carried the child under her heart. And it does not go out of her heart ever again. Not even when it is dead. All this the man does not know; he knows nothing. He does not know the difference before love and after love, before motherhood and after motherhood. He can know nothing. Only a woman can know that and speak of that. That is why we won't be told what to do by our husbands. A woman can only do one thing. She can respect herself. She can keep herself decent. She must always be as her nature is. She must always be maiden and always be mother. Before every love she is a maiden, after every love she is a mother. In this you can see whether she is a good woman or not.

Let these words of a noble Abyssinian woman, quoted by Frobenius in one of his finest books, *Der Kopf als Schicksal* (p. 88), stand as a motto in preparation and confirmation of what is said in the sequel. I did not know them when I wrote my study of the Kore. They are meant at the same time to stand in remembrance of a great man, whose life's work is an abiding stimulus to all those concerned with anthropology and mythology.

1. *Anadyomene*

The Florentine Renaissance came to love the Homeric hymns even more than the two great epics. Marsilius Ficinus, the translator of Plato, began by translating the Homeric and Orphic hymns. We know that he also sang them in the antique manner to the accompaniment of a lute. Angelo Poliziano, another leading spirit of Florentine humanism, paraphrased a hymn to Aphrodite—neither the greatest nor the least of those ascribed to Homer—in his own verses. We could say that he painted it in the style of the Quattrocento were it not for the painter who actually did so, with Poliziano's poetic assistance: Botticelli.[1] *The Birth of Venus* is not a good name for this picture. It is rather Aphrodite's arrival in Cyprus according to the Homeric hymn, or, in accordance with the significance of this masterpiece and the rôle it has played in our civilization, Aphrodite's arrival among *us*. Botticelli's picture contains at least as much living mythology as the Homeric hymn.[2]

Aphrodite's *birth* is different: brutal and violent, and departing from the style of Homeric poetry in just as archaic a manner as from the style of Botticelli. In both cases the mutilation of Uranos, the casting of his manhood into the sea, the whole terrible foregoing history, the titanic mythology of the world's beginnings—all this was swept aside. The unity of that mythological moment when begetter and begotten were one in the womb of the water[3] had been broken up even in Hesiod and become a historical process. In Hesiod, too, we hear of Aphrodite drifting, drifting on the waves, as Maui did in the myth of the Polynesians.[4] At last the white foam gave birth to the girl who took her name from it: ἀφρός is foam and Aphrodite the goddess. This ancient etymology, accepted by Hesiod, derived its credibility from a grand mythological vision that must be still older: from the picture of Anadyomene, the goddess risen from the waves. Representations of Aphrodite's *arrival* are later. The mild breeze carries the great goddess,

[1] Details in A. Warburg, *Die Erneuerung der heidnischen Antike*, pp. 6ff.
[2] "Mythology" in the sense defined in the Prolegomena, supra.
[3] Cf. supra, p. 56.
[4] Cf. supra, p. 47.

already born, to one of her sacred islands, or, in Botticelli's picture, to firm ground.

The soft foam that cushions Aphrodite is a symbol of her birth, and fits in with the Homeric style just as the mussel-shell does with Botticelli's. In the Roman poets we read that Venus was born of a mussel-shell, or that she journeyed in a mussel-shell over the sea. Ancient representations show her as if growing out of a mussel. We need not surmise with H. Usener, the eminent philologist, that the growth of the pearl was at the bottom of the symbol.[5] Later, this image was blended with the archaic foam-image. Originally yet another kind of mussel, by no means so noble, was the creature sacred to Aphrodite in Cnidos.[6] The mussel in general constitutes a most graphic example and expression, appealing at once to the senses, of the aphrodisian properties of the "humid element." The Homeric poem was too spiritual to employ this symbol. Poliziano was too sensual to be able to forget it. Venus steps out of her mussel-shell in Botticelli in such a way that you can see immediately: it belongs to the goddess, yet she is leaving it behind her as she leaves behind the whole of primitive mythology, which Poliziano nevertheless relates according to Hesiod.

From the high sea, stepping out of a mussel-shell, borne along by the wind and received by the gaily clad goddess of earth, Aphrodite Anadyomene arrives. She is an aspect of the primordial maiden, Protogonos Kore. Botticelli's picture helps us, as modern men, to conjure up the vision of Anadyomene. And she must be conjured up if we want to understand the goddesses of the Greeks. She is the closest to the origins.

2. *The Paradox of the Mythological Idea*

To the religious-minded man of the Greek world, his divinities had always appeared in classical perfection since the time of Homer. And undoubtedly they appeared not as the fictions or creations of art but as living deities who could be believed in. They can best be understood as eternal *forms*, the great world-realities. "The reason for the mightiness of all these

---

5 Cf. Usener, *Vorträge und Aufsätze* (pp. 119ff.) for the classical references.
6 Pliny, *Historia naturalis*, IX, 80.

figures lies in their truth."[7] As psychologists we may stress the fact that this truth is always a *psychic reality;* as historians we may add that the psychic reality of such a truth, as indeed of all truth, *changes with time;*[8] as biologists we may call the alteration of the power that so moves us *natural decay,* but the essentially convincing inner structure of the classical Greek divinities remains unshakable for all time.

We have a handy comparison in the kind of formula that gives us a clear picture of the balance of tremendous cosmic forces, that catches the world in each of its aspects as though in a *border-line situation* and presents it to the mind as though the least disturbance of that balance would bring about a universal collapse. Every natural law is just such a balanced aspect of the world and is immediately intelligible as the mathematical formulation of a border-line situation.

So it is with the figures of gods. In *Apollo* sublimest clarity and the darkness of death face one another, perfectly poised and equal, on a border-line;[9] in *Dionysus,* life and death;[10] in *Zeus,* might and right[11]—to name only the three greatest. In relation to the cosmos as a whole, these divinities are merely certain aspects of it; in themselves they are wholes,[12] "worlds" which have aspects in their turn, and contradictory aspects for the very reason that their structure combines contradictions in perfect equilibrium.

Such gods can only be understood *as spiritual ideas;* in other words, they can only be known by immediate revelation.[13] They cannot emerge step by step from something quite different. And conversely, we cannot imagine or believe in a god who did not appear to the *spirit,* who was not an immediate spiritual revelation. The very possibility of the Greek divinities, the reason for their credibility, consists in the fact that they are *ideal.*

If the historian ventures to adopt an attitude in accord with

---

[7] W. F. Otto, *Der europäische Geist und die Weisheit des Ostens* (1931), p. 21.

[8] Kerényi, *Apollon* (1941), pp. 15ff.; *La Religione antica,* pp. 1ff.; *Die antike Religion,* p. 45.

[9] *Apollon,* pp. 37ff.

[10] W. F. Otto, *Dionysos* (1933), p. 186.

[11] *Die antike Religion,* pp. 78f.

[12] Otto, *The Homeric Gods,* p. 241.

[13] Otto, *Dionysos,* p. 29; Kerényi, *Die antike Religion,* p. 3.

this knowledge; if he is bold enough to take the things of the spirit spiritually, and religion religiously, he immediately lights on a paradox. He can easily go so far back into the prehistory of the Greek gods that the balance we have spoken of dissolves before his eyes and all certain outlines vanish. *Artemis,* for instance, is to be found in the untamedness of young animals and equally in the terrors of birth. In the classical figure of this goddess, the wildness and the terrors meet at a border-line: they are in equilibrium.[14] The further we penetrate into her prehistory, the more the outlines connected with the name of "Artemis" evaporate. The border-line situation widens into a border-*region* midway between motherhood and maidenhood, *joie de vivre* and lust for murder, fecundity and animality. The more we realize that the divinity of the gods can only be experienced spiritually, in the illumination of an *idea,* by direct revelation, the more we sense a difficulty. The majority of investigators shrink from recognizing *ideal* figures in the gods, thinking of much that is the reverse of ideal in the early history of Greek religion so far as known.

It is a paradox, but nothing impossible, that we meet here: the revelation of something that is dark in comparison with an idea, but ideal in comparison with blind feeling—the revelation of something *still unopened, like a bud.* All the most ancient mythological ideas are buds of this sort. Above all, the idea of genesis and origin—an idea which every living thing experiences in its own genesis and, to that extent, realizes in fact. Mythologically, the idea is embodied in miraculous "primal beings," either in such a way that in them father and child, prime begetter and prime begotten, are one and the same, or that the fate of the woman becomes the symbol and expression of all genesis and origination. Zeus, Apollo, Dionysus, Hermes, Asklepios, Heracles—all may be regarded as having evolved out of a mythological *primordial child,* who originally comprised both begetter and begotten.[15] The same idea, seen as the woman's fate, presented itself to the Greeks in equally budlike form. The budlike quality of it is expressed in the name often given to its personification: *Kore,* which is simply the goddess "Maiden."

14 *Apollon,* p. 72.
15 Cf. supra, the sections (6–9, in I) on the first four divinities.

The Kore-goddess throws light on the old mythological idea in its budlike capacity to unfold and yet to contain a whole compact world in itself. The idea can also be likened to a nucleus. We have to understand, as it were, the structure hidden in the "abyss of the nucleus." In so doing, we must not forget the figure of Anadyomene. We shall have an assurance that our understanding is true to life if this ideal structure, as we conceive it, remains compatible with her image.

3. Maiden-Goddesses

Maiden-goddesses are far more typical of Greek religion than boy-gods or even, perhaps, divine youths. Divine maidens are in fact so typical of this religion that it cannot be called either a "Father religion" or a "Mother religion," or yet a combination of both. It is as though the Olympian order had thrust the great Mother Goddesses of olden time into the background for the sole purpose of throwing the divine Korai into sharper relief. In the innermost circle of the hierarchy of Greek gods— both on Olympus and in the lesser world of many a Greek city —it was not *Hera,* Zeus' spouse, who shared dominion with him so much as the androgynous figure of Pallas Athene.

In the Peloponnese she was also adored as "Mother Athene,"[16] and to the Athenians she was very much the "Mother."[17] Nevertheless, this designation does not affect her essence, which cannot be better expressed than by the word "Kore." She was called by this more often than by the other name for virgin— *parthenos.* The very coins that bore her image were known as *korai* in Athenian parlance.[18] Her "maidenhood," however, was not thought of in connection with the mother whose daughter she might have been. The goddess Metis, who might have been her mother, vanished in Zeus, and Pallas Athene sprang from her father.[19] Still less was her "maidenhood" understood in connection with a man, for whom she might have been intended or to whom she might have fallen like any other maiden. The Greek idea of divinity seems first to have freed itself from

16 Pausanias, V, 3, 3.
17 Euripides, *Heraclidae,* 771.
18 Hyperides, in Pollux, IX, 74.
19 Hesiod, *Theogony,* 886ff.

sexuality in the maidenhood of Athene, without, however, forfeiting a characteristic otherwise peculiar to male divinities like Zeus and Apollo, namely intellectual and spiritual power.[20]

In the outer circle of the Olympian hierarchy there reigns yet another maiden—Artemis. She too is both Kore and Parthenos. But *her* maidenhood expresses something different from Athene's.[21] Her world is the wide world of Nature, and the brute realities balanced in her—unsubdued virginity and the terrors of birth—have their dominion in a *purely naturalistic, feminine world*. Athene's maidenhood excluded the very possibility of her succumbing to a man; with Artemis, on the other hand, her maidenhood presupposes this possibility. The connection between Artemis the Kore and her mother is looser than between the Kore Persephone and Demeter. Yet Leto is not forgotten when we evoke a vision of Artemis: she is there, enjoying the spectacle of Artemis dancing.[22] The great mythological poets of antiquity, like Aeschylus,[23] and the experts on old mythologems, like Callimachus,[24] ventured to hint that it was a question of only one Kore and one mother, namely Demeter's daughter, be she called Artemis or Persephone.

Persephone, generally called Kore or Pais (ἡ παῖς) by the Greeks, differs from Athene in the same way as Artemis. She is a Kore not because she is above all feminine connections—with mother or husband—but because she embodies these connections as two forms of being each carried to extremes and balanced against one another. One of the forms (daughter with mother) appears as life; the other (young girl with husband) as death. Mother and daughter form a living unity in a borderline situation—a natural unit which, equally naturally, carries within it the seeds of its own destruction. As a maiden, Persephone is an Artemisian figure. She might well have been one of the companions of Artemis who were untrue to their maidenhood and thus paid the penalty of death. This is what in fact happens (though she herself is guiltless) because it is in her nature to happen.

---

[20] Cf. Otto, *The Homeric Gods,* pp. 54f.
[21] Ibid., pp. 89f.
[22] *Odyssey,* VI, 106.
[23] Herodotus, II, 156; Wilamowitz, *Hellenistische Dichtung,* II, p. 48.
[24] Schneider, *Callimachea,* II, pp. 197ff.

Athene and Artemis as the playmates of Persephone, who were present at her rape[25]—thus the myth unites the three variations on the theme of the Kore in a single incident. Artemis and Persephone are like two sides of the same reality. Artemis is the active one. She carries death in herself in the form of murder; according to Homer she was a lioness to women,[26] and in Arcady and Attica she was a bear.[27] Persephone is completely passive. She was picking flowers when she was raped by the Lord of the Dead. They were heavily scented flowers, stupefying flowers like the narcissus.[28] Poets have never failed to catch the significance of this scene. For one of them[29] the flowers were "hell-hounds on her heels"; for another[30] it was a case of "Persephone gathering flowers, herself a fairer flower." The Kore is a creature destined to a flower-like existence which cannot be better described than by one of the poets mentioned:[31]

> . . . a little torrent of life
> leaps up to the summit of the stem, gleams, turns
>   over round the bend
> of the parabola of curved flight,
> sinks, and is gone, like a comet curving into the invisible.

Such would seem to be the essence of Persephone: a lingering on the borders of Hades, a fleeting moment of climax, no sooner here than gone. This Kore would be a perfectly *ideal* figure, a poetic image as clear and pure as a mathematical formula, if it were all nothing but an allegory. An allegory of woman's fate: the borders of Hades an allegory of the border-line between maidenhood and the "other" life, and the seducer, King of the Underworld, an allegory of the earthly bride-groom and husband. But it is not so. As the relics of the Persephone cult show, the meaning is the other way about. She was worshipped in the most serious manner as the *Queen of the*

25 Homeric Hymn to Demeter, 424. Parallels in Allen and Sikes, *The Homeric Hymns;* cf. also L. Malten, "Altorphische Demetersage," pp. 422ff.
26 *Iliad,* XXI, 483.
27 L. R. Farnell, *The Cults of the Greek States,* II, pp. 435 ff.
28 Hymn to Demeter, 7; Preller, *Griechische Mythologie,* I, p. 760.
29 D. H. Lawrence, "Purple Anemones."
30 Milton, quoted in Allen and Sikes, verse 17.
31 D. H. Lawrence, "Fidelity," in his book *Pansies.*

Dead, and the rape of the bride was an allegory of death. Lost maidenhood and the crossing of the borders of Hades are allegorical equivalents—the one can stand for the other equally well.

This kind of equivalence only exists in a given sphere, in an immediately recognizable spiritual connection that can combine very different things, such as marriage and death, in one *comprehensive idea.* Mythological ideas are like the compact buds of such connections. They always contain *more* than the non-mythological mind could conceive. This is also true of the Kore, whom we have so far been considering only in her most *human* form. Here, then, is our Persephone: a creature standing unsubdued on a pinnacle of life and there meeting her fate —a fate that means death in fulfilment and dominion in death.

4. *Hecate*

The oldest account of the rape of the Kore is at the beginning of the Homeric hymn to Demeter. The unknown poet sets out to sing of Demeter, the great Mother Goddess, "of her and her daughter." The "two goddesses" (τὼ δεώ), so they were called at Eleusis, the sacred place whose fame the hymn declares. They are to be thought of as a *double figure,* one half of which is the ideal complement of the other. Persephone is, above all, her *mother's* Kore: without her, Demeter would not be a *Meter.*

Persephone appears in just as ideal a light in another connection as well—as the half of another double figure, the Rulers of the Underworld. Here, as *her bridegroom's Kore,* she belongs (much as the equivalent Thessalian figure was called "Admetus' Kore")[32] to her husband, Hades, to whom she was given by Zeus. The triad consisting of Mother, Kore, and Seducer has a clear and natural place in Zeus' world-order. Clarity and naturalness and a well-defined place in Zeus' world are characteristic of the Homeric style of the hymn.

But a third goddess has a notable part to play beside mother and daughter. According to the hymn, Persephone was raped somewhere in the distance, on the flat ground near the mytho-

32 Hesychius, s.v.

logical Mount Nyssa, where she was playing with the daughters of Oceanus. The scene, however, is still of our world, the world in which our sun shines, to whom Demeter can appeal as the surest eye-witness of the rape. Like the sun, this third goddess appears to belong to the Demeter-Persephone world: *Hecate.* She is in her cave when the sun sees the seduction. All she hears are the cries of the seduced. She is often held to be the representative of the moon, particularly as she is closely related to this heavenly body in other ways.[33]

On the other hand she would seem to be the *double of Demeter herself.* She hears the victim's voice, just as Demeter hears it. She meets Demeter "with a light in her hand" and asks about the seducer in words which, according to an Orphic version of the hymn, are Demeter's own. Then, the poet says, they both go to seek the sun, the eye-witness. There are, however, two versions of the mythologem, one of which leads Demeter,[34] the other Hecate,[35] to the Underworld in search of Persephone. After mother and daughter are reunited, Hecate once more appears in the hymn in order to receive the Kore and remain her companion always: Hecate and Persephone are as inseparable as Persephone and Demeter. *Gaia,* the Earth Mother, has no connection whatever with Demeter in the hymn; she is the seducer's accomplice. So Hecate's close relationship with the double figure of Demeter and the Kore is all the more striking.

A compact group, a triad of unmistakable individuals, this is how the hymn shows the three goddesses: Mother, Daughter, and the moon-goddess Hecate. They are easily confused on sacred monuments, because the torch appears to be the attribute of each of them. This emblem accords with the epithet *phosphoros,* which is applied to Hecate more than once.[36] She is thus explicitly called the "bringer of light." The torch she carries is described in the hymn as σέλας, "light," but not as a means of purification, which is how many moderns are inclined to take this palpable symbol. "Light-bringing" is no doubt an

[33] Cf. Farnell, II, 598 f.
[34] Kerényi, "Zum Vorständnis von Vergilius Aeneis B. VI," p. 422, confirmed by a fragment from the poet Philikos; cf. A. Körte, *Hermes,* pp. 450f.
[35] Callimachus in Scholium to Theocritus, II, 12; Schneider, p. 691.
[36] Scholium to Theocritus, II, 12; Euripides, *Helen,* 569 (fr. 959).

essential part of the goddess's nature, but the torch is characteristic not only of Hecate, it also plays an important part in the Demeter and Persephone cult. One torch, two torches held by the same goddess, three torches in a row,[37] or the "crossed torch" with four lights, all these occur as attributes of both Demeter and Persephone;[38] and this variety of forms proves that we are dealing with some sort of expression rather than an application; a symbol, not a means to a practical end. In the hymn itself Demeter appears with two burning torches.[39] Further investigation outside the confines of the strictly Homeric Zeus-world convinces us that we are not far wrong in our surmise that Hecate is a second Demeter.

As Greek religion developed, there appeared, even in places where the overlordship of Zeus so characteristic of the Homeric religion was of long standing, certain divinities who, on the fringes of the Hellenic cultural world, had retained all their pre-Homeric, pristine freshness. Thus the great goddess of the town of Pherai in Thessaly—*Pheraia*—came to Athens as a "foreign" divinity. In this torch-bearing goddess the Athenians recognized their own Hecate,[40] whereas in her Thessalian home Pheraia was none other than Demeter herself.[41] Pheraia's daughter was also known as Hecate, a different Hecate from the great goddess of Pherai, though obviously resembling her mother.[42] Demeter and her daughter display, in a more primitive form than the Homeric and Attic one, features that permit both of them to appear as Hecate. Or, looking at it from the other point of view, we could say: the Greeks attached the name "Hecate" to a goddess who united in herself affinities with the moon, a Demetrian nature, and Kore-like characteristics—not only those of Persephone but of *Artemis* as well. She was invoked as the daughter of Demeter and the daughter of Leto.[43]

[37] Picture of a sacrifice to Persephone in an Attic vase-painting, L. Deubner, *Attische Feste*, fig. 2.
[38] Kerényi, "ΑΝΟΔΟΣ-Darstellung in Brindisi," p. 279.
[39] Line 48. Similarly Hecate in a *relievo* in Thasos, cf. Farnell, II, Pl. XXXIX a.
[40] Hesychius, s.v.
[41] Eckhel, *Doctrina Nummorum Veterum*, II, p. 147; cf. Lobeck, *Aglaophamus*, II, p. 1213. Cf. also P. Philippson, *Thessalische Mythologie*, pp. 69ff.
[42] Scholium to Lycophron, *Alexandra*, 1180.
[43] Euripides, *Ion*, 1048; *Phoenissae*, 108.

Hecate and Artemis, Trivia and Diana are used so often as equivalent names in ancient literature that we cannot regard this as wholly groundless, any more than we can the familiar equation of Persephone with the moon[44] and Diana with Luna.[45]

The budlike idea of the connection between three aspects of the world—maiden, mother, and moon—hovers at the back of the triad of goddesses in the Homeric hymn. Hecate has a subordinate part to play in keeping with her position on the fringes of the Zeus-world. And yet she still retains, even under Zeus' rule, the characteristics of that archaic figure who preceded the historical Hecate. One such characteristic, and the chief among them, is the *triple form* which appears relatively late in artistic representations of the goddess,[46] but is indirectly confirmed by Hesiod. The poet of the *Theogony* acclaims her as the mighty Mistress of *three* realms—earth, heaven, and sea.[47] He also says that the goddess already had this dominion in the time of the Titans, before Zeus and his order. The new ruler of the world honoured her by leaving her in her former majesty.

The classical figure of Hecate stands stiff and strange in the Greek world, built up on a triangle, and with faces turned in three directions. They tried to get rid of the stiffness of these Hecate statues by breaking up the triune goddess into three dancing maidens. Later times were to stick more rigidly to the characteristic number 3 than did the classical age of Hesiod. The fact that *Hecateia* were set up at the crossing of three roads and that these places were held especially sacred to Hecate does not militate against the Hesiodic or cosmic conception of the number 3: all crossings of three roads point clearly and obviously enough to the possibility of dividing the world into three parts. At the same time Hecate, as Mistress of the Spirits, warned the Greeks that a threefold division would necessarily leave, side by side with the ordered world of Zeus, a chaotic region in which the amorphousness of the primitive world

---

[44] Kerényi, *Pythagoras und Orpheus,* pp. 47ff.
[45] P. Kretschmer, "Dyaus, Zεύς, Diespiter und die Abstrakta im Indogermanischen," pp. 111ff.
[46] Farnell, II, pp. 449ff.
[47] Hesiod, *Theogony,* 411ff.

could live on as the Underworld. The Greeks took Hecate's triplicity as something underworldly.

But in earlier times, before Hecate's three faces had petrified into the well-known *Hecateia*, these three aspects, it seems, were so many aspects or realms of the world, so many possible developments of one and the same compact, budlike idea. Hence we see the inner connection between Demeter, the Kore, and Hecate—and thus the profoundest idea of the mythologem as unfolded in the hymn—in the figure of what is *apparently* the least of the goddesses, the most subordinate of the three.

Besides her Kore quality, her affinity with the moon and with a primitive world of ghosts, a sort of motherliness also pertains to the idea of Hecate. Like Artemis or Mother Earth herself, she was κουροτρόφος, *nurse and nourisher* of all those born after her.[48] In the hymn it is Demeter that appears in this role, as nurse of the king's youngest son in Eleusis. And it is to *her* figure that our concern with Hecate now leads us. In her as well those elements are contained which, besides those already mentioned, constitute the fundamental idea of the hymn. We must not forget for an instant that it is not the idea of the classical or still later Hecate that comes closest to this fundamental idea, but of an original *Demeter and Hecate in one person.*

5. *Demeter*

The sphere of human realities, such as maidenhood and motherhood, is enlarged in the Demeter hymn insofar as it now, thanks to Hecate, suggests a relationship to the moon. At the same time Demeter herself seems to lead us back to something purely human. "La déesse mère vouée à l'éternel regret de sa fille disparue" is how a historian of Greek sculpture describes the celebrated seated statue of her found in Cnidos.[49] These words might also characterize the Demeter of the hymn. The poet describes Persephone's rape at the beginning of the poem, and from then on it is full of her divine mother's pain and grief. Even in their reunion there is still a portion of bitterness, for Persephone has eaten, while with her husband, of the pome-

[48] Hesiod, *Theogony*, 450ff., scholium to Aristophanes, *Wasps*, 804.
[49] Collignon, *Histoire de la sculpture grecque*, II, p. 362.

granate and has to spend a third of every year with him.[50] The mother never quite succeeds in getting her daughter back again.

Human sorrow, yet not *merely* human. For the goddess lets no crops grow during her daughter's absence, and by means of the earth's unfruitfulness she compels the gods to restore her daughter. And she it is who, appeased, lets fruit and flowers grow once more. She "lets" all this "come up,"[51] she who is adored as Anesidora, Chloe ("the Green One"), and Karpophoros ("Bringer of Fruit"). As Horephoros she also brings the favourable season. Science is in the greatest doubt whether she should be identified with the earth or with the grain, or should be regarded as a subterranean power. There are adherents to all three views among the learned. In order to decide for one or the other we must have a clear understanding of the Homeric poet's point of view.

Demeter describes herself in the hymn as being "of the greatest use and the greatest joy to gods and men."[52] There is not a word about her having *taught* men the use of agriculture and the joys of the grain. She could have done—and, according to other sources, did—this just as Aphrodite taught *her* particular "works"—love—had she felt any special desire to do so. Aphrodite is all love, the great goddess who is the cosmic principle and ideal illustration of her works, which she alone makes possible. Once Aphrodite has become a psychic reality, love is the unavoidable and obvious thing. Equally obviously, the idea of Demeter includes, for the Homeric poet, the idea of agriculture, and her fate the fate of the grain.

Neither does the goddess *show* men what has to be done with the grain. What she does show, after the earth has yielded up its fruit, are the *mysteries of Eleusis*. The mythical king of that place and his sons learn from her the secret usages of the cult, which the poet may not disclose. He who has seen the unutterable works of Demeter is fortunate: the uninitiate will enjoy no such lot in the darkness of death.[53]

---

50 According to later tradition (Ovid and Hyginus), *half* the year. We are not concerned with this easily understandable version here, since it is obviously not the primary one.
51 Hymn to Demeter, 471, ἀνῆκεν.
52 Ibid., 268f.
53 Ibid., 473–480.

So much we learn from the Homeric poet. For him, grain is the self-evident gift of the goddess. What Demeter shows to mortals over and above this is something worthy of note but not to be named, the ἄρρητον. The hymn is completely unthinkable without this allusion to the mysterious, supreme gift of the goddess. But we do not need to write a poem just to say something self-evident and already tacitly assumed, as is this connection between Demeter and the grain.[54] It is no less fundamental to the hymn than the other connections we have mentioned, between marriage and death and maiden and moon. On this self-evident foundation rests the special thing that the goddess does and shows. One of the symbols that was displayed in the Eleusinian mysteries on Demeter's instructions was a single ear of grain.[55] So the *self-evident* gift of the goddess serves to express what was revealed only to the *initiate*. The core of the Demetrian idea has *grain and motherhood* as its natural sheath and disguise. All three aspects—Mother Goddess, Corn Goddess, and Goddess of esoteric mysteries—belong to the figure of Demeter; none of them can be thought away, and the latter two in particular are closely connected in the hymn.

The strange conduct of Demeter as a nurse seems, in the hymn, to rest likewise on these two aspects. When, still unknown, the goddess came to Eleusis she offered her services as nurse to the friendly daughters of the king. These gave her the king's youngest son, Demophoön, to look after. Every night she laid him secretly in the fire—a singular method of obtaining immortality for her charge! The Homeric poet likens the child so placed to a flaming brand or torch (δαλός). He may have been thinking of the great part the torch played in the nocturnal celebrations at Eleusis. The mythological picture of the child in the fire[56] is in accord with the fact that in the mysteries the birth of a divine child was celebrated with the shining of a great light. Caught in her strange and awful act, the goddess speaks, in words of mystic revelation, of the *ignorance* of men.[57]

54 Because of this, the analysis put forward by Wilamowitz (*Der Glaube der Hellenen*, II, pp. 47ff.) falls to the ground.

55 Hippolytus, *Elenchos*, V, 8, 39.

56 Cf. supra, pp. 35ff., Kullervo; and Kerényi, *Niobe*, pp. 75f., 259.

57 Hymn to Demeter, 256f. The words used here by Demeter are taken up in the Orphic version (fr. 49, 95f.), in a later Orphic poem (fr. 233), and in the *Carmen aureum Pythagorae*, 54f.

Had they understanding of good and evil, she says, they would also understand the significance of that apparently deadly deed.

The meaning of it—good concealed in evil—is *immortality*. There can be no doubt of that. It is scarcely necessary to point out that Demeter's behaviour is not "anthropomorphic." To be laid in the fire and yet to remain alive, indeed to win immortality—that is no human fate. Does the goddess, perhaps, overstep the bounds of the humanly possible by reason of her sovereignty in that other domain of hers, which includes the *fate of the grain?* And not only by reason of her *power*, but because of her *form?* It would seem so, when we consider that the Demetrian fruit is perfected for human nourishment *in the fire*. Whether it is parched or baked as bread, death by fire is the fate of the grain. Nevertheless, every sort of grain is eternal. "I am not dead"—so sings the Maize God of the Cora Indians of Mexico after he is given over to the fire.[58] "My younger brothers (mankind) appear but once. Do they not die forever? But I never die; I appear continually. . . ." Among another tribe of Mexican Indians, the Tahumares, new-born boys undergo, on the third day, a rite very similar to what the Cora Indians do to the cobs that signify the Maize God: they make a great fire out of the stalks and carry the child three times through the smoke in all four directions. They do this, so runs the explanation today, in order that the child may thrive and be successful in life, i.e., in "raising corn."[59]

Of all the analogies that have been collected[60] this seems to fit best. Demeter treats Demophoön as though he were grain. Not, however, in order to make a successful farmer out of him. The Demophoön incident points as clearly as does the whole hymn to the fact that immortality is one of Demeter's gifts and that this immortality is akin to that of the grain. Old questions at once arise: Is Demeter's motherhood to be understood metaphorically? Was not the goddess, before she became completely anthropomorphic, a "Corn Mother," the ripe corn being taken as a maternal entity? And consequently, is not her daughter only apparently a maiden, but in reality a kind of plant? In late

[58] K. T. Preuss, *Der religiöse Gehalt der Mythem,* p. 8.
[59] C. Lumholtz, *Unknown Mexico,* I, p. 272.
[60] Frazer, in his edition of Apollodorus (1921), II, pp. 311f.

antiquity the word κόρη was explained as the feminine form of κόρος (sprout).[61] Another old interpretation is in the same spirit, which saw in Demeter's ravished daughter the grain for sowing.[62] The disappearance of both as though in death and their resurrection-like return said much in favour of this view. Yet even in antiquity such interpretations were merely rationalistic explanations which reversed the religious meaning: for the religious-minded man the *grain* expressed an inexpressible divine reality rather than that the goddess, Demeter's daughter, expressed the grain. The Kore figure of Persephone may have been the allegorical equivalent of the grain, but they are so equivalent that each can stand for the other. Both allude only to that unutterable thing hinted at in the very name of this Kore—ἄρρητος κούρα: the Maiden not to be named.[63]

Mother divided from daughter, and the mown ear, are two symbols of something unspeakably painful that is hidden in the Demeter-aspect of the world; but also of something very consoling. Demeter contains this consolation in herself and reveals it in Eleusis. Seen as a whole, the Demetrian idea is not confined to purely human forms and relations, nor is it exhausted in the great reality of the grain. But in this non-human reality the idea is more comprehensive than it is in its purely human forms. The grain-figure is essentially the figure of both origin and end, of mother and daughter; and just because of that it points beyond the individual to the universal and eternal. It is always *the grain* that sinks to earth and returns, always the grain that is mown down in golden fullness and yet, as fat and healthy seed, remains whole, mother and daughter in one.

The symbolical value of the grain in the Demeter religion is vouched for in every way. The mown ear in Eleusis, five beautiful stalks of wheat in a little temple depicted on a vase[64] —there is evidence enough. The two great goddesses (also called

---

[61] Porphyry, in Eusebius, *Praeparatio Evangelica*, III, 11, 7, 9.

[62] Cicero, *De natura deorum*, II, 66.

[63] Euripides, *Helen*, 1307 (fr. 63); Carcinus in Diodorus Siculus, V, 5, 1; cf. ἄφραστος in Hesychius, s.v., and Ἑκάτη Ἄφραστος, *Jahrbuch für Phil.*, Suppl., XXVII (1900), 111.

[64] Farnell, III, Pl. 111b, with Lenormant's explanation in Daremberg and Saglio, *Dictionnaire des antiquités grecques et romaines*, I, p. 1066.

Δαμάτερες, in the plural)[65] are not diminished in their aspect as grain; on the contrary they become greater, more comprehensive, more cosmic. Herein lies the real religious value of everything in the fate of the grain that reminded the Greeks of the fate of Persephone. And what did not remind them of it? There was hardly anything that did not do so. The only thing that is impossible is to reduce the whole mythologem of mother and daughter, and the innumerable associations that unfold in it like a bud, *merely* to the fate of the grain and to understand it purely allegorically. The mythological idea does not keep strictly to any natural process; it is enriched by them and enriches them in turn. It takes from nature but gives back again, and this is the sense in which we are to think of the relationship between the Persephone myth and the fate of the grain.

In Attica, besides the lesser mysteries in Agrai and the great mysteries in Eleusis, there were various other festivals connected with Persephone. Two of them fell at the time of the sowing: the Eleusinian mysteries and a women's festival, the Thesmophoria, from which men were excluded. Both involved fasting, following the example of Demeter's fast; and thus both were in some way connected with the disappearance of the Kore, which occasioned the fasting. Hence it was the sowing of the grain that reminded the Greeks of the Kore's rape.

The link between sowing the grain and vanishing in the underworld is confirmed by a further correspondence of myth and cult. The Orphic variants of the mythologem relegated the events in the Homeric hymn to a very primitive setting.[66] A swineherd comes in, with the name of *Eubuleus* (a name also of Hades); he is the witness of the rape, because his pigs were swallowed up by the earth along with Persephone. This story is borne out—as the sources themselves show[67]—by the fact that *young pigs* were cast into pits in honour of the two goddesses. We learn this in connection with the Thesmophoria; but it would be clear enough in any case that an analogy existed between the cavalier treatment of pigs and the sowing of the grain.

The pig is Demeter's sacrificial animal. In one connection,

65 Nilsson, "Die eleusinischen Gottheiten," p. 87.
66 Cf. Malten, pp. 429ff.
67 Clement of Alexandria, *Protrepicus*, II, 17, 1; Rabe, scholium to Lucian, p. 275.

where it is dedicated to the Eleusinian mysteries, it is called δέλφαξ,[68] the "uterine animal" of the earth, just as the dolphin was the "uterine animal" of the sea.[69] It was customary for Demeter to receive a gravid sow as a sacrificial offering.[70] The mother animal is a fit offering to the Mother Goddess, the pig in the pit a fit offering to her vanished daughter. As symbols of the goddesses, *pig* and *grain* are perfect parallels. Even the decomposed bodies of the pigs were drawn into the cult: the noisome remains were fetched up again, put on the altar, and used to make the sowing more fruitful.[71] If, then, the pig-and-grain parallel lays stress on corruption, it will no doubt remind us that the grain *decays* under the earth and thus, in this state of fruitful death, hints at the Kore dwelling in the realm of the dead.

So the Demeter idea is not lacking in the element of corruption coupled with the Kore's subterranean abode. Seen in terms of the Persephone myth, the fruitful death of the grain, religiously emphasized by the particulars of the pig-sacrifice, acquires a symbolic value, just as it is used as a parable for another idea: "Verily I say unto you, except a corn of wheat fall into the ground and die, it abideth alone: but if it die, it bringeth forth much fruit."[72] The corn and the pig buried in earth and left to decay point to a mythological happening and, interpreted accordingly, become transparently clear and hallowed.

The happenings of the natural process and the development of the mythological idea coincide thus far and no further. Persephone spends a *third* of every year in the underworld. Does the "fruitful death" of the grain last that long? The new crop sprouts much earlier;[73] and Demeter, the mother proud of her daughter (the ripened grain), appears much later in her golden garment of ears. According to the myth, the ripened wheat grains would have to fall to earth, the scene of their death and resurrection, immediately after their separation from

[68] Epicharmus, fr. 100.
[69] Cf. supra, p. 50.
[70] Farnell, pp. 330, 91; 365, 246.
[71] Scholium to Lucian, loc. cit.
[72] John, 12:24.
[73] This objection comes from Nilsson, p. 107.

the "mother." Under the original conditions, when grain grew wild, this was in fact the case. The corresponding mythologem is probably just as old and is closer to the natural process than to the artificial process. True, even in early antiquity the grain was kept in storage chambers and containers almost as in a tomb, the seed-corn generally for four months;[74] but it was preserved *from* decay and coming to life again. This has nothing to do with the myth. The grain in the vaults of Eleusis was part of the *temple treasure* of Demeter and meant to keep for a long time.

Hence the third of the year cannot be explained as a mere allegory of the agricultural process. The threefold division is inextricably bound up with the primitive form of the goddess Demeter, who was also Hecate, and Hecate could claim to be mistress of the three realms. In addition, her relations to the moon, the grain, and the realm of the dead are three fundamental traits in her nature. The goddess's sacred number is the special number of the underworld: 3 dominates the chthonic cults of antiquity.[75] The division of the year into three in the Persephone myth corresponds not to a natural process but to a mythological idea.

6. *Persephone*

A divinity with a number of aspects is very apt to appear only in the *one* aspect under which he or she is being regarded at the moment. So it is with the primary goddess, who could equally well be called Hecate. In her Persephone aspect she exemplifies the Greek idea of *non-being;*[76] in her Demeter aspect she is a Hellenic form of the idea of the All-Mother. Those of us who are inclined to regard the Greek divinities as unmixed types must, in this case, accustom themselves to a duality of fundamentally different goddesses. But they must also realize that the idea of non-being in Greek religion forms the root-aspect of being.[77] This realization will enable them to

74 Here, with Cornford, Nilsson (op. cit., p. 108) finds the explanation of the Persephone myth.
75 H. Diels, *Sibyllinische Blätter,* p. 40.
76 Kerényi, *Die antike Religion,* pp. 220ff.
77 Kerényi, *Dionysos und das Tragische in der Antigone,* p. 10.

understand the deep-rooted identity of those two different and yet so closely related figures. Those, on the other hand, who do not incline to this view are tempted to assume a superficial and subsequent merging of two originally independent goddesses.

For this subsequent merging there is of course no evidence whatever, and the connection between the goddesses is anything but superficial. In the very place where, according to modern assumptions, this "superficial" connection is supposed to have been made, namely Eleusis, we see how intimately the Kore and Demeter are in fact connected. The daughter as a goddess originally quite independent of her mother is unthinkable; but what *is* thinkable, as we shall see, is the original *identity* of mother and daughter. Persephone's whole being is summed up in an incident that is at once the story of Demeter's own sufferings. The daughter's being is revealed like a flash in her mother's, only to be snuffed out the next moment:

> turns over round the bend
> of the parabola of curved flight,
> sinks, and is gone. . . .

The Kore who appears with Demeter is comparable with the *Hebe* who appears with the great goddess *Hera*. In ancient Arcadia[78] Hera had three forms: maiden ($\pi\alpha\tilde{\iota}\varsigma$), fulfilled woman ($\tau\epsilon\lambda\epsilon\acute{\iota}\alpha$), and woman of sorrows ($\chi\acute{\eta}\varrho\alpha$). As $\tau\epsilon\lambda\epsilon\acute{\iota}\alpha$ she has in Hebe *her own maiden self,* "Ηρα παῖς, for constant companion.[79] That is the static or plastic way of putting what is told in dynamic mythological form in the story of Hera emerging from her bath in the spring Kanathos ever again as a virgin.[80] As Hebe's mother she always has Hebe in herself; and as $\chi\acute{\eta}\varrho\alpha$ she is endowed with characteristics that remind us of the grieving and recriminatory Demeter.

The comparison with Hera and her daughter may be allowed to stand as a mere analogy, and the question of whether they are both to be regarded as developments of the same mytho-

---

[78] In Stymphalis; Pausanias, VIII, 22.
[79] Or, from Hebe's point of view: "It is as though Hebe had separated herself only gradually from the goddess to become her daughter and an independent divinity, as though in the beginning she had been a manifestation of Hera herself." P. Philippson, *Griechische Gottheiten in ihren Landschaften (Symbolae Osloenses,* suppl. fasc. IX, 1939), p. 48.
[80] Pausanias, II, 38, 2.

logical idea may be left undiscussed. Archaic Demeter figures are vivid proof that they always contain their own maiden form. Arcadia was familiar with two such Demeters, or rather with one that had two names: a dark, age-old goddess whose bitter rancour makes her kin both to the Ἥρα χήρα and to the sorrowful Eleusinian mother.[81] In Phigalia she was called the Black One (Δημήτηρ μέλαινα) in Thelpusa, Demeter Erinys. Both places had the same legend about her, a legend that expresses the deep-rooted identity of the original Demeter and the original Kore mythologically, but none the less clearly.

This is the mythologem of the marriage of the reluctant goddess, and the best-known variation of it came at the beginning of the cyclical epic, *Cypria*.[82] Here the bride—the original Kore—was called *Nemesis;* the bridegroom and seducer, *Zeus.* Pursued by the god's desire, the goddess transforms herself into various beasts of the earth, sea, and air. In this last mutation, as wild birds of the primeval swamp—she as a goose, he as a swan—the two divinities celebrate their marriage by rape. For this marriage was and remained a rape. The goddess was not to be softened by love; she succumbed to violence and therefore became the eternal avenger—Nemesis. The Kore to whom she gave birth was called *Helen.* The daughter had Artemisian traits from her Artemisian mother, Zeus' unwilling bride; and Aphrodisiac traits that were the reason for her being continually ravished. But in her ravishment and revenge, to which so many mortals fell victim, her mother's nature was only repeating itself. Helen is the eternally youthful Nemesis, spoiling for a rape and always wreaking her vengeance afterwards.

A similar story was told in Arcadia of the Demeter whose cognomen *Erinys* is the same as Nemesis. She, too, was pursued by a god—Poseidon, whose name simply means that he became Demeter's spouse.[83] She, too, transformed herself into the shape of an animal in order to escape from her seducer. Our source only speaks of her transformation into a mare, in which shape

---

81 Pausanias, VIII, 25 and 42, our source for what follows. The credibility of Pausanias' description of the Demeter statue in Phigalia is vouched for by the mythologem and art relics as against Wilamowitz, *Der Glaube der Hellenen* I, pp. 402f.

82 Kerényi, *Die Geburt der Helena*, pp. 9ff.

83 Kretschmer, "Zur Geschichte der grechischen Dialekte," pp. 28ff.

she was overpowered by Poseidon the *horse*. Her image in the Phigalian cave, however, was distinguished not only by a horse's head with "snakes and other animals growing out of it," but by a dolphin and a bird as well, apparently a dove. An aquatic animal and a creature of the air would therefore seem to indicate the two other realms in which, apart from the earth, the pursued goddess might have undergone transformations. The Kore who was born of this Nemesis-like marriage was called "Mistress" (Δέσποινα) in Phigalia—that is, with one of Persephone's ritual names. Our source further remarks that in Phigalia the daughter was *not* a horse, that in Thelpusa she was a being "not to be named" before the uninitiate, and that she had a brother there who was the horse *Areion*. So the original Demeter seems to have been reborn in her mysterious daughter with the horse-brother just as Nemesis was in Helen.

Strangest of all is the explanation of the goddess's dark Erinys aspect. She is wroth because of the rape of her daughter and *at the same time* because of the marriage by rape which she herself had to undergo. In the legend that has come down to us, it is said that she was overpowered by Poseidon while she was looking for her ravished daughter. This mythological elaboration *doubles* the rape, for the goddess experienced the rape in *herself,* as Kore, and not in a separate girl. A daughter with the name of "Mistress" or "She who is not to be named" was born of this rape. The goddess becomes a mother, rages and grieves over the Kore who was ravished *in her own being,* the Kore whom she immediately recovers, and in whom she gives birth to *herself* again. The idea of the original Mother-Daughter goddess, at root a single entity, is at the same time the idea of *rebirth.*

To enter into the figure of Demeter means to be pursued, to be robbed, raped, to fail to understand, to rage and grieve, but then to get everything back and be born again. And what does all this mean, save to realize the universal principle of life, the fate of everything mortal? What, then, is left over for the figure of Persephone? Beyond question, that which constitutes the structure of the living creature *apart from* this endlessly repeated drama of coming-to-be and passing-away, namely the *uniqueness* of the individual and its *enthralment to non-being.* Uniqueness and non-being understood not philosophically but envisaged corporeally in figures, or rather as these are envisaged in the formless, unsubstantial realm of Hades. There Persephone reigns, the eternally unique one who is no more. Her uniqueness, so we could put it philosophically, forms the τι— that something in regard to which even non-being *is* (ἐστὶ κατά τι).[84] Had that uniqueness not been, had nothing ever stirred and started up in non-being, then the realm of Hades would not exist; in relation to pure nothing it would not be at all, not even an aspect of the past.

Homer conceives the realm of Hades as amorphously as it was possible for a Greek—that is to say, as poor in form and without any contours, with no connecting lines. He has no use for the method employed in archaic art to express the dead and the deadly: the creation of terrifying monsters and hybrids. Apparitions of this kind are as little suited to his style as to his conception of the shadowy realm. It is no awful shape that prevents the soul of Patroclus from passing through the gate of Hades and across its river. (The gate of Hades, the river, and even the House of Hades in which Patroclus' soul wanders, are all fluid, not marked off from one another; only in comparison with the realm of the living are they something wholly different.) Instead of a single terrifying shape, the whole kingdom of the dead rises up to oppose the entry of the soul of one not yet buried—the shadowy, amorphous kingdom seen as the congregation of all the souls: τῆλέ με εἴργουσι ψυχαί εἴδωλα καμόντων.[85]

Taken individually, the souls are not amorphous: they are the *images of the departed* (εἴδωλα καρόντων), but not corpselike images. They have nothing of the "living corpse" about them[86] which figures in the ghost stories of so many peoples. The soul of Patroclus still has the lovely eyes of the hero, though in the corpse these have long since decayed.[87] The εἴδωλα in the realm

---

[84] The Platonic expression is here used in the same sense as in *Die antike Religion*, p. 234.

[85] *Iliad*, XXIII, 72.

[86] Nor anything of the "corpse spiritualized or dematerialized in some mysterious way," as W. F. Otto (*Die Manen*, p .37) expresses the idea that, in his view, best corresponds to the Homeric "shade."

[87] Compare with this the terrible state Hector was in when his spirit appeared to Aeneas in Virgil, *Aeneid*, II, 270ff. As F. Altheim once observed to me, it is as though the Romans clung even in death to the *historical* figure, the Greeks to the *ideal* one.

of the dead represent as it were the *minimum conceivable amount of form;* they are the image with which the deceased individual, through his uniqueness, has enriched the world.[88] Over the countless "images" of all that has once been, now heaped together and merged into an indeterminate featureless mass, there reigns *Persephone*—the eternally unique.

Whenever she is mentioned in the Iliad, she receives the title of ἐπαινή ("awful"), which implies praise and fear of her in equal measure; and she is indissolubly linked to the ruler of the dead. Her husband is sometimes called Hades, sometimes the *Zeus of the Underworld.* The wife of this Zeus undoubtedly counts as a great goddess, to whom all mortals are subject just as they are to that other Zeus—the ruler of the world seen in his deadly aspect. She has dominion over the manifold powers of death. Here we have the terrible aspects of Persephone, which are merely hinted at in Homeric poetry and are only associated with her—or with her and her husband as an indivisible pair—by implication. The association does not give rise to the firm outlines of a concrete figure, a monstrous figure, say, like the Black Demeter in Phigalia. Homer does not draw any frightening apparition for us, but he brings out the association all the more clearly. In the ninth book of the Iliad it is unmistakable. On one occasion the *Erinyes* are invoked in the plural. The curse, however, is heard and fulfilled not by a vague throng of vengeful spirits but by the underworldly Zeus and Persephone.[89] The second time the curse is addressed to the rulers of the Underworld. The utterer of the curse beats the earth with her hands. She is heard by Erinys, the mist-wandering goddess who dwells in the gloomy nether regions of Erebos.[90]

There are two ways of considering connections like this between Erinys and the rulers of the Underworld. One way be-

---

[88] According to the Pythagoreans, the image of the unique mixture of elements that produced the individual passes to the moon, never to be replaced (Kerényi, *Pythagoras und Orpheus,* 2nd edn.; p. 59). Every individual being is accordingly preserved not only in the *past* of a world temporally conceived (consisting of what *has been* and *is*), but in a definite portion of the spatial universe as well. Another such storage-place is the House of Hades, the *thesaurus Orci* of the Romans.

[89] *Iliad,* IX, 454–457.

[90] Ibid., 569–572.

gins with the dispersed state of the various aspects of the gods and believes in a *subsequent* mythological combination of them, with the result that mythology is understood at best as a co-ordinating and embellishing activity of the mind. Our way is opposed to this. It begins with the mythological ideas, which are easily recognized by their pristine *richness and many-sidedness.* Mythology is then understood as the mind's *creation* of gods in the sense that something real and valid is brought into the world.[91] Realities that disclose themselves to the mind are timeless. The *forms* in which they disclose themselves are stages in a process of (budlike) unfolding, and every unfolding tends ultimately towards dissolution. The primary thing for us is not this final state, not the Erinyes as spirits of vengeance, or Demeter and Persephone existing independently side by side, but the historical *Demeter Erinys* who contains in herself her own Kore figure—Persephone.

The Odyssey furnishes proof that the deadly powers associated with the Homeric Underworld may be regarded as allusions to this goddess. One such power, the power to terrify, to petrify with fright, to *turn to stone,* is possessed by the *Gorgon's head.* Odysseus is thinking of this when he sees the countless host of the dead approaching him: perhaps Persephone has sent the Gorgon's head from Hades![92] The mass of shades and the frightful apparition are respectively the *indefinite* and the *definite* manifestation of the realm of the dead. Though this realm is the domain of Persephone and her husband, the definite form of it points to the original Demeter.

Gorgon-like features are in fact displayed by the Black Demeter, who had a legend in common with Demeter Erinys. The horse-headed goddess was further characterized by having "snakes and other animals growing out of her head." The Gorgon's head in conjunction with a horse's body can be seen in an archaic representation of the killing of Medusa.[93] The Gorgon-headed Medusa was, like Demeter, Poseidon's bride. Like her, she gave birth to a horse—Pegasus—and to a mysterious son with the name of Chrysaor, the cognomen of Demeter Chrysaor.

91 Kerényi, *Apollon,* 120; *Die antike Religion,* p. 65.
92 *Odyssey,* XI, 634f.
93 Boeotian wine-jar in relief in Paris, cf. R. Hampe, *Frühe griechische Sagenbilder in Böotien,* Pls. 36 and 38.

Closer scrutiny shows that the most important features in the fate of Persephone are also common to Medusa: she too was the only member of a divine triad—the trinity of Gorgons—to succumb to death *by violence*.[94]

The Kore's rape and the killing of Medusa are further connected by the name of the killer. Persephone (in Homer, "Persephoneia," Attic "Perrephatta") may well be a pre-Hellenic word that has been given Greek form; it is most probably connected with the name of Medusa's killer *Perseus*,[95] and can be understood in Greek as "she who was killed by Perseus."[96] Perseus has various things in common with Hades; for one thing he wore Hades' cap that made him invisible, and in Lerna he was actually identical with Hades. He immersed Dionysus in the waters, which in this case probably signified the Underworld.[97] The similarity between the fates of Dionysus and Persephone does not rest on this alone. We shall not pursue it further here, but shall keep to one aspect of the Medusa-killing.

The Gorgon's head was cut off with a *sickle*, an ancient mythological weapon with which Uranos was mutilated by Kronos.[98] If anything can throw light on the *meaning* of the use of this instrument and no other, it is the simple fact that from the remotest times this moon-shaped instrument has been used for the cutting of that which *bears the seed*, i.e., the standing corn. It is almost as if something *lunar* were fated to die by something *moon-shaped*. At any rate, certain features in Medusa's fate transparently connect this goddess with the bride, grain, and death aspects of Persephone.

Or, looking at it the other way round, we could say that through the figure of Persephone, the stately Queen of Hades, we glimpse the Gorgon. What we conceive philosophically as the element of *non-being* in Persephone's nature appears, mythologically, as the hideous Gorgon's head, which the goddess sends forth from the Underworld and which she herself bore in her archaic form. It is not, of course, *pure* non-being, rather

---

[94] Hesiod, *Theogony*, 276–282; Apollodorus, *Bibliotheca*, II, 4, 2.

[95] Wilamowitz, *Der Glaube der Hellenen*, I, pp. 108f.; further details in Altheim, "Persona," pp. 45f.

[96] Like Θεόπομπος in the connotation "he who is sent by God."

[97] C. Robert, *Die griechische Heldensage*, I, p. 243.

[98] Hesiod, *Theogony*, 174–181.

the sort of non-being from which the living shrink as from something *with a negative sign:* a monstrosity that has usurped the place of the unimaginably beautiful, the nocturnal aspect of what by day is the most desirable of all things.

If we wanted to answer the question of the origin of this symbol, we should have to go more deeply into the antecedents of the other two great Kore figures, Artemis and Athene. There, too, we would meet with the Gorgon's head. Athene wears it on her breast, and Medusa appears on archaic monuments as a primitive form of Artemis, the mistress of wild animals.[99] She also has the wings of Nemesis. In her most ancient aspect as Medusa and Nemesis, Artemis proves to be identical with the original Demeter and thus with Persephone. The picture of the killing of Medusa—the most ancient form of Persephone's fate —on the pediment of the archaic temple to Artemis in Corfu commemorates this primitive mythological state.[100]

From it, the classical figure of Persephone rises up pure and beautiful, Artemisian and Aphrodisiac at once, another Helen, herself the daughter of Nemesis. Her Gorgonesque features remain in the background. On the wonderful little votive tablet in a temple to Persephone in Lower Italy[101] the Kore's departure is depicted as well as her rape. It is worthy of Aphrodite herself: winged cupids draw the chariot of the goddess. One would think that it was not Persephone celebrating her triumph, but Aphrodite. And indeed reference could be made to *Aphrodite Epitymbidia* or *Tymborychos*,[102] goddess of the tombs and the dead. In Persephone the sublimest beauty as well as the most hideous ugliness has its foundation. Non-being can put on an alluring face, and the goddess of the dead can appear in the form of an hetaera. Such were the sirens, Circe and Calypso, but not the Grecian Persephone. The foundation of her aphrodisiac beauty lies in what we have called her *uniqueness.*

---

99 Kerényi, *Die Geburt der Helena,* p. 19; cf. *Journal of Hellenic Studies,* 1885, Pl. LIX.

100 The inscriptions mention Artemis; cf. Kaiser Wilhelm II's *Erinnerungen an Korfu,* p. 105.

101 Lokroi Epizephyroi, cf. Quagliati, "Rilievi votivi arcaici," p. 188.

102 Plutarch, *Quaestiones Romanae,* XXIII; Clement of Alexandria, *Protrepicus,* XXXVIII.

In a world of living and dying, that is, in the world of Demeter and Persephone, there is an intimate connection between uniqueness and beauty. We can regard it from the point of view of beauty alone, as Winckelmann did, thinking unconsciously of Persephone when he said: "Strictly speaking, a beautiful person is beautiful for a moment only." Or we can regard it from the point of view of that instant after which non-being comes, like a dark abyss. At such moments the beautiful shines out in all its supreme radiance, and even a mortal maiden—Antigone advancing towards her bridal chamber, the grave—is then in the likeness of "beautiful Persephone."[103]

7. *Indonesian Kore Figures*

The paradox of mythological ideas, the *fons et origo* of our discussion, seems to have complicated itself to the point of unintelligibility. We have assumed, at the back of the double-figure of Demeter and the Kore, an idea which embraces both and which, budlike, compact of the strangest associations, unfolds into three divinities—Hecate, Demeter, and Persephone. It is not the unfolding that is unintelligible; the possibility of this is grounded on numerous mythological examples, the hybrid and changeling forms of the original Demeter or Nemesis. What are difficult to understand, because they appear to have no precedent, are the strange associations.

There is, for instance, the strange equation of marriage and death, the bridal chamber and the grave. Marriage in this connection has the character of murder: the brutal ravisher is the god of death himself. On the other hand, marriage retains its proper and primary meaning as the union of man and woman. But not only does it call forth the lamentations of the celebrants, it also calls forth obscene speech and laughing at obscene actions. Demeter herself furnishes an example of this, as also of lamentation, when she permits herself to be moved to mirth by a shameless old woman. (In the hymn the name of the old woman, *Iambe,* is suggestive of indecent speech, while the

---

[103] Kerényi, *Dionysos und das Tragische in der Antigone,* pp. 12ff.; *Die antike Religion,* p. 239. Virgil (*Aeneid*, VI, 142) calls Persephone *pulchra Proserpina;* καλά and καλλίστα are titles of Artemis, cf. Preller, *Griechische Mythologie,* p. 301, n. 3.

name she has in the Orphic variations,[104] *Baubo* or "belly," suggests indecent behaviour.) We can speak of a connection between *death and fertility,* and conceive fertility in such a crude way that a gravid sow may serve as its symbol.

Another peculiar association is that between the ambiguous incident of the Kore's rape and Hecate. At the centre of Hecate's sphere of influence there stands the moon. What the moon sheds her light on is in its turn highly ambiguous: on the one hand we have motherly solicitude and the growth of all living things, on the other more indecency and deadliness[105]— not in the sense of the bride dying in order to give life, but in the sense of witchcraft and ghosts. Proper to Hecate is the *dog,* the animal howling in the moonlight, which, for the Greeks, symbolized the last word in obscenity. One could define the world of Hecate as the *lunar aspect of the Demeter world.* But we must add that it is at the same time a distorted aspect of the world of the mighty huntress and *dancer* Artemis. Fertility and death are somehow related to those aspects of the world ruled by the moon.

A third strange association is with the *plant that serves mankind as food.* This is not a question simply of allegories (for even the grain-symbol cannot, by itself, comprise the whole idea of the primary goddess who is mother and daughter in one), nor of a causal connection between the moon and certain phenomena of human and vegetable life. The moon in this case is not a *primum movens;* she suffers just like man or plant. It is rather a question of some *occurrence in our cosmos* which mythology expresses equally in the symbol of the moon, the woman, and the grain. In so doing it speaks of the one under the image of the other. For this purpose it is particularly fond of the Kore figure.

Not only is this the case with the Greeks but also in a part of the world as far removed from old Mediterranean culture as the Indonesian archipelago. Kores are to be found there which show that what seemed unintelligible to us existed not once only and not only in one particular mythology. These Kores came unexpectedly to light as the result of a Frobenius expedition to the island of Ceram. The leader of the expedi-

104 *Orphicorum fragmenta* (ed. Kern), 52.
105 For what follows see *Apollon,* pp. 150ff.

tion and editor of the whole collection of myths, Dr. Jensen, could not anticipate what an impression of uncanny similarity his *Hainuwele,* the divine maiden after whom he named the new collection,[106] would make on those who were already engaged on a study of Persephone. All the more important are the observations with which he prefaces his volume.

These observations are based not on the Indonesian material alone but also on other and much more comprehensive ethnological findings, mostly African. Dr. Jensen observes first that the majority of peoples cannot think of the fact of death without thinking of the fact of procreation and the increase of mankind. Thus the Ceramese say that the first men could not die so long as they had not eaten of the coconut. And only when they did this could they marry. "Wherever the connection between death and fertility is explicit in the myths," so Dr. Jensen says in his second observation, "emphasis is laid on the connection between men and plants." In this sense we have to understand the fact that in the great *Hainuwele* mythologem the first death among men was a murder, and that only since then have there been useful plants. To this we must add the close relationship between the maiden Hainuwele and the moon. The complete picture that results is as follows: "At the centre of the Ceramese mythological view of the world there is a connection between death and procreation, and this, as with so many peoples of the earth, is seen and experienced in the image of the *plant* as a form of being, and in the phenomenon of the dying and returning *moon.*"

The ethnologist thus confirms, from the religious views of many different peoples, the whole system of associations on which the Persephone mythologem is based. Even more surprising than the correspondence of principle is the correspondence of detail in the Indonesian myth of the Kore, which points not merely to the same fundamental budlike idea but to a far-reaching similarity in its unfolding. This is particularly striking when we compare the two main variations: the seduc-

---

106 *Hainuwele: Volkserzählungen von der Molukken-Insel Ceram,* collected and edited by A. E. Jensen and H. Niggemeyer with illustrations by A. Hahn. Jensen's Introduction and the Hainuwele mythologem also in "Eine ostindinesische Mythe als Ausdruck einer Weltanschauung," pp. 199 ff.; cf. Jensen, *Das religiöse Weltbild einer frühen Kultur; Die drei Ströme.*

tion of *Rabie* and the killing of *Hainuwele*. *Rabie* is the name of the moon-maiden. Hainuwele is sometimes called Rabie-Hainuwele; but in her there is more of an identity with the plant, while Rabie is evidently more of a lunar character.

Rabie is wooed by *Tuwale,* the sun-man. Her parents won't give her to him. They put a dead pig in her place in the bridal bed. Tuwale thereupon returns the marriage portion and goes away. A few days later Rabie leaves the village and stands on the roots of a tree. "As she was standing there," so the story continues, "the roots sank slowly into the ground and *Rabie sank with them.* Try as she would she could not get out of the earth and sank deeper and deeper. She cried for help and the villagers came running. They tried to dig Rabie out, but the more they struggled the deeper she sank. When she had gone in up to her neck she said to her mother: 'Tuwale is fetching me! Kill a pig and make ready a feast, for I am dying. When it is evening three days from now, look up at the sky, all of you, and you will see me appearing as a light.' Her parents and the villagers went home and killed a pig. They held a feast of the dead for Rabie that lasted three days, and on the third day they all looked up at the sky. Then, for the first time, the full moon rose in the east."[107]

In the Hainuwele mythologem proper the name of the father, *Ameta,* which contains the signification "dark" or "night," is the first thing that points to the lunar character of the girl; the second thing is the appearance of a pig. In another story[108] the moon-maiden takes refuge in a *pond* after her sun-moon marriage, disappears in it, and goes on living as a pig with her child, also a pig. The Hainuwele mythologem begins as if the heroine, "coconut-palm branch"—for that is the meaning of the word "Hainuwele"—were the Kore Rabie who had now reappeared on the scene, the moon-maiden whose second form was a pig.

All this happened a long time ago when there were nine families of men and nine sacred dancing-places. That they were no ordinary mortals but divine beings is shown by their subsequent fate: after they became mortal only a few of them were destined to live as human beings, the rest changed themselves

107 *Hainuwele,* pp. 48ff.
108 Ibid., p. 235.

into animals and ghosts. Among these first men was Ameta, the lonely man of the night who had neither wife nor children. "One day he went hunting with his dog. After a little while the dog scented a pig in the wood and followed it to a pond. The pig ran into the water, but the dog remained standing on the bank. Soon the pig could swim no more and was drowned. Meanwhile Ameta came along and fished out the dead pig. He found a coconut on the end of the pig's tusk. But in those days there were no coconut-palms on the earth."

Ameta took the coconut home. He covered it up as they used to cover new-born children in Ceram, and planted it. In a miraculously short space of time it grew into the first coco-nut-palm: it reached its full height in three days, and in three more days it had blossomed. On one of the leaves, on which fell a drop of Ameta's blood, the maiden Hainuwele was formed in twice three days. And three days later she was already of an age to be married—a Kore. If we wished to describe her nature with a Greek name we could say that she was the feminine *Plutos,* richness itself. She bestowed everything beautiful and good so generously on men that they—killed her. This surprising *dénouement* is neither logical nor psychological; it is genuinely mythological. Only thus can we see the significance of this Kore: "The buried parts of Hainuwele's body turned into things that had not existed on earth before, above all the tuberous fruits on which mankind has chiefly lived ever since."

The killing of Hainuwele is a remarkable ritual repetition of the Kore's rape as suffered also by Rabie. Tuwale caused Rabie to sink into the earth, or else she sank into a river[109] or into a lake, just as the pig did with the coconut. One is reminded of the Sicilian scene of the Kore's rape, Lake Pergusa, where Persephone was playing with her companions when Hades appeared and carried her off. Hainuwele's descent into the earth was made at the ninth of the nine dancing-places, and during the ninth night of the great Maro Dance. The dance itself is the means of her descent. Men and women linked alternately form a huge ninefold spiral. It is a *labyrinth,*[110] the primordial image and later the replica of that through which men have to pass when they die in order to reach the Queen of Hades and

109 Ibid., p. 54.
110 Cf. the native drawing, ibid., p. 65.

be ordained to human existence again. Hainuwele stands in the middle of the labyrinth, where a deep hole has been dug in the earth. In the slow convolutions of the spiral dance, the dancers press closer and closer towards her and finally push her into the pit. "The loud three-voiced Maro chant drowns the maiden's cries. They heap earth upon her, and the dancers stamp it down firmly over the pit with their dancing feet."

Thus Hainuwele was danced underground, or in other words the labyrinthine dance bore her under the earth. This form of dance is not without analogies in antique religion. There are accounts of the introduction of a chorus of maidens in Persephone's honour in Rome which led us to conclude that similar dances were performed in the Greek or Graeco-Italian Kore cults.[111] The accounts refer to the number of dancers: they were thrice nine, and there is also mention of a rope which they held in their hands in order to form a continuous chain. It is difficult to think of this as a dead-straight line with no windings at all. Scholars have pointed out that dances were performed in Delos with the help of such a rope.[112] The most important of these dances was the one that Theseus is supposed to have danced with his companions on the Apollonian isle after he had extricated them from the labyrinth.[113] It was done in honour of Aphrodite, by which was meant Ariadne, whose nature coincides both with Aphrodite's and Persephone's.[114] The dance was called the Crane Dance and its convolutions were so involved that our chief source calls them an imitation of the windings of the labyrinth.[115] In this ritual dance the rope probably played the same part as the thread in the fable of Ariadne.[116] For the Greeks the spiral was the key-figure of the labyrinth, though it is usually stylized in angular form.[117] On Delos they used to dance in honour of a god who had come into

[111] Livy, XXVII, 37; cf. Altheim, *Terra Mater*, pp. 1ff.

[112] Diels, *Das Labyrinth* (Festgabe Harnack), p. 91; Altheim, p. 4.

[113] Cf. F. Weege, *Der Tanz in der Antike*, p. 61.

[114] Otto, *Dionysos*, pp. 169ff.

[115] Plutarch, *Theseus*, 21.

[116] Cf. L. Pallat, *De fabula Ariadnea*, p. 6.

[117] Cf. M. Büdinger, *Die römischen Spiele und der Patriciat*, p. 49; Pallat, pp. 4f., not refuted by R. Eilmann, *Labyrinthos* (1931), pp. 68ff. Further details in my *Labyrinth-Studien*.

the world near the sacred palm-tree—the young Apollo. When a childgod was born, whether Zeus or Dionysus, mythological beings danced in a ring round the new-born. A dance like the Ceramese Maro Dance, if danced in honour of Persephone, would have to go as it were in the *wrong direction,* that is, to the left, the direction of death. And in fact the horns of the altar round which the Crane Dance was performed point in this direction.[118] Probably the dance, too, went the same way.

The Maro Dance was also performed to the left, as the Greeks would have considered proper in a cult of the Underworld. But in the Hainuwele mythologem the death-direction is the same as the *birth-direction.* Only after Hainuwele's murder could men die, and only then could they be born again. At the end of the mythologem the Indonesian Kore appears who now becomes the Queen of Hades—the Kore *Satene.* She was the youngest fruit of the first banana-tree, and ruled over the first men while yet they had committed no murder. On account of the murder of Hainuwele she became angry and set up a great gate on one of the nine dancing-places. "It consisted of a nine-fold spiral arranged like the men in the Maro Dance." It was the gate of Hell and at the same time the gate to human life. For only those who had passed through the gate to Satene could remain men in the future, but she herself had dwelt on the Mountain of Death ever since the first murder, and men had to die in order to come to her. The killing of Hainuwele was the way to humanity, and the dance to death was a dance to birth.

Thus the testimony offered by the Indonesian Kore mythologem. It covers all the strange associations, even the strangest of them: the association of birth and death. Nor is it unimportant that precisely this connection is brought out by a *dance.* The number on which the Maro Dance is based—3 and 3 times 3—and probably the spiral as well, have their counterparts in the domain of Persephone; and we know that the secret of Eleusis could be betrayed by dancing more readily than by speaking. The word for betraying the mysteries was ἐξορχεῖσθαι— to reveal by indiscreet gestures. We have an example of how a mystery of this kind, a very profound and important one, is still danced today.

[118] Plutarch, *Theseus;* W. A. Laidlaw, *A History of Delos,* p. 52, 10.

8. *The Kore in Eleusis*

A mythological figure stands before us in all its richness. We can call it a primordial figure because it is not exclusive to Greek mythology. In its primordial, paradoxical form it does not belong to the Olympian mythology at all. If we wanted to give it a name—not, admittedly, exhausting its significance but at least a name *a potiore*—those signifying "Mother" would come less into consideration: Demeter less than Kore, "Primordial Mother" less than "Primordial Maiden." The name Δημήτηρ, even if the Δη is really equivalent to Γῆ, proves no more than that one aspect of the lunar rather than terrestrial Primordial Maiden happened to coincide with the maternal aspect of the earth. The maiden of primordial mythology may have harboured the cares and sorrows of motherhood in her nature, but the patient earthly endurance of the absolute mother is wholly lacking to her. It is not without reason that Gaia aids and abets the seducer in the Homeric hymn. From the Earth Mother's point of view, neither seduction nor death is the least bit tragic or even dramatic. The Demeter myth, on the contrary, the unfolding of her nature, is full of drama.

In the hymn, Rhea, the great mother of the gods, the mother also of Zeus and Demeter, is closer to her daughter than the Earth Mother. Zeus sends her to pacify Demeter. The Homeric poet sorts out the aspects of the two mothers in this way: Rhea is calm and calming, Demeter passionate. The Pythagoreans held the two to be identical,[119] doubtless on the ground that their natures were akin. This kinship is by no means confined to motherhood. The equivalent of Rhea in Asia Minor, Cybele, the mother of the gods, exhibits a passionateness amounting to ecstasy. On the other hand, as mistress of wild animals, she is by nature akin to Artemis, and Artemis moreover in her original form. The original Artemis and the original Demeter prove in their turn to be very closely related, indeed in their pristine state (the mythological idea of the Primordial Maiden) to be identical. All roads lead to this primary figure.

No more than we can expect to find this original mythological state on Homer's Olympus should we be surprised to meet

[119] Kerényi, *Pythagoras und Orpheus*, p. 37.

136

it in Eleusis. Scholars have always looked for something extremely ancient in the Eleusinian cult. Archaeologists have
disinterred Mycenaean fragments of the Greek-temple type
from under the sacred Telesterion;[120] historians of religion
have endeavoured to discover elements of the ancient Cretan
religion in Eleusis.[121] The cult's own traditions and modern
research both place the origins of the mysteries in very remote
times.

Our present starting-point is mythologems whose originality
is no less self-evident than the Mycenaean and Cretan style is
to the archaeologist. In this way we made the acquaintance of
the mythologem telling of the marriage of Nemesis, and also
of the Arcadian version of the Demeter myth. Both were characterized by a certain *dreamlike* unfolding of the drama. The
primordial god and goddess undergo endless transformations
before they come together; the maiden dies, and in her place
there appears an angry goddess, a mother, who bears the Primordial Maiden—*herself*—again in her daughter. The scene of
the drama is the universe, divided into three just as the goddess
herself is threefold: original Kore, mother, and daughter. But
the universe could only come to be the scene of such a drama
because man had assimilated the whole world and lent it the
animation and fluidity of his own mind, or, to put it differently,
because the lively and versatile spirit of man had faced the universe and permeated it with itself. The archaic attitude combines open acceptance of reality with this kind of confrontation.

The fluidity peculiar to the original mythological state presupposes a oneness with the world, a perfect acceptance of all
its aspects. Basing ourselves on the Arcadian mythologem
we said earlier that by entering into the figure of Demeter we
realize the universal principle of life, which is to be pursued,
robbed, raped, to *fail to understand,* to rage and grieve, but
then to get everything back and be born again. To our certain
knowledge of the Eleusinian mysteries belongs precisely this
fact, that the participants identified themselves with Demeter.

[120] K. Kuruniotis, "Das eleusinische Heiligtum von den Aufgängen bis zur
vorperikleischen Zeit," pp. 52ff.
[121] A. W. Persson, "Der Ursprung der eleusinischen Mysterien," pp. 287ff.; C.
Picard, "Die Grosse Mutter von Kreta bis Eleusis," pp. 91ff.

The formula for the initiate's confession has been preserved: "I have fasted; I have drunk the mixed drink; I have taken out of the *cista* [little chest], worked with it, and then laid it in the basket and out of the basket into the *cista*." However mysterious the second half of the formula is, the first half is clear enough. It is not a question of entering into divine childhood but of divine *motherhood*. The initiate entered into the figure of Demeter by doing what the sorrowing and wrathful goddess did: fasted and then drank the mixed drink. The mysterious business with the *cista* and the basket can only be something that Demeter did in the royal household at Eleusis, some action in the service of the queen.[122]

Anyone could be initiated into the mysteries of Eleusis who spoke Greek and was not guilty of the shedding of blood, men and women alike. Men, too, entered into the figure of Demeter and became one with the *goddess*. To recognize this is the first step towards an understanding of what went on in Eleusis. There is historical evidence to show that the initiate regarded himself as a goddess and not as a god—the coins of the Emperor Gallienus, which give him the title of *Galliena Augusta*. The explanation of this official title is to be found in the fact that Gallienus attached particular weight to his having been initiated into the mysteries of Eleusis.[123] There are other proofs that men incarnated themselves in the goddess of the Demeter religion. In Syracuse, at the shrine of Demeter and Persephone, men took the great oath clad in the purple robe of the goddess and with her burning torch in their hands. From Plutarch's *Dion*[124] it appears that in Syracuse this was the garb of the *mystagogos*, master of the initiation. The same mysteries existed in the Arcadian Pheneos as in Eleusis, and there the priest wore the mask of Demeter Kidaria[125] in the "greatest mystery." It was a far from friendly face, more like some ghastly apparition which one can only imagine as Gorgonesque.

The procession that came to Eleusis with burning torches in a night of the autumn month of Boedromion to celebrate

122 Cf. S. Eitrem, who, in "Eleusinia—les Mystères et l'agriculture," pp. 140ff., stresses the agricultural side of the rite.
123 A. Alföldi, "Zur Kenntnis der Zeit der römischen Soldaten-kaiser," p. 188.
124 Plutarch, *Dion*, 56.
125 Pausanias, VIII, 15; cf. Kerényi in "Man and Mask," p. 155.

the "great mysteries" was made up of men and women who
followed the Demetrian path. The festival proper began in
Athens on Boedromion 16th, when the initiates were called
together and everybody else was excluded. On the 17th the
celebrants were summoned to the sea, into the purifying element. On the 19th the procession started, in order to reach
Eleusis by night. The view best corresponding to the classical
texts is that the procession consisted of celebrants who had
already been initiated into the "lesser mysteries" of Agrai.[126]

One became an initiate, μύστης, through the μύησις. Water and
darkness played the chief part. In Agrai, a suburb of Athens,
the water came from the Ilissus and the initiation was held in
honour of Persephone, though the "lesser" mysteries were at
the same time in honour of Demeter,[127] and Hecate too is
proved to have been operative in Agrai.[128] It was above all the
"underworldly Persephone," the Queen of the Dead, to whom
the road of this initiation led.[129] The head of the initiant was
wrapped in darkness just as in antiquity brides and those vowed
to the Underworld were veiled.[130] The word for "to initiate,"
μυεῖν, means "to close," and is used for eye and mouth alike. The
initiate, μυούμενος, remained passive, but the closing of the eyes
and the entry into darkness is something active. The word
μύστης is a *nomen agentis*. The passivity of Persephone, of the
bride, the maiden doomed to die, is re-experienced by means
of an *inner act*—if only an act of surrender. Our sources speak
of an "imitation of Dionysian happenings."[131] As a sacrificial
victim and one who is doomed, Dionysus is the male counterpart of Persephone.

126 Plato, *Republic,* 364E; *Gorgias,* 497C with scholium; Plutarch, *Demetrius,*
26. Only the most important references are mentioned. For material concerning
the "lesser" and "great" mysteries, cf. Deubner, *Attische Feste,* pp. 69ff.; Farnell,
III, pp. 343ff.; P. Foucart, *Les Mystères d'Eleusis;* O. Kern, *Die griechischen
Mysterien der klassischen Zeit;* Pauly-Wissowa, *Realencyclopädie,* XVI, col. 1211;
and Kerényi, *Die Geburt der Helena,* pp. 42ff.
127 Bekker, *Anecdota,* I, 326, 24; cf. Hesychius, s.v. Ἀγραὶ.
128 Plutarch, *De Herodoti malignitate,* 26; *Corpus Inscriptionum Atticarum,*
II, 1590; Furtwängler, "Die Chariten der Akropolis," p. 197.
129 Hippolytus, *Elenchos,* V, 8, 43.
130 Diels, *Sibyllinische Blätter,* p. 122; Deubner, fig. 7; Rizzo, "Il Sarcafago di
Torre Nova," pp. 103ff.; for Heracles in Agrai, cf. Diodorus Siculus, IV, 14.
131 Stephanus Byzantinus, s.v. Ἀγραί.

Thus far does our information go concerning the beginning of the experiences now to be continued in Eleusis, the beginning of a process that culminated in the "great mysteries." Μύησις has, significantly enough, the meaning of the Latin *initia*, "beginning," or more accurately "entry." This ceremony in Agrai is probably connected with the fact that the celebrants took their way to Eleusis decked with myrtle and carrying torches of myrtle,[132] for the myrtle belongs to both Aphrodite and the dead.[133] We shall not, however, lay overmuch stress on these details, although doubtless no detail is without meaning— neither the jug in the hands of the men, nor the vessel for carrying light and seed on the heads of the women, nor the pilgrim's staff and scrip.[134] We intend to keep only to the τέλος, the consummation of the τελετή or celebration in Eleusis itself. The actions in that celebration had to be suffered as passively as the μυεῖν. They were called τελεῖν, "leading to the τέλος, the goal." They took place mainly in the great sacred edifice, the Telesterion. The τέλος was only to be attained by means of the *epopteia,* the supreme vision, but not by any means on the first trip to Eleusis. At least one other participation in the mysteries was essential for this.[135]

Can we ascertain anything at all about this *telos,* the supreme vision? "Everything depended on what the *epoptes* were permitted to see"—in these words Wilamowitz sums up our positive and negative knowledge.[136] "The whole procedure was a δρησμοσύνη (service) entrusted to the hierophant, and what *he* revealed was the principal thing." (The name "hierophant" means the "priestly demonstrator" of the holy mysteries.) Wilamowitz also admits the parts played by the *dadouchos,* the priestly torchbearer, and by the light in the mysterious goings-on in the Telesterion. He continues: "There does not seem to have been much music. At the invocation to the Kore, the hierophant clashed a cymbal. It is futile to attempt to visualize what was

132 H. G. Pringsheim, *Archäologische Beiträge zur Geschiche des eleusinischen Kulte,* pp. 16ff.
133 Cf. I. Murr, *Die Pflanzenwelt in der griechischen Mythologie,* pp. 84ff.
134 Cf. votive tablet of Niinnion, *Ephemeris Archaeologica,* 1901, Pl. 1; Deubner, fig. 5, 1.
135 Plutarch, *Demetrius,* 26.
136 *Der Glaube der Hellenen,* II, p. 57.

shrouded in mystery. To turn the δρησμοσύνη into a mimic representation of the Kore's rape is as frivolous a device as to turn the ritual formulae that were inevitably spoken at the monstrance of the ἱερά into a sermon by the hierophant."

An important step towards a correct understanding of the Eleusinian mysteries is the negative recognition that the δρησμοσύνη introduced by Demeter—the first of the three components in the celebration of the mysteries, respectively δρώμενα, λεγόμενα, and δεικνύμενα (the doing, the saying, and the showing)—was *not a stage-play*. The archaeological findings are decisively against the supposition of a mystery-theatre, either in the Telesterion or outside it. And not a single text speaks a word in its favour. For the δρᾶμα μυστικόν, in the metaphorical sense of the Church Father Clement of Alexandria,[137] admits very well of other kinds of dramatic representations besides the mimic drama after the manner of a profane pantomime, with the story of the Homeric hymn, perhaps, for a text. The mythologem of the Kore's rape was known in several versions; had it been presented simply as a pantomime there would have been nothing in the least mysterious about it. The Eleusinian mystery was not to be betrayed by the mere *telling* of the Kore's rape but by profaning the Eleusinian way of representing it, namely the Eleusinian *dance*. The Indonesian Maro Dance gave us an idea of this kind of dramatic representation.[138] Can *that* be called a "mimic drama"? If so, it is an extremely stylized one which may be reminiscent of the oldest dances in the tragic chorus, but not of the tragedy itself. It was also characteristic of the Eleusinian mystery-dance that at certain stages it turned into a torch-dance.[139] Clement gives the δρᾶμα μυστικόν a more accurate name when he uses the word δᾳδουχεῖν, "to carry a torch."

We can, indeed, form no conception of what was "shrouded in mystery," or rather of the *Eleusinian manner* of representing that particular idea, *one* of whose modes of representation—

[137] *Protrepticus*, 12, 2; cf. Wilamowitz, II, p. 481; and Lobeck, *Aglaophamus* (1829), II, p. 1263.
[138] Plutarch's description of the πλάναι and περιδρομαί of the initiates in his *De anima* (Stobaeus, *Florilegium*, 120, 28) is strongly reminiscent of the labyrinth dances; cf. Pallat, p. 3, n. 1.
[139] Lactantius, *Institutiones divinae*, Epit. 18, 7.

among many others possible—was the story of the Kore's rape in the Demeter hymn. We know several versions of this and know the basic idea brought out in the mythologems. We also know that in Eleusis that idea lost everything confusing and painful and became a *satisfying* vision. The Eleusinian experience began with sorrow, the wandering quest that corresponded to the πλάνη, to the wanderings of Demeter herself and her lamentations; and it probably began outside Eleusis with the fasting of the celebrants. Eleusis was the place of the εὕρεσις, the finding of the Kore. In this finding something was *seen*— no matter through what symbols—that was objective and subjective at once. Objectively, the idea of the goddess regaining her daughter, and therefore *herself,* flashed on the experient's soul. Subjectively, the same flash of revelation showed him his own continuity, the continued existence of all living things. The not-knowing, the failure to understand that attached to the figure of the grieving Demeter, ceased. The paradox contained in the living idea—that, in motherhood, death and continuity are one in the losing and finding of the Kore—is now resolved.

The finding was preceded, apart from the search, by something else of a mysterious nature which was done and experienced with doused torches in the dark. This was the marriage by violence, not, as one might expect, the Kore's, but that of Demeter herself and Zeus.[140] It must have been a true Nemesis- or Erinys-marriage, for the goddess was given a name akin to both: *Brimo.* The situation corresponds exactly to the Arcadian mythologem, although the consummation of it is different—not theriomorphic but anthropomorphic. (A Christian source[141] names the hierophant and the priestess of Demeter as the celebrants of the sacred marriage.) The exact correspondence is confirmed by later and in part hostile accounts on the basis of which we can reconstruct the sequence of events as follows: union of the Kore with Hades, mourning and search, sacred marriage of the mourning and searching goddess, recovery.

Another confirmation is the name *Brimo.* The word βρίμη means "the power to arouse terror"; βριμᾶσθαι, "to rage"; βριμάζειν, "to roar or snort." Here, then, we have not only the

---

140 Tertullian, *Ad nationes,* 2, 7: "Cur rapitur sacerdos Cereris, si non tale Ceres passa est?" Cf. Clement of Alexandria, *Protrepticus,* 2, 15.
141 Asterius, *Homilies,* X, Migne, *P. G.,* vol. 40, col. 324.

same wrathful bride of Zeus whom we have met in the mythologems as Nemesis and Demeter Erinys and Demeter Melaina, but a being who has her rightful place in the Underworld just like the Erinyes or the Gorgon's head.[142] Were we not told that Demeter is called by this name in her own mysteries,[143] we should have to conclude that Brimo is Persephone in one of her terrible, underworldly aspects. However, we also know that in the *idea* that must be at the bottom of the Eleusinian mysteries as well as of the Demeter hymn, both things can be true at once: Brimo is as much Demeter as Persephone. Besides which, she is also Hecate.[144] As a matter of fact, she is Demeter, Persephone, and Hecate rolled into one. Demeter's most elementary form bears the name of Brimo; it was also the name of *Pheraia,* the torch-bearing goddess seated on a running horse.[145] (We recall the connection between the original Demeter and the horse.) The marriage of this Brimo, by Lake Boibeis in Thessaly, was a marriage of Persephone.[146] The name of the lake (the inhabitants said *Boibe* instead of *Phoibe*) reveals that we are dealing with the same primordial Kore who is also called Artemis. The Eleusinian poet Aeschylus knew of the identity of Artemis and Persephone, and Callimachus mentioned it in his Attic Epyllion *Hekale.* The primary figure with the name—among so many others—of Brimo, and with these Demeter-Hecate-Artemis aspects, was not merely a Thessalian phenomenon. She appears in the ancient mystery cults of Eleusis as well.

It was undoubtedly after the search and the sacred marriage that a great light shone and the cry of the hierophant resounded: "The great goddess has borne a sacred child: Brimo has borne Brimos!"[147] Which of them bore the child—the mother or the daughter? On the basis of the evidence that in Eleusis Brimo is Demeter, and on the basis of the Arcadian mythologem, it can only be the angry and sorrowing mother; and the child can only be her reborn daughter, who in Arcadia

---

142 Lucian, *Menippus,* 20.
143 Clement of Alexandria, op. cit.
144 Apollonius Rhodius, *Argonautica,* III, 861, with scholium.
145 Preller, I, p. 327.
146 Cicero, *De natura deorum,* III, 22; Propertius, II, 2, 11; Lobeck, p. 1213; cf. Kerényi, *Asklepios,* pp. 91f.
147 Hippolytus, *Elenchos,* V, 8: ἱερὸν ἔτεκε πότνια κοῦρον Βριμὼ Βριμόν.

was likewise called Despoina, "Mistress." The hierophant, however, did not proclaim the birth of a Kore but of a κοῦρος—a
divine boy. And that does not conflict with our idea. For Brimo
is not Demeter *only*, as distinct from Persephone; she is non-
differentiated mother *and* daughter. The child is likewise undifferentiated—it is only *what is born,* the fruit of birth. The all-
embracing idea of *birth,* of the everlastingly repeated beginning
of life, united mother, daughter, and child in a single unit
pregnant with meaning. The meaning of the birth is not the beginning of all things, not the unique, the original beginning,
but *continuity* in an uninterrupted sequence of births. In the
identity of mother and daughter, the eternally child-bearing
mother manifests herself as an eternal being, and it is into her
being and her destiny that the celebrants enter. The child is the
sign that this duration is more than individual; that it is continuity and continual rebirth in one's own offspring.

Post-Homeric poets spoke of the confidence that was vouchsafed to the celebrants in Eleusis. In the hymn, the good fortune of the initiate was defined negatively: never will the uninitiate who have not shared the Eleusinian experience attain
what the participants attain in the darkness of death.[148]
Sophocles calls those "thrice happy" who have reached the
telos in Eleusis and seen it: for them alone is there life in
death; for the rest Hades is fell and joyless.[149] The Lesbian
poet Krinagoras promises the initiate a life without care, without the care of death, and a passing "with a lighter heart."[150]
Elsewhere too there is mention of the hope (ἔλπις) of the celebrants, which need not necessarily refer to bliss in the Christian
sense.[151] Those of the ancients who concerned themselves most
with the fate of the soul, the Pythagoreans, combined the doctrine of metempsychosis with the doctrine that the "images" of
the departed remained with Persephone.[152] The principal thing
in Eleusis was not metempsychosis but birth as a more than individual phenomenon, through which the individual's mortality

---

[148] Lines 480–82.
[149] Fragment 752.
[150] *Anthologia Palatina*, XI, 42.
[151] Isocrates, *Panegyricus,* 28; Cicero, *De legibus,* II, 375; Plutarch, *De facie in orbe lunae,* 943D.
[152] *Pythagoras und Orpheus* (2nd edn.), pp. 47ff.

was perpetually counterbalanced, death suspended, and the continuance of the living assured. Perhaps Pindar is the most explicit when he says: "Happy he who, having witnessed such things, goes under the earth: he knows life's end and knows its Zeus-given *beginning*."[153] In the Demeter myth, Zeus reigns over the world of the gods not only as father; he is also the eternal procreator: father of Persephone, father of Brimos, and father too of the child who, according to the Orphic tradition, is born of Persephone—Zagreus.

The Eleusinian *mythologem* says that Eleusis was the place of the εὕρεσις, the refinding of the Kore. According to the *idea* on which the mythologem was based, Eleusis was the *place of birth*, of that ever-recurrent cosmic event which guaranteed the continuance of life in Attica, indeed in the whole world. To Greek ears the name "Eleusis" sounded something like the word for "arrival." Most probably, however, it is connected with the name of the birth-goddess *Eileithyia*, who was also worshipped in Agrai.[154] The spread of her cult to Crete, the Aegean islands, and the Peloponnese seems to indicate that this goddess played a more important part in the pre-Grecian religion of the Aegean world than in the Greek religion proper. Her name is held to be pre-Greek.[155] At any rate, she could not have been regarded by the Greeks as the maieutic goddess pure and simple if the great cosmic event of birth had not belonged originally to her sphere. And if we identify her chiefly with Artemis, we know that the original Artemis was not different from the original Demeter at the time when Demeter may have encountered the pre-Grecian birth-goddess. In view of such considerations we have to imagine the original Demeter as coming from the north in the earliest history of the Eleusinian cult. Her connection with the horse testifies to this. If science is not in error in its assumption of the pre-Greek character of Eileithyia, and if things are not even more complicated than we suppose today, we can say that the age-old Greek goddess of eternal birth and rebirth in Eleusis took the place of a pre-Greek goddess whose nature was akin to hers.

153 *Fragmenta*, 137A.
154 *Corpus Inscriptionum Atticarum*, II, 1590; III, 319.
155 Cf. M. P. Nilsson, *The Minoan-Mycenaean Religion and its Survival in Greek Religion*, pp. 447ff.

Hence the most probable historical hypothesis merely confirms what, on the ground of the mythological and literary evidence (which corresponds to the basic idea of the mythologems), we have already discovered to be the primary Eleusinian theme, a theme that the mysteries presented in their own special, and to us unknown, way. With this theme are connected the Eleusinian paintings on two celebrated vases. Naturally enough, the theme is presented and modified in the manner of vase-painting, but even so the variations bear clear witness to the principal thing, which was *the birth of a divine child*.

On one of the vases (from Rhodes), a goddess is rising out of the earth, and handing the divine child, seated in a horn of plenty, to another goddess.[156] The child's situation shows that it is valued as the fruit of the earth. The other vase (from Kerch) shows the divine child twice, the centre of two scenes.[157] In the one scene, where Hermes receives the newborn child from a goddess rising out of the earth, the child has become rather indistinct, owing to the state of the painting. In the other it stands between the two Eleusinian goddesses in the likeness of a little ephebe with a cornucopia in his hand. Some people see him as *Plutos,* Plenty, of whom it is said in the *Theogony* that he was born of Demeter's marriage with the mortal hero Iasion.[158] The symbolical character of the child is unmistakable. The symbol can also be interpreted to mean *Plutos,* for this may be just as much a variation of the child of the mysteries as the marriage with Iasion is a variation of the sacred marriage. The more abstract the pictorial expression (which is certainly different from the mystical)—so abstract, indeed, that child and cornucopia appear to be no more than hieroglyphic signs—the more appropriate it is to the primary Eleusinian theme: the vision of birth as a source from which life, growth, and replenishment spring in inexhaustible plenty.

Probably connected with this theme is also the part played by the Athenian child in the Eleusinian mysteries, the παῖς ἀφ' ἑστίας. It was taken from hearth and home and initiated

---

156 Farnell, Pl. XXIb.

157 Ibid., Pls. XVIII and XXIa.

158 Lines 969–71; cf. Hymn to Demeter, 486–89, and *Anthologia Lyrica Graeca* (ed. Diehl), II, 182, 2.

(μυηθεὶς ἀφ' ἑστίας)—never more than *one* child, which was destined for the part by a combined process of sortilege and fate. Its task was to carry out a *dromenon* exactly as directed. Probably the child represented all the initiates, and a particularly favourable result was expected from the punctilious execution of its duties, a "mollification of the Divine," as a late source puts it.[159] We do not hear anything more precise about this rôle, but the most plausible supposition is that which best corresponds to the idea underlying the mysteries, namely that the παῖς ἀφ' ἑστίας represented the successors of those who had already entered into the fate of the angry and sorrowing goddess. In that event it is not without significance that the rôle of the child was restricted neither to the male nor the female sex. Boys and girls alike were accorded the distinction of the child-initiate and were thereafter immortalized by statues.[160]

The Kore was lost and sought—but how she was found, even the identity of what was found, remains a secret for us and was probably the deepest secret of all for the initiates. The identity, too, of the εὕρεσις and the birth is a mystery. However, confirmation is found in the scene on the Kerch vase of Hermes receiving the child, where a woman with a cymbal is seated to one side; for we know that the Kore was invoked with a cymbal. Even more mysterious is the child. In Phigalia, Demeter's daughter, who was born of her violent marriage with Poseidon, was called simply "Mistress." In Thelpusa she was not to be named at all before the uninitiate, though her brother, born at the same time, was called the horse Areion. The description of her who was sought as ἄρρητος κούρα, "the maiden not to be named," by Euripides and a younger tragedian, seems to refer to that unutterable something which was also expressed in the child Brimos. The name Brimos points to a figure arousing fear and dread like his mother Brimo. A Christian apologist has preserved an Orphic tradition according to which the child of Zeus and Rhea-Demeter, the Kore or Persephone, had four eyes and two faces.[161] A "Tetrakore," that is, a Kore with four eyes (for the pupils are also called κόρη), appears in an inscrip-

[159] Porphyry, *De abstinentia*, IV, 5.
[160] Pringsheim, p. 118.
[161] Athenagoras, 20 (Migne, *P. G.*, vol. 6, 929).

tion in Asia Minor.[162] Apart from this the mysterious child had
horns.[163] According to another tradition Zagreus, son of Zeus
and Persephone, was a "horned child."[164] Dionysus and the
Kore seem to go very closely together in their most secret form.
Nor were they first associated in late speculations, for in the
Roman triad Ceres-Liber-Libera, where Ceres corresponds to
Demeter and Dionysus is called Liber, the Kore appears as the
female form of Liber—as *Libera*.[165] This points to the bisexuality of mythological beings which has already been shown to
hold of Dionysus.[166] Neither bisexuality nor the other miraculous features associated with Persephone's child Zagreus are irreconcilable with the mysterious nature of Brimos. More we
cannot say.

The birth of Brimos was only one of the Eleusinian symbols,
only *one* unfolding of the budlike idea that envisaged the continuity of life in the unity of maiden, mother, and child, a
being that dies, gives birth, and comes to life again. Another
symbol was the object of the celebrants' loftiest vision: the
δεικνύμενον that followed the δρώμενον. This passed off not with
a loud cry, like the proclamation of the birth of Brimos, but ἐν
σιωπῇ; *silently* a mown ear of grain was exhibited. It was a symbol and example of how things come to be in death and birth;
a symbol of Persephone's fate, which is the whole meaning of
Demeter's fate too.

What happened afterwards, on the last day of the mysteries,
recalled the primal element, the original source of all birth,
the element that purifies everything because everything is reborn in it: water. Though we know little of "what was said"
in the mysteries, the λεγόμενον, we do know this: that looking
up to heaven they cried ὕε, "let it rain," and looking down to
earth they cried κύε.[167] The second word means not only "conceive!" "be fruitful!"; it has more the meaning of *"make* fruit-

<hr>

[162] *Corpus Inscriptionum Graecarum,* n. 4000; Usener, *Kleine Schriften,* IV, p.
353.
[163] Athenagoras, cf. *Orphic Hymns,* XXIX, 11.
[164] Nonnus, *Dionysiaca,* VI, 264.
[165] Altheim, p. 34.
[166] Cf. supra, pp. 53ff., 66f.
[167] Proclus, *In Platonis Timaeum commentarii,* 293C.

ful!" and in this case it means the effect of water working in the earth. That both words refer to water is proved by the inscription on the rim of an Athenian fountain, where yet a third imperative is added: ὑπερχύε—"foam over!"[168] In view of the fountain's natural connection with water, this interpretation is as appropriate to the mysteries as it is to the fountain in front of the Dipylon. For on the last day, two vessels shaped "like spinning-tops" were filled and set up in Eleusis, one facing the east, the other facing the west. While a certain λεγόμενον was being recited, the two vessels were tipped over.[169]

There is no reason to doubt that it was water and no other liquid that flowed to east and west out of the overturned vessels, that is, in the directions of birth and death. The two aspects of the primal element were thus called to mind. Nor can it be doubted that the thought of fertility was present in this ceremonial act. Possibly the double word ὕε κύε was uttered at the overturning of the vessels. The details are uncertain, but the basic idea is all the more certain: the primal element was expected to go on working for the realization of this idea, the idea of *eternal birth*.

How the cosmos co-operated in the mystery-night between the 19th and 20th Boedromion is described for us by Euripides in one of the choruses to his tragedy *Ion*.[170] It is the night on which the celebrants dance round the "fountain in the square of beautiful dances" with torches in their hands, and "the starry heaven of Zeus begins to dance also, the moon and the fifty daughters of Nereus, the goddesses of the sea and the everflowing rivers, all dance in honour of the golden-crowned maiden and her holy mother." The primal element dances with the celebrants and the whole universe. Now we understand why the Orphic hymn to the Nereids declares that the water-goddesses were the first to celebrate the mysteries of Dionysus and Persephone.[171] The basic theme of both these mysteries was the eternal coming of life from death; the repeated celebration of the mystery continued this cosmic event; consequently the first

[168] Usener, p. 315.
[169] Athenaeus, 496A.
[170] Lines 1078–86.
[171] *Orphic Hymns*, XXIV, 10f.

celebration coincided with the first birth. If one mentally dissociated oneself from the spots sacred to the mysteries in Greece, and steeped oneself in the pure mythological idea of divine birth, then that primal celebration of the mystery could only be thought of as taking place in the primal element, where alone, according to the mythologems of so many peoples, the Primordial Child was born. And though in Eleusis it was not the divine child who arose out of the water, they did not forget the primal element.

The mythological idea to which we have devoted these considerations appears to have had a twofold form in Eleusis: it was an event and it was also a figure. The event was the birth of a divine child. The figure was a goddess whom we have called the Primordial Maiden, an archetype that contained all the dramatic possibilities associated with Persephone's fate, from being born to giving birth. That fate was determined for all time by Persephone's character as a Kore, and by a certain trait in the original Kore who unfolded into Artemis as well as into Persephone, and whose salient feature was an *elemental virginity*. The Primordial Maiden can only be conceived as a primal being born of the primal element. And in fact, in the mysteries celebrated in the Attic village of Phlya, the Kore had a name which was generally borne only by the primal being Eros: *Protogone*.[172] Not only was she the ἄρρητος κούρα of the mysteries, she was also the πρωτόγονος κούρα, the "first born."[173] Her virginity, and hence the virginity of all the Kores in the world of the Greek gods, is not anthropomorphic but a quality of the unadulterated primal element which had given her birth. She is its own feminine aspect, as it were.

Naturally the primal element has another aspect, which, projected into a human figure, is more hetaera-like than virginal: the promiscuity of life in the water and the swamps. For all that, Hera rose out of the pure element—the water of the Kanathian fount—renewed as a virgin. Demeter Erinys bathed in the river Ladon after her anger had passed, and became Demeter Lusia: her new title signified renewal through purification by water. The close ties which, as Hecate, the original

172 Pausanias, I, 31, 4.
173 Pausanias, IV, 1, 8.

Kore had with the sea are shown by the fact that fish were sacrificed to her, namely gurnards and barbels.[174] In the Eleusinian mysteries fish, especially gurnards, were sacred; the initiates were not allowed to eat them.[175]

Moreover, it was in keeping with the immemorial figure who reigned in Eleusis that the rising of a goddess from the sea should be represented in connection with the mysteries: the *birth of Aphrodite,* the divine maiden in whom Greek mythology commemorates the first appearance of this kind from the sea. The source that bears explicit witness to this is the latest of all.[176] It is related of the beautiful Phryne that she showed herself naked in the sea to the celebrants at Eleusis.[177] She was thus inadvertently representing Anadyomene. Whether this exhibition was, strictly speaking, part of the cult is difficult to decide.[178] If it was, then it probably made no difference that Phryne was a courtesan; the point was that her body gleamed in dewy virginal perfection as she rose out of the wet. Apelles is said to have made his Aphrodite Anadyomene after such a vision.[179] As a reminder of the cult, this episode forms a charming pendant to the primary mythological theme unfolded in the mysteries, but its meaning is the same.

9. *The Eleusinian Paradox*

The experiences of the initiates in Eleusis had a rich mythological content, expressed, for instance, by the dazzling and sensuous image of Anadyomene rising from the waves. On the other hand, it could also be expressed in the plainest and simplest way. From the sacred records of a religion totally different in style—Buddhism—we learn of a remarkable "sermon" preached by its founder. One day the Buddha silently held up a flower before the assembled throng of his disciples.

---

174 F. J. Dölger, ΙΧΘΥΣ, II, pp. 316ff.
175 Ibid., pp. 331ff.
176 Psellos, cf. Kern, p. 71.
177 Athenaeus, 590f.; Kern, p. 72.
178 It goes against this view that Phryne did the same thing at the great feast of Poseidon.
179 Athenaeus, loc. cit.

This was the famous "Flower Sermon."[180] Formally speaking, much the same thing happened in Eleusis when a mown ear of grain was silently shown. Even if our interpretation of this symbol is erroneous, the fact remains that a mown ear was shown in the course of the mysteries and that this kind of "wordless sermon" was the sole form of instruction in Eleusis which we may assume with certainty.

Nonetheless, the difference between the two "sermons" is more characteristic than their similarity. The Buddha was concerned with the individual and his unique road, along which he may come to his own deliverance. He had discovered the truth in a great flash of revelation: all men are originally possessed of the wisdom, virtue, and form of the One Who Is. And just as all men are Buddha, so are all things—plants, trees, the whole earth. Thereupon he preached this truth for forty-five years. In his "Flower Sermon," words were finally transcended. His silence was meant to imply the profoundest revelation of the truth, for it was all-embracing and the source of his whole teaching. Characteristically enough, the "Flower Sermon" went uncomprehended by all save one disciple.

In Eleusis, on the other hand, they were, as far as we can see, concerned with a common standpoint whereby all the participants would suddenly understand—through immediate vision and insight. For this there was no need to transcend words. We do not know whether words played any considerable part in the initiation rites at Eleusis and Agrai. It is hardly likely that there was anything of a sermon. Liturgical exclamations occurred, but nothing in the way of a "speech" is preserved in the records. It was essentially a wordless initiation that led to a knowledge which it was neither necessary nor possible to clothe in words. We have to assume, in the history of the Eleusinian mysteries, a certain period during which the ear of grain, under whatever circumstances it was shown, was transparently clear in meaning to the celebrants. We must take it as axiomatic that such a transparent meaning was there in the very fact of the mystery-festival being celebrated and experienced at all. It is inconceivable that people *never* found any meaning in the things they witnessed with such deep reverence.

180 For what follows, cf. Schûei Ohasama, *Zen,* p. 3. Our interpretation of the "Flower Sermon" applies to Zen Buddhism and not to Hinayana Buddhism.

To them it was self-evident once they had adopted the common standpoint of the wordlessly initiated.

A further difference is no less instructive. The flower that the Buddha held up and showed to his disciples as a sermon was the broadest hint imaginable that all things are Buddha, hence that all things were just as much silent revealers of the truth as he was himself. It was a very suggestive and yet enigmatic gesture, which can also be understood in other ways. But the ear of grain in Eleusis sums up a certain aspect of the world, the Demetrian aspect. The two goddesses and their fate are variations of this symbol, more elaborate, spiritually more formed and developed; and the birth as a divine event is yet another kind of summary. The Buddha could equally well have held up something else, a stone or a bit of wood, with the same significance as the flower. But in Eleusis budlike summings-up and goddesses in all their perfection form a single, unequivocal, coherent group. They set one another off and coalesce at the same time. And the thing that unites them like a common root is no less positive. Through all of them, through the grain of wheat and the Mother-Daughter goddess, the same vision opens, the vision, if I may repeat myself, into the "abyss of the nucleus." Every grain of wheat and every maiden contains, as it were, all its descendants and all her descendants—an infinite series of mothers and daughters in one. An "infinite series"— that is as modern a way of putting it as the "abyss of the nucleus."[181] We are reminded of Pascal's "infinities": the infinitely great and the infinitesimally small. What we see in Eleusis—not, however, broken up in this way but summed up in clear figures—is something uniform and quite definite: the infinity of supra-individual organic life.

The celebrant of the mysteries saw and passively experienced the supra-individual; he was not redeemed by it, rather he was secure and happy in it, because in it he won to a wordless wisdom. If we want to gain some approximate understanding of the Eleusinian experience, we must contrast it not only with Buddhist experiences but with modern European experiences as well; we shall have to put the paradox of it as sharply as possible. The Eleusinians experienced a more than individual

[181] Cf. the Prolegomena, p. 8.

fate, the fate of organic life in general, as their own fate. As Hellenes they were not conscious so much of the "abyss" that opened in their own being, as of the "being" into which that abyss opened. The "infinite series" meant, to them, nothing less than infinite being—being pure and simple. They experienced being, the nucleus of the nucleus, so to speak, as their own being. The knowledge of it did not turn into discursive thought or words. Had it done so, the paradox of this experience could have been expressed as the individual's "experience" of the supra-individual, his having all being for his own. The seeing and the thing seen, knowing and being, are, as everywhere in Greek life and thought, blended into a unity.[182] They even claimed for the visionary knower a special position with regard to being: happy he who has seen such things, says the poet; his lot after death will be different from that of others. He personally will possess the duration that logically belongs only to the impersonal nucleus, to unseeing, unknowing organic life —insofar as such duration really means "continuity."

In that wordless knowing and being the first two elements of this paradox—having a supra-individual fate as one's own fate, and all being as one's own being—are not really contradictory. As organic beings we do in fact possess both. Only the third element seems to be in conflict with reality, the conviction that the full and happy possession of all being as one's own is vouchsafed solely to those who have "seen" in Eleusis, and "know." The dependence of being on knowing is something that goes beyond the Greek unity of these two. Such a conviction is of a more universally human character where belief in one's own continued existence is concerned. Upon it are based the instructions in the Orphic "passports" for the dead, that the deceased shall choose the fountain of Mnemosyne, remembrance, and not the fountain of Lethe, forgetfulness.[183] And, to take a Buddhist example, the whole *Tibetan Book of the Dead* is founded upon it.[184] Is this no more than a foolish clutching at consciousness on the part of mortal man? Might it not be that the break-through to wordless knowledge really is the climax of our whole existence, which does indeed sever the participant

182 Kerényi, *Die antike Religion*, p. 114.
183 Fr. 32, a–b (ed. Kern).
184 Ed. W. Y. Evans-Wentz.

in such a "vision" fundamentally from the non-participants, and distinguish their natures for all time?

It was not our aim to resolve and iron out the logical contradictions inherent in mythological experiences and "budlike" ideas. Mythology remains for us, as for Schelling,[185] "a phenomenon which in profundity, permanence, and universality is comparable only with Nature herself." We wanted—to sum up the essentials in Schelling's words—our explanation "to do justice to the subject, not to level it down, simplify, or garble it just to make it easier." We did not ask "which view of the phenomenon must be taken in order to offer a convenient explanation in accordance with some philosophy or other, but, on the contrary, what philosophy is required if we are to be equal to our subject, on the same level with it. Not *how* the phenomenon must be turned and twisted, oversimplified or distorted, so as to appear explicable at all costs by means of principles which we are determined not to overstep, but—*in what direction* we must enlarge our thoughts in order to stand in fit relationship to the phenomenon. Whoever, and for whatever reason, shrinks from such an amplification of his thoughts should at least be honest enough, instead of pulling the phenomenon down to the level of his own conceptions and trivializing it, to count it among those things, of which there are still a great many for all men, that he does not understand; and if he is incapable of proving adequate to the phenomena in question, he should at least guard against uttering something totally inadequate."

[185] For this and the following passage see *Philosophie der Mythologie,* pp. 136f.

THE PSYCHOLOGICAL ASPECTS
OF THE KORE

BY C. G. JUNG

Not only is the figure of Demeter and the Kore in its three-fold aspect as maiden, mother, and Hecate not unknown to the psychology of the unconscious, it is even something of a practical problem. The "Kore" has her psychological counterpart in those archetypes which I have called the *self* or *supraordinate personality* on the one hand, and the *anima* on the other. In order to explain these figures, with which I cannot assume all readers to be familiar, I must begin with some remarks of a general nature.

The psychologist has to contend with the same difficulties as the mythologist when an exact definition or clear and concise information is demanded of him. The picture is concrete, clear, and subject to no misunderstandings only when it is seen in its habitual context. In this form it tells us everything it contains. But as soon as one tries to abstract the "real essence" of the picture, the whole thing becomes cloudy and indistinct. In order to understand its living function, we must let it remain an organic thing in all its complexity and not try to examine the anatomy of its corpse in the manner of the scientist, or the archaeology of its ruins in the manner of the historian. Naturally this is not to deny the justification of such methods when applied in their proper place.

In view of the enormous complexity of psychic phenomena, a purely phenomenological point of view is, and will be for a long time, the only possible one and the only one with any prospect of success. "Whence" things come and "what" they are, these, particularly in the field of psychology, are questions which are apt to call forth untimely attempts at explanation. Such speculations are moreover based far more on unconscious philosophical premises than on the nature of the phenomena themselves. Psychic phenomena occasioned by unconscious processes are so rich and so multifarious that I prefer to *describe* my findings and observations and, where possible, to classify them—

that is, to arrange them under certain definite types. That is the method of natural science, and it is applied wherever we have to do with multifarious and still unorganized material. One may question the utility or the appropriateness of the categories or types used in the arrangement, but not the correctness of the method itself.

Since for years I have been observing and investigating the products of the unconscious in the widest sense of the word, namely dreams, fantasies, visions, and delusions of the insane, I have not been able to avoid recognizing certain regularities, that is, *types*. There are types of *situations* and types of *figures* that repeat themselves frequently and have a corresponding meaning. I therefore employ the term "motif" to designate these repetitions. Thus there are not only typical dreams but typical motifs in the dreams. These may, as we have said, be situations or figures. Among the latter there are human figures that can be arranged under a series of archetypes, the chief of them being, according to my suggestion,[1] the *shadow*, the *wise old man*, the *child* (including the child hero), the *mother* ("Primordial Mother" and "Earth Mother") as a supraordinate personality ("daemonic" because supraordinate), and her counterpart the *maiden*, and lastly the *anima* in man and the *animus* in woman.

The above types are far from exhausting all the statistical regularities in this respect. The figure of the Kore that interests us here belongs, when observed in a man, to the *anima* type; and when observed in a woman to the type of *supraordinate personality*. It is an essential characteristic of psychic figures that they are duplex or at least capable of duplication; at all events they are bipolar and oscillate between their positive and negative meanings. Thus the "supraordinate" personality can appear in a despicable and distorted form, like for instance Mephistopheles, who is really more positive as a personality than the vapid and unthinking careerist Faust. Another negative figure

[1] To the best of my knowledge, no other suggestions have been made so far. Critics have contented themselves with asserting that no such archetypes exist. Certainly they do not exist, any more than a botanical system exists in nature! But will anyone deny the existence of natural plant-families on that account? Or will anyone deny the occurrence and continual repetition of certain morphological and functional similarities? It is much the same thing in principle with the typical figures of the unconscious. They are forms existing *a priori*, or biological norms of psychic activity.

is the Tom Thumb or Tom Dumb of the folktales. The figure corresponding to the Kore in a woman is generally a double one, i.e., a mother and a maiden, which is to say that she appears now as the one, now as the other. From this I would conclude, for a start, that in the formation of the Demeter-Kore myth the feminine influence so far outweighed the masculine that the latter had practically no significance. The man's role in the Demeter myth is really only that of seducer or conqueror.

As a matter of practical observation, the Kore often appears in woman as an *unknown young girl,* not infrequently as Gretchen or the unmarried mother.[2] Another frequent modulation is the *dancer,* who is often formed by borrowings from classical knowledge, in which case the "maiden" appears as the *corybant, maenad,* or *nymph.* An occasional variant is the nixie or water-sprite, who betrays her superhuman nature by her fishtail. Sometimes the Kore- and mother-figures slither down altogether to the animal kingdom, the favourite representatives then being the *cat* or the *snake* or the *bear,* or else some black monster of the underworld like the crocodile, or other salamander-like, saurian creatures.[3] The maiden's helplessness exposes her to all sorts of *dangers,* for instance of being devoured by reptiles or ritually slaughtered like a beast of sacrifice. Often there are bloody, cruel, and even obscene *orgies* to which the innocent child falls victim. Sometimes it is a true *nekyia,* a descent into Hades and a quest for the "treasure hard to attain," occasionally connected with orgiastic sexual rites or offerings of menstrual blood to the moon. Oddly enough, the various tortures and obscenities are carried out by an "Earth Mother." There are *drinkings of blood* and *bathings in blood,*[4] also cruci-

---

[2] The "personalistic" approach interprets such dreams as "wish-fulfilments." To many, this kind of interpretation seems the only possible one. These dreams, however, occur in the most varied circumstances, even in circumstances when the wish-fulfilment theory becomes entirely forced or arbitrary. The investigation of motifs in the field of dreams therefore seems to me the more cautious and the more appropriate procedure.

[3] The double vision of a salamander, of which Benvenuto Cellini tells in his autobiography, would be an anima-projection caused by the music his father was playing.

[4] One of my patients, whose principal difficulty was a negative mother-complex, developed a series of fantasies on a primitive mother-figure, an Indian woman,

fixions. The maiden who crops up in case histories differs not inconsiderably from the vaguely flower-like Kore in that the modern figure is more sharply delineated and not nearly so "unconscious," as the following examples will show.

The figures corresponding to Demeter and Hecate are supra-ordinate, not to say over-life-size "Mothers" ranging from the Pietà type to the Baubo type. The unconscious, which acts as a counterbalance to woman's conventional innocuousness, proves to be highly inventive in this latter respect. I can recall only very few cases where Demeter's own noble figure in its pure form breaks through as an image rising spontaneously from the unconscious. I remember a case, in fact, where a maiden-goddess appears clad all in purest white, but carrying a black monkey in her arms. The Earth Mother is always chthonic and is occasionally related to the moon, either through the blood-sacrifice already mentioned, or through a child-sacrifice, or else because she is adorned with a sickle moon.[5] In pictorial or plastic representations the Mother is dark deepening to *black,* or *red* (these being her principal colours), and with a primitive or animal expression of face; in form she not infrequently resembles the

---

who instructed her on the nature of woman in general. In these pronouncements a special paragraph is devoted to blood, running as follows: "A woman's life is close to the *blood.* Every month she is reminded of this, and birth is indeed a bloody business, destructive and creative. A woman is only *permitted* to give birth, but the new life is not *her* creation. In her heart of hearts she knows this and rejoices in the grace that has fallen to her. She is a little mother, not the *Great Mother.* But her little pattern is like the great pattern. If she understands this she is blessed by nature, because she has submitted in the right way and can thus partake of the nourishment of the Great Mother. . . ."

[5] Often the moon is simply "there," as for instance in a fantasy of the chthonic mother in the shape of the "Woman of the Bees" (Josephine D. Bacon, *In the Border Country,* pp. 14ff.): "The path led to a tiny hut of the same colour as the *four great trees* that stood about it. Its door hung wide open, and in the middle of it, on a low stool, there sat an old woman wrapped in a long cloak, looking kindly at her. . . ." The hut was filled with the steady *humming of bees.* In the corner of the hut there was a deep cold *spring,* in which "a white moon and little stars" were reflected. The old woman exhorted the heroine to remember the duties of a woman's life. In Tantric yoga an "indistinct hum of swarms of love-mad bees" proceeds from the slumbering Shakti (*Shat-Chakra Nirupana,* in Avalon, *The Serpent Power,* p. 29). Cf. infra, the dancer who dissolves into a *swarm of bees.* Bees are also, as an allegory, connected with Mary, as the text for the consecration of the Easter candle shows. See Duchesne, *Christian Worship: Its Origin and Evolution,* p. 253.

neolithic ideal of the "Venus" of Brassempouy or that of Willendorf, or again the sleeper of Hal Saflieni.[6] Now and then I have come across *multiple breasts*, arranged like those of a sow. The Earth Mother plays an important part in the woman's unconscious, for all her manifestations are described as "powerful." This shows that in such cases the Earth Mother element in the conscious mind is abnormally weak and requires strengthening.

In view of all this it is, I admit, hardly understandable why such figures should be reckoned as belonging to the type of "supraordinate personality." In a scientific investigation, however, one has to disregard moral or aesthetic prejudices and let the facts speak for themselves. The *maiden* is often described as not altogether human in the usual sense; she is either of unknown or peculiar origin, or she looks strange or undergoes strange experiences, from which one is forced to infer the maiden's extraordinary, myth-like nature. Equally and still more strikingly, the Earth Mother is a divine being—in the classical sense. Moreover, she does not by any means always appear in the guise of Baubo, but, for instance, more like Queen Venus in the *Hypnerotomachia Poliphili*, though she is invariably heavy with destiny. The often unaesthetic forms of the Earth Mother are in keeping with a prejudice of the modern feminine unconscious; this prejudice was lacking in antiquity. The underworld nature of Hecate, who is closely connected with Demeter, and Persephone's fate both point nevertheless to the dark side of the human psyche, though not to the same extent as the modern material.

The "supraordinate personality" is the total man, i.e., man as he really is, not as he appears to himself. To this wholeness the unconscious psyche also belongs, which has its requirements and needs just as consciousness has. I do not want to interpret the unconscious personalistically and assert, for instance, that fantasy-images like those described above are the "wish-fulfilments" due to repression. These images were as such never conscious and consequently could never have been repressed. I understand the unconscious rather as an *impersonal* psyche common to all men, even though it expresses itself through a

[6] See Neumann, *The Great Mother*, Pls. 1a, 3. This entire work elucidates the present study.

personal consciousness. When anyone breathes, his breathing is not a phenomenon to be interpreted personally. The mythological images belong to the structure of the unconscious and are an impersonal possession; in fact, the great majority of men are far more *possessed by* them than possessing them. Images like those described above give rise under certain conditions to corresponding disturbances and symptoms, and it is then the task of medical therapy to find out whether and how and to what extent these impulses can be integrated with the conscious personality, or whether they are a secondary phenomenon which some defective orientation of consciousness has brought out of its normal potential state into actuality. Both possibilities exist in practice.

I usually describe the supraordinate personality as the "self," thus making a sharp distinction between the ego, which, as is well known, extends only as far as the conscious mind, and the *whole* of the personality, which includes the unconscious as well as the conscious component. The ego is thus related to the self as part to whole. To that extent the self is supraordinate. Moreover, the self is felt empirically not as subject but as object, and this by reason of its unconscious component, which can only come to consciousness indirectly, by way of projection. Because of its unconscious component the self is so far removed from the conscious mind that it can only be partially expressed by human figures; the other part of it has to be expressed by objective, abstract symbols. The human figures are father and son, mother and daughter, king and queen, god and goddess. Theriomorphic symbols are the dragon, snake, elephant, lion, bear, and other powerful animals, or again the spider, crab, butterfly, beetle, worm, etc. Plant symbols are generally flowers (lotus and rose). These lead on to geometrical figures like the circle, the sphere, the square, the quaternity, the clock, the firmament, and so on.[7] The indefinite extent of the unconscious component makes a comprehensive description of the human personality impossible. Accordingly, the unconscious supplements the picture with living figures ranging from the animal to the divine, as the two extremes outside man, and rounds out the animal extreme, through the addition of

[7] *Psychology and Alchemy,* Part II.

vegetable and inorganic abstractions, into a microcosm. These addenda have a high frequency in anthropomorphic divinities, where they appear as "attributes."

Demeter and Kore, mother and daughter, extend the feminine consciousness both upwards and downwards. They add an "older and younger," "stronger and weaker" dimension to it and widen out the narrowly limited conscious mind bound in space and time, giving it intimations of a greater and more comprehensive personality which has a share in the eternal course of things. We can hardly suppose that myth and mystery were invented for any conscious purpose; it seems much more likely that they were the involuntary revelation of a psychic, but unconscious, pre-condition. The psyche pre-existent to consciousness (e.g., in the child) participates in the maternal psyche on the one hand, while on the other it reaches across to the daughter psyche. We could therefore say that every mother contains her daughter in herself and every daughter her mother, and that every woman extends backwards into her mother and forwards into her daughter. This participation and intermingling give rise to that peculiar uncertainty as regards *time:* a woman lives earlier as a mother, later as a daughter. The conscious experience of these ties produces the feeling that her life is spread out over generations—the first step towards the immediate experience and conviction of being outside time, which brings with it a feeling of *immortality.* The individual's life is elevated into a type, indeed it becomes the archetype of woman's fate in general. This leads to a restoration or *apocatastasis* of the lives of her ancestors, who now, through the bridge of the momentary individual, pass down into the generations of the future. An experience of this kind gives the individual a place and a meaning in the life of the generations, so that all unnecessary obstacles are cleared out of the way of the life-stream that is to flow through her. At the same time the individual is rescued from her isolation and restored to wholeness. All ritual preoccupation with archetypes ultimately has this aim and this result.

It is immediately clear to the psychologist what cathartic and at the same rejuvenating effects must flow from the Demeter cult into the feminine psyche, and what a lack of psychic hygiene characterizes our culture, which no longer knows the kind of wholesome experience afforded by Eleusinian emotions.

I take full account of the fact that not only the psychologically minded layman but the professional psychologist and psychiatrist as well, and even the psychotherapist, do not possess an adequate knowledge of their patients' archetypal material, in so far as they have not specially investigated this aspect of the phenomenology of the unconscious. For it is precisely in the field of psychiatric and psychotherapeutic observation that we frequently meet with cases characterized by a rich crop of archetypal symbols.[8] Since the necessary historical knowledge is lacking to the physician observing them, he is not in a position to perceive the parallelism between his observations and the findings of anthropology and the humane sciences in general. Conversely, an expert in mythology and comparative religion is as a rule no psychiatrist and consequently does not know that his mythologems are still fresh and living—for instance, in dreams and visions—in the hidden recesses of our most personal life, which we would on no account deliver up to scientific dissection. The archetypal material is therefore the great unknown, and it requires special study and preparation even to collect such material.

It does not seem to me superfluous to give a number of examples from my case histories which bring out the occurrence of archetypal images in dreams or fantasies. Time and again with my public I come across the difficulty that they imagine illustration by "a few examples" to be the simplest thing in the world. In actual fact it is almost impossible, with a few words and one or two images torn out of their context, to demonstrate anything. This only works when dealing with an expert. What Perseus has to do with the Gorgon's head would never occur to anyone who did not know the myth. So it is with the individual images: they need a context, and the context is not only a myth but an individual anamnesis. Such contexts, however, are of enormous extent. Anything like a complete series of images would require for its proper presentation a book of about two hundred pages. My own investigation of the Miller fantasies

8 I would refer to the thesis of my pupil Jan Nelken, "Analytische Beobachtungen über Phantasien eines Schizophrenen," as also to my own analysis of a series of fantasies in *Symbols of Transformation*.

gives some idea of this.[9] It is therefore with the greatest hesitation that I make the attempt to illustrate from case-histories. The material I shall use comes partly from normal, partly from slightly neurotic, persons. It is part dream, part vision, or dream mixed with vision. These "visions" are far from being hallucinations or ecstatic states; they are spontaneous, visual images of fantasy or so-called *active imagination*. The latter is a method (devised by myself) of introspection for observing the stream of interior images. One concentrates one's attention on some impressive but unintelligible dream-image, or on a spontaneous visual impression, and observes the changes taking place in it. Meanwhile, of course, all criticism must be suspended and the happenings observed and noted with absolute objectivity. Obviously, too, the objection that the whole thing is "arbitrary" or "thought up" must be set aside, since it springs from the anxiety of an ego-consciousness which brooks no master besides itself in its own house. In other words, it is the inhibition exerted by the conscious mind on the unconscious.

Under these conditions, long and often very dramatic series of fantasies ensue. The advantage of this method is that it brings a mass of unconscious material to light. Drawing, painting, and modelling can be used to the same end. Once a visual series has become dramatic, it can easily pass over into the auditive or linguistic sphere and give rise to dialogues and the like. With slightly pathological individuals, and particularly in the not infrequent cases of latent schizophrenia, the method may, in certain circumstances, prove to be rather dangerous and therefore requires medical control. It is based on a deliberate weakening of the conscious mind and its inhibiting effect, which either limits or suppresses the unconscious. The aim of the method is naturally therapeutic in the first place, while in the second it also furnishes rich empirical material. Some of our examples are taken from this. They differ from dreams only by reason of their better form, which comes from the fact that the contents were perceived not by a dreaming but by a waking consciousness. The examples are from women in middle life.

[9] Cf. *Symbols of Transformation*. H. G. Baynes' book, *The Mythology of the Soul*, runs to 939 pages and endeavours to do justice to the material provided by only two cases.

1. Case X (spontaneous visual impressions, in chronological order)

i. *"I saw a white bird with outstretched wings. It alighted on the figure of a woman, clad in blue, who sat there like an* antique statue. *The bird perched on her hand, and in it she held a grain of wheat. The bird took it in its beak and flew into the sky again."*

For this X painted a picture: a blue-clad, archaically simple "Mother"-figure on a white marble base. Her maternity is emphasized by the large breasts.

ii. *A bull lifts a child up from the ground and carries it to the antique statue of a woman. A naked young girl with a wreath of flowers in her hair appears, riding on a white bull. She takes the child and throws it into the air like a ball and catches it again. The white bull carries them both to a temple. The girl lays the child on the ground, and so on (initiation follows).*

In this picture the *maiden* appears, rather in the form of Europa. (Here a certain school knowledge is being made use of.) Her nakedness and the wreath of flowers point to Dionysian abandonment. The game of ball with the child is the motif of some secret rite which always has to do with "child-sacrifice." (Cf. the accusations of ritual murder levelled by the pagans against the Christians and by the Christians against the Jews and Gnostics; also the Phoenician child-sacrifices, rumours about the Black Mass, etc., and "the ball-game in church.") [10]

iii. *"I saw a golden pig on a pedestal. Beast-like beings danced round it in a circle. We made haste to dig a hole in the ground. I reached in and found water. Then a man appeared* in a golden carriage. *He jumped into the hole and began swaying back and forth, as if dancing. . . . I swayed in rhythm with him. Then he suddenly leaped out of the hole, raped me, and got me with child."*

X is identical with the young girl, who often appears as a *youth,* too. This youth is an animus-figure, the embodiment of the masculine element in a woman. Youth and young girl together form a syzygy or *coniunctio* which symbolizes the essence

[10] Cf. "On the Psychology of the Trickster-Figure."

of wholeness (as also does the Platonic hermaphrodite, who later became the symbol of perfected wholeness in alchemical philosophy). X evidently dances with the rest, hence "*we* made haste." The parallel with the motifs stressed by Kerényi seems to me remarkable.

iv. "*I saw a beautiful youth with golden cymbals, dancing and leaping in joy and abandonment. . . . Finally he fell to the ground and buried his face in the flowers. Then he sank into the lap of a* very old mother. *After a time he got up and jumped into the water, where he sported like a* dolphin. . . . *I saw that his hair was golden. Now we were leaping together, hand in hand. So we came to a* gorge. . . ." In leaping the gorge the youth falls into the chasm. X is left alone and comes to a river where a white sea-horse *is waiting for her with a golden boat.*

In this scene X is the youth; therefore he disappears later, leaving her the sole heroine of the story. She is the child of the "very old mother," and is also the dolphin, the youth lost in the gorge, and the bride evidently expected by Poseidon. The peculiar overlapping and displacement of motifs in all this individual material is about the same as in the mythological variants. X found the youth in the lap of the mother so impressive that she painted a picture of it. The figure is the same as in item i; only, instead of the grain of wheat in her hand, there is the body of the youth lying completely exhausted in the lap of the gigantic mother.

v. *There now follows a sacrifice of sheep, during which a game of ball is likewise played with the sacrificial animal. The participants* smear themselves with the sacrificial blood, *and afterwards bathe in the pulsing gore. X is thereupon transformed into a* plant.

vi. *After that X comes to a* den of snakes, *and the snakes wind all round her.*

vii. *In a den of snakes beneath the sea there is a* divine woman, *asleep.* (She is shown in the picture as much larger than the others.) *She is wearing a blood-red garment that covers only the lower half of her body. She has a dark skin, full red lips, and seems to be of great physical strength. She kisses X, who is obviously in the role of the young girl, and hands her as a present to the many men who are standing by, etc.*

This chthonic goddess is the typical Earth Mother as she appears in so many modern fantasies.

viii. *As X emerged from the depths and saw the light again, she experienced a kind of illumination: white flames played about her head as she walked through waving* fields of grain.

With this picture the Mother-episode ended. Although there is not the slightest trace of any known myth being repeated, the motifs and the connections between them are all familiar to us from mythology. These images present themselves spontaneously and are based on no conscious knowledge whatever. I have applied the method of active imagination to myself over a long time and have observed numerous symbols and symbolic associations which in many cases I was only able to verify years afterwards in texts of whose existence I was totally ignorant. It is the same with dreams. Some years ago I dreamed for example that: *I was climbing slowly and toilsomely up a mountain. When I had reached, as I imagined, the top, I found that I was standing on the edge of a plateau. The crest that represented the real top of the mountain only rose far off in the distance. Night was coming on, and I saw, on the dark slope opposite, a brook flowing down with a metallic shimmer, and two paths leading upwards, one to the left, the other to the right, winding like serpents. On the crest, to the right, there was a hotel. Down below, the brook ran to the left with a bridge leading across.*

Not long afterwards I discovered the following "allegory" in an obscure alchemical treatise. In his *Speculativae philosophiae* [11] the Frankfurt physician Gerard Dorn, who lived in the second half of the sixteenth century, describes the "Mundi peregrinatio, quam erroris viam appellamus" (Tour of the world, which we call the way of error) on the one hand and the "Via veritatis" on the other. Of the first way the author says:

The human race, whose nature it is to resist God, does not cease to ask how it may, by its own efforts, escape the pitfalls which it has laid for itself. But it does not ask help from Him on whom alone depends every gift of mercy. Hence it has come about that men have built for themselves a great Workshop on the left-hand side of the road . . . presided over by Industry. After this has been attained, they turn aside from Industry and bend their steps towards the

[11] *Theatrum chemicum*, I (1602), pp. 286ff.

second region of the world, making their crossing *on the bridge of infirmity.* . . . But because the good God desires to draw them back, He allows their infirmities to rule over them; then, seeking as before a remedy in themselves [industry!], they flock *to the great Hospital likewise built on the left,* presided over by Medicine. Here there is a great multitude of apothecaries, surgeons, and physicians, [etc.].[12]

Of the "way of truth," which is the "right" way, our author says: ". . . you will come to the camp of Wisdom and on being received there, you will be refreshed with food far more powerful than before." Even the brook is there: ". . . a stream of living water flowing with such wonderful artifice from the mountain peak. (From the Fountain of Wisdom the waters gush forth.)" [13]

An important difference, compared with my dream, is that here, apart from the situation of the hotel being reversed, the river of Wisdom is on the right and not, as in my dream, in the middle of the picture.

It is evident that in my dream we are not dealing with any known "myth" but with a group of ideas which might easily have been regarded as "individual," i.e., unique. A thorough analysis, however, could show without difficulty that it is an archetypal image such as can be reproduced over and over again in any age and any place. But I must admit that the archetypal nature of the dream-image only became clear to me when I read Dorn. These and similar incidents I have observed repeatedly not only in myself but in my patients. But, as this

[12] "Humanum genus, cui Deo resistere iam innatum est, non desistit media quaerere, quibus proprio conatu laqueos evadat, quos sibimet posuit, ab eo non petens auxilium, a quo solo dependet omnis misericordiae munus. Hinc factum est, ut in sinistram viae partem officinam sibi maximam exstruxerint . . . huic domui praeest industria, etc. Quod postquam adepti fuerint, ab industria recedentes *in secundam mundi regionem* tendunt: *per infirmitatis pontem* facientes transitum.* . . . At quia bonus Deus retrahere vellet, infirmitates in ipsis dominari permittit, tum rursus ut prius remedium [industria!] a se quaerentes, *ad xenodochium etiam a sinistris constructum* et permaximum confluunt, cui medicina praeest. Ibi pharmacopolarum, chirurgorum et physicorum ingens est copia." (p. 288.)

[13] ". . . pervenietis ad Sophiae castra, quibus excepti, longe vehementiori quam antea cibo reficiemini. . . . viventis aquae fluvius tam admirando fluens artificio de montis apice. (De Sophiae fonte scaturiunt aquae!) " Slightly modified by the author. Cf. Dorn, pp. 279–80.

example shows, it needs special attention if such parallels are not to be missed.

The antique Mother-image is not exhausted with the figure of Demeter. It also expresses itself in Cybele-Artemis. The next case points in this direction.

2. *Case Y (dreams)*

i. *"I am wandering over a great mountain; the way is lonely, wild, and difficult. A woman comes down from the sky to accompany and help me. She is all bright with light hair and shining eyes. Now and then she vanishes. After going on for some time alone I notice that I have left my stick somewhere, and must turn back to fetch it. To do this I have to pass a terrible monster, an enormous bear. When I came this way the first time I had to pass it, but then the sky-woman protected me. Just as I am passing the beast and he is about to come at me, she stands beside me again, and at her look the bear lies down quietly and lets us pass. Then the sky-woman vanishes."*

Here we have a maternally protective goddess related to bears, a kind of Diana or the Gallo-Roman Dea Artio. The sky-woman is the positive, the bear the negative aspect of the "supraordinate personality," which extends the conscious human being upwards into the celestial and downwards into the animal regions.

ii. *"We go through a door into a tower-like room, where we climb a long flight of steps. On one of the topmost steps I read an inscription: 'Vis ut sis.' The steps end in a temple situated on the crest of a wooded mountain, and there is no other approach. It is the shrine of* Ursanna, *the bear-goddess and Mother of God in one. The temple is of red stone. Bloody sacrifices are offered there. Animals are standing about the altar. In order to enter the temple precincts one has to be transformed into an animal—a beast of the forest. The temple has the form of a cross with equal arms and a circular space in the middle, which is not roofed, so that one can look straight up at the sky and the constellation of the Bear. On the altar in the middle of the open space there stands the moon-bowl, from which smoke or vapour continually rises. There is also a huge image of the goddess, but it cannot be seen clearly. The worshippers, who have been changed into animals and to whom I also belong, have to touch the goddess's foot with their own foot, whereupon the image gives them a sign or an oracular utterance like 'Vis ut sis.' "*

In this dream the bear-goddess emerges plainly, although her statue "cannot be seen clearly." The relationship to the self, the supraordinate personality, is indicated not only by the oracle "Vis ut sis" but by the quaternity and the circular central precinct of the temple. From ancient times any relationship to the stars has always symbolized eternity. The soul comes "from the stars" and returns to the stellar regions. "Ursanna's" relation to the moon is indicated by the "moon-bowl."

The moon-goddess also appears in children's dreams. A girl who grew up in peculiarly difficult psychic circumstances had a recurrent dream between her seventh and tenth years: *"The moon-lady was always waiting for me down by the water at the landing-stage, to take me to her island."* Unfortunately she could never remember what happened there, but it was so beautiful that she often prayed she might have this dream again. Although, as is evident, the two dreamers are not identical, the *island motif* also occurred in the previous dream as the inaccessible mountain crest.

Thirty years later, the dreamer of the moon-lady had a dramatic fantasy:

"I am climbing a steep dark mountain, on top of which stands a domed castle. I enter and go up a winding stairway to the left. Arriving inside the dome, I find myself in the presence of a woman wearing a head-dress of cow's horns. I recognize her immediately as the moon-lady *of my childhood dreams. At her behest I look to the* right *and see a dazzlingly bright sun shining on the other side of a deep chasm. Over the chasm stretches a narrow, transparent bridge, upon which I step, conscious of the fact that in no circumstances must I look down. An uncanny fear seizes me, and I hesitate. Treachery seems to be in the air, but at last I go across and stand before the sun. The sun speaks: 'If you can approach me nine times without being burned, all will be well.' But I grow more and more afraid, finally I do look down, and I see a black tentacle like that of an octopus groping towards me from underneath the sun. I step back in fright and plunge into the abyss. But instead of being dashed*

to pieces I lie in the arms of the Earth Mother. When I try to look into her face, she turns to clay, and I find myself lying on the earth."

It is remarkable how the beginning of this fantasy agrees with the dream. The moon-lady above is clearly distinguished from the Earth Mother below. The former urges the dreamer to her somewhat perilous adventure with the sun; the latter catches her protectively in her maternal arms. The dreamer, as the one in danger, would therefore seem to be in the role of the Kore.

Let us now turn back to our dream-series:

iii. *Y sees two pictures in a dream, painted by the Scandinavian painter Hermann Christian Lund.*

I. "*The first picture is of a Scandinavian peasant room. Peasant girls in gay costumes are walking about arm in arm (that is, in a row). The middle one is smaller than the rest and, besides this, has a hump and keeps turning her head back. This, together with her peculiar glance, gives her a witchlike look.*"

II. "*The second picture shows a dragon with its neck stretched out over the whole picture and especially over a girl, who is in the dragon's power and cannot move, for as soon as she moves, the dragon, which can make its body big or little at will, moves too; and when the girl wants to get away it simply stretches out its neck over her, and so catches her again. Strangely enough, the girl has no face, at least I couldn't see it.*"

The painter is an invention of the dream. The animus often appears as a painter or has some kind of projection apparatus, or is a cinema-operator or owner of a picture-gallery. All this refers to the animus as the function mediating between conscious and unconscious: the unconscious contains pictures which are transmitted, that is, made manifest, by the animus, either as fantasies or, unconsciously, in the patient's own life and actions. The animus-projection gives rise to fantasied relations of love and hatred for "heroes" or "demons." The favourite victims are tenors, artists, movie-stars, athletic champions, etc. In the first picture the maiden is characterized as demonic, with a hump and an evil look "over her shoulder." (Hence amulets against the evil eye are often worn by primitives on the nape of the neck, for the vulnerable spot is at the back, where you can't see.)

In the second picture the "maiden" is portrayed as the innocent victim of the monster. Just as before there was a relationship of identity between the sky-woman and the bear, so here between the young girl and the dragon—which in practical life is often rather more than just a bad joke. Here it signifies a widening of the conscious personality, i.e., through the helplessness of the victim on the one hand and the dangers of the humpback's evil eye and the dragon's might on the other.

iv (part dream, part visual imagination). *"A magician is demonstrating his tricks to an Indian prince. He produces a beautiful young girl from under a cloth. She is a dancer, who has the power to change her shape or at least hold her audience spell-bound by faultless illusion. During the dance she dissolves with the music into a swarm of bees. Then she changes into a leopard, then into a jet of water, then into an octopus that has twined itself about a young pearl-fisher. Between times, she takes human form again at the dramatic moment. She appears as a she-ass bearing two baskets of wonderful fruits. Then she becomes a many-coloured peacock. The prince is beside himself with delight and calls her to him. But she dances on, now naked, and even tears the skin from her body, and finally falls down—a naked skeleton. This is buried, but at night a lily grows out of the grave, and from its cup there rises a* white lady, who *floats slowly up to the sky."*

This piece describes the successive transformations of the illusionist (artistry in illusion being a specifically feminine talent) until she becomes a transfigured personality. The fantasy was not invented as a sort of allegory; it was part dream, part spontaneous imagery.

v. *"I am in a church made of grey sandstone. The apse is built rather high. Near the tabernacle a girl in a red dress is hanging on the stone cross of the window. (Suicide?)"*

Just as in the preceding cases the sacrifice of a child or a sheep played a part, so here the sacrifice of the maiden hanging on the "cross." The death of the dancer is also to be understood in this sense, for these maidens are always doomed to die, because their exclusive domination of the feminine psyche hinders the individuation process, that is, the maturation of personality. The "maiden" corresponds to the anima of the man and makes use of it to gain her natural ends, in which illusion plays the greatest role imaginable. But as long as a woman is content to be a *femme à homme,* she has no feminine individuality. She is empty and merely glitters—a welcome vessel for masculine projections. Woman as a personality, however, is a very different thing: here illusion no longer works. So that when the question of personality arises, which is as a rule the painful fact of the second half of life, the childish form of the self disappears too.

All that remains for me now is to describe the Kore as observable in man, the *anima.* Since a man's wholeness, in so far as he is not constitutionally homosexual, can only be a masculine personality, the feminine figure of the anima cannot be catalogued as a type of supraordinate personality but requires a different evaluation and position. In the products of unconscious activity, the anima appears equally as maiden and mother, which is why a personalistic interpretation always reduces her to the personal mother or some other female person. The real meaning of the figure naturally gets lost in the process, as is inevitably the case with all these reductive interpretations whether in the sphere of the psychology of the unconscious or of mythology. The innumerable attempts that have been made in the sphere of mythology to interpret gods and heroes in a solar, lunar, astral, or meteorological sense contribute nothing of importance to the understanding of them; on the contrary, they all put us on a false track. When, therefore, in dreams and other spontaneous products, we meet with an unknown female figure whose significance oscillates between the extremes of goddess and whore, it is advisable to let her keep her independence and not reduce her arbitrarily to something known. If the unconscious shows her as an "unknown," this attribute should not be got rid of by main force with a view to arriving at a "rational" interpretation. Like the "supraordinate personality," the anima is bipolar and can therefore appear positive one moment and negative the next; now young, now old; now mother, now maiden; now a good fairy, now a witch; now a saint, now a whore. Besides this ambivalence, the anima also has "occult" connections with "mysteries," with the world of darkness in general, and for that reason she often has a religious tinge. Whenever she emerges with some degree of clarity, she always has a peculiar relationship to *time:* as a rule she is more or less immortal, because outside time. Writers who have tried their hand at this figure have never failed to stress the anima's peculiarity in this respect. I would refer to the classic descriptions in Rider Haggard's *She* and *The Return of She,* in Pierre Benoît's *L'Atlantide,* and above all in the novel of the young American author, William M. Sloane, *To Walk the Night.* In all these accounts, the anima is outside time as we know it and consequently immensely old or a being who belongs to a different order of things.

Since we can no longer or only partially express the archetypes of the unconscious by means of figures in which we religiously believe, they lapse into unconsciousness again and hence are unconsciously projected upon more or less suitable human personalities. To the young boy a clearly discernible anima-form appears in his mother, and this lends her the radiance of power and superiority or else a daemonic aura of even greater fascination. But because of the anima's ambivalence, the projection can be entirely negative. Much of the fear which the female sex arouses in men is due to the projection of the anima-image. An infantile man generally has a maternal anima; an adult man, the figure of a younger woman. The senile man finds compensation in a very young girl, or even a child.

3. *Case Z*

The anima also has affinities with animals, which symbolize her characteristics. Thus she can appear as a snake or a tiger or a bird. I quote by way of example a dream-series that contains transformations of this kind: [14]

i. *A white bird perches on a table. Suddenly it changes into a fair-haired seven-year-old girl and just as suddenly back into a bird, which now speaks with a human voice.*

ii. *In an underground house, which is really the underworld, there lives an old magician and prophet with his "daughter." She is, however, not really his daughter; she is a dancer, a very loose person, but is blind and seeks healing.*

iii. *A lonely house in a wood, where an old scholar is living. Suddenly his daughter appears, a kind of ghost, complaining that people only look upon her as a figment of fancy.*

[14] Only extracts from the dreams are given, so far as they bear on the anima.

iv. *On the façade of a church there is a Gothic Madonna, who is alive and is the "unknown and yet known woman." Instead of a child, she holds in her arms a sort of flame or a snake or a dragon.*

v. *A black-clad "countess" kneels in a dark chapel. Her dress is hung with costly pearls. She has red hair, and there is something uncanny about her. Moreover, she is surrounded by the spirits of the dead.*

vi. *A female snake comports herself tenderly and insinuatingly, speaking with a human voice. She is only "accidentally" shaped like a snake.*

vii. *A bird speaks with the same voice, but shows herself helpful by trying to rescue the dreamer from a dangerous situation.*

viii. *The unknown woman sits, like the dreamer, on the tip of a church-spire and stares at him uncannily across the abyss.*

ix. *The unknown woman suddenly appears as an old female attendant in an underground public lavatory with a temperature of 40° below zero.*

x. *The unknown woman leaves the house as a* petite bourgeoise *with a female relation, and in her place there is suddenly an over-life-size goddess clad in blue, looking like Athene.*

xi. *Then she appears in a church, taking the place of the altar, still over-life-size but with veiled face.*

In all these dreams [15] the central figure is a mysterious feminine being with qualities like those of no woman known to the dreamer. The unknown is described as such in the dreams themselves, and reveals her extraordinary nature firstly by her power to change shape and secondly by her paradoxical ambivalence. Every conceivable shade of meaning glitters in her, from the highest to the lowest.

Dream i shows the anima as elflike, i.e., only partially human. She can just as well be a bird, which means that she may belong wholly to nature and can vanish (i.e., become unconscious) from the human sphere (i.e., consciousness).

Dream ii shows the unknown woman as a mythological figure from the beyond (the unconscious). She is the *soror* or *filia mystica* of a hierophant or "philosopher," evidently a parallel to

[15] The following statements are not meant as "interpretations" of the dreams. They are intended only to sum up the various forms in which the anima appears.

those mystic syzygies which are to be met with in the figures of Simon Magus and Helen, Zosimus and Theosebeia, Comarius and Cleopatra, etc. Our dream-figure fits in best with Helen. A really admirable description of anima-psychology in a woman is to be found in Erskine's *Helen of Troy*.

Dream iii presents the same theme, but on a more "fairytale-like" plane. Here the anima is shown as rather spookish.

Dream iv brings the anima nearer to the Mother of God. The "child" refers to the mystic speculations on the subject of the redemptive serpent and the "fiery" nature of the redeemer.

In *dream v*, the anima is visualized somewhat romantically as the "distinguished" fascinating woman, who nevertheless has dealings with spirits.

Dreams vi and vii bring theriomorphic variations. The anima's identity is at once apparent to the dreamer because of the voice and what it says. The anima has "accidentally" taken the form of a snake, just as in *dream i* she changed with the greatest ease into a bird and back again. As a snake, she is playing the negative role, as a bird the positive.

Dream viii shows the dreamer confronted with his anima. This takes place high above the ground (i.e., above human reality). Obviously it is a case of dangerous fascination by the anima.

Dream ix signifies the anima's deep plunge into an extremely "subordinate" position, where the last trace of fascination has gone and only human sympathy is left.

Dream x shows the paradoxical double nature of the anima: banal mediocrity and Olympian divinity.

Dream xi restores the anima to the Christian church, not as an icon but as the altar itself. The altar is the place of sacrifice and also the receptacle for consecrated relics.

To throw even a moderate light on all these anima associations would require special and very extensive investigation, which would be out of place here because, as we have already said, the anima has only an indirect bearing on the interpretation of the Kore figure. I have presented this dream-series simply for the purpose of giving the reader some idea of the empirical material on which the idea of the anima is based.[16] From this series and others like it we get an average picture of that strange factor which has such an important part to play in the

[16] Cf. "Concerning the Archetypes, with special reference to the Anima Concept."

masculine psyche, and which naïve presumption invariably identifies with certain women, imputing to them all the illusions that swarm in the male Eros.

It seems clear enough that the man's anima found occasion for projection in the Demeter cult. The Kore doomed to her subterranean fate, the two-faced mother, and the theriomorphic aspects of both afforded the anima ample opportunity to reflect herself, shimmering and equivocal, in the Eleusinian cult, or rather to experience herself there and fill the celebrants with her unearthly essence, to their lasting gain. For a man, anima experiences are always of immense and abiding significance.

But the Demeter-Kore myth is far too feminine to have been merely the result of an anima-projection. Although the anima can, as we have said, experience herself in Demeter-Kore, she is yet of a wholly different nature. She is in the highest degree *femme à homme,* whereas Demeter-Kore exists on the plane of mother-daughter experience, which is alien to man and shuts him out. In fact, the psychology of the Demeter cult bears all the features of a matriarchal order of society, where the man is an indispensable but on the whole disturbing factor.

EPILEGOMENA

BY C. KERÉNYI

The Miracle of Eleusis

Contemporaneously with the studies of the numerous aspects of the Kore figure presented in this volume, attempts have been made by scholars of note to bring the secret of the Eleusinian mysteries somewhat nearer to modern man. Only now, by way of a supplement, is it possible to take up a position in respect of them. I shall not enter here into questions of detail which were purposely avoided in the Kore study proper. In one instance alone does it seem necessary to take up a position, and that is where the results of our study had almost been reached by someone else and where he who had almost reached them yet failed to take the last and decisive step. Today I believe that I can directly prove the justice of this last step—the basic identity of mother and daughter—from an ancient record. I should also like to give reasons why I cannot take another step along with him—the step not to "wordless knowledge" but to a "miracle." All this seems to me so much the more needful since it was a man like Walter F. Otto who omitted to take the former, decisive step and yet ventured the latter one as regards the "miracle."[1]

What is the basis of our insight into the fundamental identity of Demeter and Persephone? It is based on psychic reality and on the tradition that testifies to the existence of this psychic reality in antiquity. Professor Jung has thrown light on its psychologically real basis. He has certainly not said the last word, but enough to show that research is not going in a "speculative" direction when it starts out from mythological "ideas." The ancient records were and remain the deciding factor. They afford indirect proof of that basic identity.

Direct proof would be the admission of this identity by an initiate. Instead of which we find in Eleusis the remains of a cult proving that the initiates paid homage to *two* goddesses, mother and daughter. On the other hand this pair of divinities

[1] "The Meaning of the Eleusinian Mysteries."

forms a unit the essential nature and uniqueness of which give us pause. No one has put just this point as sharply as Otto. "How is it," he asks, "that Demeter comes to have this daughter? Indeed, what does it mean that she is so closely connected with a daughter at all?" He compares the relations of other daughters to their divine parents and finds none of them so intimate. "Even Athene, who sprang from the head of Zeus, is not as much of a daughter to her father as Persephone is to her mother." The fervour of their love for one another reminds us rather of divine lovers such as Aphrodite and Adonis, Cybele and Atthis, Ishtar and Tammuz, Isis and Osiris. Otto therefore emphasizes the *difference* all the more: "Demeter, mourning her daughter, is mourning some nature that is essentially akin to her, that makes the impression of a younger double. Such a relationship is very different in character from that of the others. So that, despite seeming parallels, it remains in the last analysis unique and in need of a special explanation." There is only one thing more to be added: just as all the other great goddesses always lose—and find—only their *one* beloved (Aphrodite her Adonis, Ishtar her Tammuz, etc.), so it is unthinkable that Demeter should get back *another* daughter as dear to her as the one she has lost, the Kore κατ' ἐξοχήν.

Thus we come to a piece of indirect evidence: the Arcadian mythologem of Demeter and her daughter.[2] Otto is very near to understanding their basic identity when he keeps his eye constantly on the Arcadian story as well as the Eleusinian. Mythologems told in this form are never the mystery, never the thing that is shrouded in mystery both in Arcadia and in Eleusis. In Arcadia, the characters in the divine drama (bearing in mind the later Greek romantic tales, we might also speak of a "divine novel") are the same as in Eleusis, and the *peripeteia* is the same—the sudden change from anger and grief to peace and happiness. Only the names are different, at least in part, and the mother experiences in Arcadia what the daughter experienced in Eleusis. Let us examine this critical point more closely than we did in the Kore study.

For the benefit of the uninitiated, Pausanias thus explains, by the old method of rational systematization of myth, the fact

2 Supra, pp. 121f.

that "first" (i.e., in the Eleusinian version) it was Demeter's daughter and "then" (i.e., in the Arcadian account) Demeter herself who undergoes a marriage by rape and becomes a mother: in his account of the shrine of Despoina in Lykosura he speaks expressly of Demeter having a second daughter. Despoina, he says, is Demeter's daughter by Poseidon, just as her other daughter by Zeus is generally called Kore, although Homer and Pamphos call her by the special name of Persephone. He does not dare, he says, reveal Despoina's proper name to the uninitiate. Speaking in this connection of the triad of goddesses in Lykosura—Demeter, Despoina, and Artemis Hegemone—he sees in the third of these yet another of Demeter's daughters, but only on the basis of a great authority. For this he cites Aeschylus, who is said to have learned such matters from the Egyptians (VIII, 37). By so doing he betrays nothing of the mysteries as known *to him*. (Aeschylus, a great teller of myths, probably knew much more.) It is quite unintentionally and unwittingly that he nevertheless furnishes us with a deeper insight into the nature of the connection between Artemis and Demeter. Pausanias does this by speaking of Despoina's pet *stag*—an animal otherwise sacred to Artemis (VIII, 10, 10).

The Lykosura triad—increased to a foursome by the mysterious figure of a man, Anytos the Titan—consists of separate figures that also point to an original unity and thus confirm the train of thought leading to the recognition of such a unity. There can, however, be no doubt that for Pausanias Despoina and the Kore were in no way different from Despoina and Artemis. The Arcadian triad Demeter-Despoina-Artemis (the last being the leader with the torch and two snakes in her hand) corresponds exactly to the Eleusinian triad of the Homeric hymn: Demeter-Kore-Hecate. In both cases the daughter sits in the middle of them, and in both cases there was only *one* daughter for all the Greeks. In accordance with this Pausanias also speaks, when relating the mythologem of Thelpusa, of Demeter being angry but *once* and having only *one* reason for her anger: the assault of the dark god—Poseidon in the Arcadian version. If we treat the rape of Persephone as a separate thing and regard it as another reason for Demeter's anger, then one of the two versions becomes a mere addition and the whole something that is put right afterwards.

Otto sticks to this secondary state of the records despite his esteem for the Arcadian mythologem. And he would still have the records, at least as regards their wording, in his favour were it not that just such a testimony as we could wish for has come to light. This is an inscription in a somewhat remote spot but still deriving from the time when the Eleusinian mysteries were alive. It was found on Delos in the precincts sacred to Egyptian gods.[3] Vain attempts were made to interpret the inscription as something Egyptian. For Demeter was always at home on any Greek island, and what is more she carried remains of the Isis cult with her to Eleusis. Conversely, too, where Isis was already being worshipped the Greeks liked to recall the Holy Mother of Eleusis. They even went so far as to equate the two goddesses. But the inscription is consecrated only to the Greek goddess:

$$\Delta \acute{\eta}\mu\eta\tau\varrho\text{o}\varsigma$$
$$\text{'}E\lambda\varepsilon\upsilon\sigma\iota\nu\acute{\iota}\alpha\varsigma$$
$$\varkappa\alpha\grave{\iota}\ \varkappa\acute{o}\varrho\eta\varsigma$$
$$\varkappa\alpha\grave{\iota}\ \gamma\upsilon\nu\alpha\iota\varkappa\acute{o}\varsigma$$

Only the initial Δ was lacking. For the rest it says plainly and with no need of completion that the Eleusinian Demeter was Kore and mature woman (Latin *matrona*) in one.

If a truth were in fact revealed to the celebrants in Eleusis by means of pictures, signs, or words, it must have been something absolutely novel, astounding, and not to be apprehended by reason and experience. This is Otto's opinion, and such is indeed the character of Demeter as girl and woman. Yet this truth, translated into the language of everyday and workaday reality, seems to him to be not nearly mysterious enough to form the heart of so great a mystery. To his way of thinking, the knowledge that man must die but lives on in his descendants is trivial. This is certainly true of mere "knowledge of" something. But there is a vast difference between "knowing of" something and *knowing it and being it*. It is one thing to know about the "seed and the sprout," and quite another to have

3 Published by Roussel, *Les Cultes égyptiens à Delos*, p. 199, No. 206.

recognized in them the past and future as one's own being and its continuation. Or, as Professor Jung puts it: to experience the return, the *apocatastasis,* of one's ancestors in such a way that these can prolong themselves via the bridge of the momentary individual into the generations of the future. A knowledge with this content, with the experience of *being in death,* is not to be despised.

In the light of this confluence of past and future, the "underworldly" aspect of the Eleusinian mysteries also becomes understandable, an aspect I have long felt and on which Otto now lays particular stress. It is all the more curious, then, that he should find the solution of the Eleusinian riddle not in the seed and the sprout, where a whole underworld of ancestral souls may be contained, but in a miracle. He takes the evidence of the part played by the mown ear in Eleusis as meaning that it was *harvested* "in complete stillness" and then displayed. This is one possible interpretation of the sentence in the Church Father Hippolytus (*Elenchos,* V, 8, 37), but the other interpretation is equally justifiable grammatically. Indeed the context favours the view that the liturgical act of *showing* was accomplished in "complete stillness," for immediately afterwards Hippolytus speaks of the loud cry of the hierophant who, proclaiming the divine birth, broke the mystic silence of wordless revelation.

And as a matter of fact, where could you get the ear of grain at that late season? It could be kept just as grain-wreaths are kept today all over the world wherever harvest festivals are celebrated, and the decorations preserved for months. Otto thinks of a miracle that was supposed to be repeated annually in Eleusis: "The miraculous nature of the proceedings cannot be doubted. The ear of grain sprouting and ripening with supernatural suddenness belongs to the mysteries of Demeter just as the grape that ripens in a few hours belongs to the drunken festivals of Dionysus. And that we should not content ourselves by conveniently appealing to priestly trickery is at least required of us by our respect for such men as Sophocles and Euripides, who deemed the miracle worthy of their praise. For a tragic poet the Dionysian miracle was as natural as it was possible. Moreover, we find the same botanical miracles in the Nature festivals of primitive peoples."

We might also add the miracle of Saint Januarius, repeated every year in Naples. It is immaterial how one explains it and how one explains the miracle of Eleusis—if there was one, which is not proved. The student of religion is concerned with the *meaning* of the "miracle" regardless of how it is worked. This meaning is the revelation of some power. Nor could it have been otherwise in antiquity. The miraculous meaning is further attested by a number of reports of miracles, by that Hellenistic form of aretology which dominates the foreground the more the classical gods fade, the more their power, inherent as though in the idea of them, gets lost. The miracle will cause people to talk of it, always and everywhere. The mystery is kept silent. Is not this, perhaps, the secret of every true and great mystery, that it is *simple?* Does it not love secrecy for that very reason? Proclaimed, it were but a word; kept silent, it is *being*. And a miracle, too, in the sense that *being* with all its paradoxes is miraculous. In this sense, miracles and epiphanies probably *were* witnessed in Eleusis: the miracle of *origination* seen in those figures where it revealed itself at a certain period in the world's history.

REFERENCES CITED

ABBREVIATIONS: *ArchRW* = *Archiv für Religionswissenschaft* (Freiburg i. B.). AV = Albae Vigiliae. BS = Bollingen Series. CWJ = Collected Works of C. G. Jung (New York / Princeton and London).

AARNE, ANTTI. *The Types of the Folk-Tale: A Classification and Bibliography.* Translated and enlarged by Stith Thompson. (Folklore Fellows. FF Communications, 74.) Helsinki, 1928.

ABRAHAM, KARL. *Dreams and Myths.* Translated by William A. White. (Nervous and Mental Disease Monograph Series, 15.) New York, 1913.

AGRICOLA, GEORG. *De animantibus subterraneis.* Basel, 1549.

ALFÖLDI, A. "Zur Kenntnis der Zeit der römischen Soldatenkaiser," *Zeitschrift für Numismatik* (Berlin), XXXVIII (1928), 197–212.

ALLEN, THOMAS WILLIAM, and EDWARD ERNEST SIKES (eds.). *The Homeric Hymns.* London, 1904; 2nd edn., Oxford, 1936.

ALTHEIM, FRANZ. *A History of Roman Religion.* Translated by Harold Mattingly. London and New York, 1938.

————. "Persona," *ArchRW*, XXVII (1929), 35–52.

————. *Terra Mater: Untersuchungen zur altitalischen Religionsgeschichte.* Giessen, 1931.

Anthologia Lyrica Graeca. Edited by Ernst Diehl. (Bibliotheca Scriptorum Graecorum et Romanorum Teubneriana.) Leipzig, 1925. 2 vols. [3rd edn., Leipzig, 1949–52. 3 vols.]

Artis auriferae quam chemiam vocant. . . . Basileae [Basel], [1593]. 2 vols. (Vol. I: i, "Allegoriae super librum Turbae" [pp. 139–45].) Another edition of the *Artis auriferae,* also quoted in this volume, appeared in 1572 at Basel; contains the "Tractatus aureus," pp. 641ff.

ASTERIUS OF AMASIA, SAINT. *Homilies,* X. In MIGNE, *P. G.,* vol. 40, col. 324.

ATHENAGORAS. "Legatio pro Christianis." MIGNE, *P. G.,* vol. 6.

AVALON, ARTHUR, pseud. (Sir John Woodroffe) (ed. and trans.) *The Serpent Power (Shat-chakra-nirupana and Paduka-panchaka).*

(Tantrik Texts.) London, 1919.

———— (ed.). *Shrī-chakra-sambhara Tantra.* (Tantrik Texts, 7.) London and Calcutta, 1919.

BACON, JOSEPHINE DASKAM. *In the Border Country.* New York, 1919.

BASTIAN, ADOLF. *Der Mensch in der Geschichte.* Leipzig, 1860. 3 vols.

BAYNES, H. G. *Mythology of the Soul.* London, 1940.

BEKKER, IMMANUEL. *Anecdota Graeca.* Berlin, 1814–21. 3 vols.

BENOÎT, PIERRE. *Atlantida.* Translated by Mary C. Tongue and Mary Ross. New York, 1920.

BERTHELOT, MARCELLIN. *Collection des anciens alchimistes grecs.* Paris, 1887–88. 3 vols.

BOLL, FRANZ. *Aus der Offenbarung Johannis: Hellenistische Studien zum Weltbild der Apokalypse.* Leipzig, 1914.

BORSARI, L. "Del Tempio di Giove Anxure, scoperto sulla vetta di Monte S. Angelo, presso la città," *Notizie degli scavi antichità* (Rome), 1894, pp. 96–111.

BÜDINGER, MAX. *Die römischen Spiele und der Patriciat: eine historische Untersuchung.* (Akademie der Wissenschaften in Wien, Phil.-hist. Classe. Sitzungsberichte, CXXIII: 3, 1890.) Vienna, 1891.

CARUS, CARL GUSTAV. *Psyche.* Pförzheim, 1846.

CELLINI, BENVENUTO. *Autobiography.* Translated by John Addington Symonds. London, 1949.

CLEMEN, CARL. *Die Religion der Etrusker.* Bonn, 1936.

COLLIGNON, LÉON MAXIME. *Histoire de la sculpture grecque.* Paris 1892–97. 2 vols.

COLONNA, FRANCESCO. *Hypnerotomachia Poliphili.* Venice, 1499.

COMPARETTI, DOMENICO. *Der Kalevala.* Halle, 1892.

CREUZER, FRIEDRICH. *Symbolik und Mythologie der alten Völker, besonders der Griechen.* 2nd edn., Leipzig and Darmstadt, 1819–23. 4 vols.

DEUBNER, LUDWIG. *Attische Feste.* Berlin, 1932.

DIELS, HERMANN. *Das Labyrinth.* (Festgabe Harnack.) Tübingen, 1921.

————. *Sibyllinische Blätter,* Berlin, 1890.

DÖLGER, FRANZ JOSEF. ΙΧΘΥΣ. Münster, 1922–40. 5 vols. (Vol. I, 2nd edn., 1928.)

DORN, GERHARD (Gerardus Dorneus). See *Theatrum chemicum.*

DUCHESNE, LOUIS. *Christian Worship: Its Origin and Evolution.* Translated by M. L. McClure. 5th edn., London, 1919.

[ECKHART, MEISTER.] *Meister Eckhart.* By Franz Pfeiffer. Translated by C. de B. Evans. London, 1924–52. 2 vols.

ECKHEL, JOSEPH. *Doctrina Nummorum Veterum,* II. Vindobonae [Vienna], 1792–1839. 8 vols.

EGGER, R. "Genius Cucullatus," *Wiener prähistorische Zeitschrift* (Vienna), IX (1932), 311–32.

EILMANN, RICHARD. *Labyrinthos.* (Diss. Halle.) Athens, 1931.

EITREM, SAMSON. "Eleusinia—les Mystères et l'agriculture," *Symbolae Osloenses* (Oslo. Societas graeco-latina; Klassisk Forening), XX (1940), 133–51.

Ephemeris Archaeologica (Athens), 1901, pl. I (votive tablet of Niinnion).

ERMAN, ADOLF. *Die Religion der Ägypter.* Berlin, 1934.

ERSKINE, JOHN. *The Private Life of Helen of Troy.* New York, 1925; London, 1926.

FARNELL, L. R. *The Cults of the Greek States.* Oxford, 1896–1909. 5 vols.

FENDT, LEONHARD. *Gnostische Mysterien.* Munich, 1922.

FLOURNOY, THÉODORE. *From India to the Planet Mars.* Translated by D. R. Vermilye. New York and London, 1900.

———. "Nouvelles Observations sur un cas de somnambulisme avec glossolalie," *Archives de psychologie* (Neuchâtel), I (1901): 2.

FORDHAM, MICHAEL. *The Life of Childhood.* London, 1944.

FOUCART, PAUL FRANÇOIS. *Les Mystères d'Eleusis.* Paris, 1914.

FREUD, SIGMUND. *The Interpretation of Dreams.* Translated by James Strachey et al. In: Standard Edition of the Complete Psychological Works, 4–5. London, 1953. 2 vols.

FROBENIUS, LEO. *Der Kopf als Schicksal.* Munich, 1924.

———. *Monumenta Africana der Geist eines Erdteils.* Weimar, 1939.

———. *Das Zeitalter des Sonnengottes.* Berlin, 1904. (Only Vol. I published.)

FURTWÄNGLER, ADOLF. "Die Chariten der Akropolis," *Athenische Mitteilungen (Mitteilungen des . . . Deutschen archäologischen Instituts,* Athenische Abteilung; Athens), III (1878), 182–202.

GELDNER, K. F. *Vedismus und Brahmanismus.* (Religionsgeschichtliches Lesebuch, 9. Edited by Alfred Bertholet.) Tübingen, 1928.

GELZER, H. "Zur armenischen Götterlehre," *Berichte über die*

Verhandlungen der Sächsischen Gesellschaft der Wissenschaften (Leipzig), XLVIII (1896), 99–148.

GOETHE, JOHANN WOLFGANG VON. *Farbenlehre*, in *Werke*, q.v., XVI, 233, § 916.

———. *Faust*, Part II, in *Werke*, q.v., V, 289–526.

———. *Werke*. (Gedenkausgabe.) Edited by Ernst Beutler. Zurich, 1948–54. 24 vols.

GOETZ, BRUNO. *Das Reich ohne Raum*. Potsdam, 1919; 2nd enl. edn., Constance, 1925.

GREY, Sir GEORGE. *Polynesian Mythology: An Ancient Traditional History of the New Zealand Race, as Furnished by Their Priests and Chiefs*. London, 1855. (Republ. by Whitcombe and Tombs Ltd., London, 1929.)

HAGGARD, H. RIDER. *Ayesha: the Return of She*. London, 1905.

———. *She*. London, 1887.

HAMPE, ROLAND. *Frühe griechische Sagenbilder in Böotien*. (Deutsches Archäologisches Institut.) Athens, 1936.

HARRISON, JANE ELLEN. *Prolegomena to the Study of Greek Religion*. Cambridge (Eng.), 1922.

———. *Themis: A Study of the Social Origins of Greek Religion*. Cambridge (Eng.), 1927. [2nd edn., revised and with supplementary notes, Cambridge, 1937.]

HEICHELHEIM, FRITZ MORITZ. "Genii Cucullati," *Archaeologia Aeliana* (Newcastle-on-Tyne), ser. 4, XII (1935), 187–94.

HIPPOLYTUS. *Elenchos* (Refutatio omnium haeresium). In: *Hippolytus' Werke*. Edited by Paul Wendland. (Griechische christliche Schriftsteller.) Vol. III. Leipzig, 1916. For translation, see: *Philosophumena: or, The Refutation of all Heresies*. Translated by Francis Legge. London and New York, 1921. 2 vols.

[HOHENZOLLERN], Kaiser WILHELM II. *Erinnerungen an Korfu*. Berlin, 1924.

HUIZINGA, JOHAN. *Homo Ludens: A Study of the Play-Element in Culture*. London, 1949; New York, 1950.

Hypnerotomachia Poliphili. See COLONNA.

INGRAM, JOHN H. *The Haunted Homes and Family Traditions of Great Britain*. London, 1890.

Ipolyi Arnold Népmesegyüjteménye. Edited by L. Kálmány. Budapest, 1914.

JAMES, M. R. (trans.) *The Apocryphal New Testament*. Oxford, 1924.

JENSEN, ADOLF ELLEGARD. *Die drei Ströme*. Leipzig, 1948.

———. "Eine ost-indonesische Mythe als Ausdruck einer Weltan-schauung," *Paideuma: Mitteilungen zur Kulturkunde* (Frankfurt a. M.), I (1938–40), 199–216.

———. *Das religiöse Weltbild einer frühen Kultur*. (Studien zur Kulturkunde, IX.) Stuttgart, 1948.

———. and H. NIGGEMEYER (comps. and eds.). *Hainuwele: Volks-erzählungen von der Molukken-Insel Ceram*. (Ergebnisse der Frobenius-Expedition 1937–38 in die Molukken und nach Hol-ländisch Neu-Guinea, I.) Frankfurt a. M., 1939.

JESSEN, O. "Hermaphroditos." In: PAULY-WISSOWA, q.v., VIII, cols. 714–21.

JOSSELIN DE JONG, J. P. B. "De Oorsprong van den goddelijken bedrieger," *Mededeelingen der Koninklijke Akademie van Wet-enschappen* [*te Amsterdam*], Afdeeling Letterkunde, ser. B, XLVIII (1929), No. 1, pp. 1–30.

Journal of Hellenic Studies (London), 1885, pl. LIX (A Pinax from Camirus, in the British Museum. Subject: a Gorgon). (This plate is one of a group bound separately from the text.)

JUNG, CARL GUSTAV. "The Aims of Psychotherapy." In: *The Prac-tice of Psychotherapy*. (CWJ, 16.) 1954.

———. *Aion: Researches into the Phenomenology of the Self*. (CWJ, 9, II.) 1959; 2nd edn., 1966.

———. *The Archetypes and the Collective Unconscious*. (CWJ, 9, I.) 1959; 2nd edn., 1968.

———. Commentary on "The Secret of the Golden Flower." In: *Alchemical Studies* (CWJ, 13). (See also WILHELM and JUNG, *The Secret of the Golden Flower*, q.v.)

———. "The Concept of the Collective Unconscious." In: *The Archetypes and the Collective Unconscious*, q.v.

———. "Concerning the Archetypes, with Special Reference to the Anima Concept." In: ibid.

———. "Conscious, Unconscious, and Individuation." In: ibid.

———. "On the Psychology of the Trickster-Figure." In: *The Archetypes and the Collective Unconscious*, q.v.

———. *Psychological Types*. (CWJ, 6; in prep.) (Alternate source: translation by H. G. Baynes, London and New York, 1923.)

———. *Psychology and Alchemy*. (CWJ, 12.) 1953; 2nd edn., 1968.

———. "Psychology and Religion" (The Terry Lectures). In: *Psychology and Religion: West and East*, q.v.

————. *Psychology and Religion: West and East.* (CWJ, 11.) 1958; 2nd edn., 1969.

————. *Psychology of the Unconscious.* Translated by Beatrice M. Hinkle. New York, 1916; London, 1917. (Superseded by *Symbols of Transformation,* q.v.)

————. "The Relations between the Ego and the Unconscious." In: *Two Essays on Analytical Psychology,* q.v.

————. *The Structure and Dynamics of the Psyche.* (CWJ, 8.) 1960; 2nd edn., 1969.

————. "The Structure of the Psyche." In: *The Structure and Dynamics of the Psyche,* q.v.

————. "A Study in the Process of Individuation." In: *The Archetypes and the Collective Unconscious,* q.v.

————. *Symbols of Transformation.* (CWJ, 5.) 1956; 2nd edn., 1967.

————. "The Transcendent Function." In: *The Structure and Dynamics of the Psyche,* q.v.

————. *Two Essays on Analytical Psychology.* (CWJ, 7.) 1953; 2nd edn., 1966.

Kalevala: das National-Epos der Finnen. Translation [into German] by Anton Schiefner. Edited by Martin Buber. Berlin, 1921. For English translation, see: *Kalevala: the Land of Heroes.* Translated from the original Finnish by W. F. Kirby. (Everyman's Library.) London and New York, 1907.

KERÉNYI, C. [*or* KARL]. "Altitalische Götterverbindungen," *Studi e materiali di storia delle religioni* (Rome), IX (1933), 17–28.

————. "ΑΝΟΔΟΣ-Darstellung in Brindisi, mit einem Zodiakus von II Zeichen," *ArchRW,* XXX (1933), 271–307.

————. *Die antike Religion: eine Grundlegung.* Amsterdam, 1942 [3rd edn., Düsseldorf, 1952]. (Cf. *The Religion of the Greeks and Romans* and *La Religione Antica,* qq. v.)

————. *Apollon: Studien über antike Religion und Humanität.* 2nd edn., Amsterdam and Leipzig, 1941; [3rd edn., Düsseldorf, 1953].

————. *Asklepios: Archetypal Image of the Physician's Existence.* Translated from the German by Ralph Manheim. (BS LXV:3.) New York, 1959.

————. *Dionysos und das Tragische in der "Antigone."* (Frankfurter Studien zur Religion und Kultur der Antike, XIII.) Frankfurt a. M., 1935. (Translation in preparation.)

———. "Die Geburt der Helena: eine mythologische Studie dis manibus Leonis Frobenii." *Mnemosyne: Bibliotheca classica batava* (Lugduni [Leyden]), N.S. 3, III (1939), 161–79.

———. *Die Geburt der Helena.* (AV, N.S. III.) Zurich, 1945. [N.S. IV, Zurich, 1946.]

———. *The Gods of the Greeks.* Translated by Norman Cameron. London and New York, 1951. (Penguin edn., 1958.)

———. *Hermes der Seelenführer: das Mythologem vom männlichen Lebensursprung.* (AV, N.S. I.) Zurich, 1944.

———. *Labyrinth-Studien: Labyrinthos als Linienreflex einer mythologischen Idee.* (AV, XV.) Amsterdam, 1941. [2nd edn. (AV, N.S. X.), Zurich, 1950.]

———. "Man and Mask." In: *Spiritual Disciplines.* (Papers from the Eranos Yearbooks, 4, translated by Ralph Manheim.) (BS, XXX:4.) New York, 1960.

———. *Niobe: Neue Studien über antike Religion und Humanität.* Zurich, 1949.

———. "Paideuma," *Paideuma: Mitteilungen zur Kulturkunde* (Frankfurt a. M.), I (1938–40), 157–58.

———. "Das persische Millennium im 'Mahābhārata,' bei der Sibylle und Vergil," *Klio: Beiträge zur alten Geschichte* (Leipzig), XXIX (1936), 1–35.

———. *Pythagoras und Orpheus: Präludien zu einer zukünftigen Geschichte der Orphik und des Pythagoreismus.* (AV, II.) 2nd edn., Amsterdam, 1940. [3rd edn. (AV, N.S. IX.), Zurich, 1950.]

———. *The Religion of the Greeks and Romans.* Translated by Christopher Holme. London and New York, 1962. (A revision of *Die antike Religion* and *La Religione antica,* qq. v.)

———. *La Religione antica.* Bologna, 1940. (Tr. from *Die antike Religion,* q.v.; cf. *The Religion of the Greeks and Romans.*)

———. "Satire und Satura: Zum religionsgeschichtlichen Hintergrund einer literarischen Gattung," *Studi e materiali di storia delle religioni* (Rome), IX (1933), 129–56.

———. "Telesphoros: Zum Verständnis etruskischer, griechischer, und keltisch-germanischer Dämongestalten." *Egyetemes Philologiai Közlöny* (Budapest), LVII (1933), 156ff.

———. "Was ist Mythologie?" *Europäische Revue* (Berlin), XV:1 (1939), 557–72.

———. "Zum Verständnis von Vergilius Aeneis B. VI: Randbemerkungen zu Nordens Kommentar," *Hermes,* LXVI (1931), 413–41.

KERN, O. *Die griechischen Mysterien der klassischen Zeit.* Berlin, 1927.

———. "Mysterien." In: PAULY-WISSOWA, q.v., XVI, cols. 1209ff.

———. See also *Orphicorum fragmenta.*

KIRCHER, ATHANASIUS. *Mundus subterraneus.* Amsterdam, 1678.

KOCH, CARL. *Der römische Juppiter.* (Frankfurter Studien zur Religion und Kultur der Antike, XIV.) Frankfurt a. M. 1937.

KOEPGEN, GEORG. *Die Gnosis des Christentums.* Salzburg, 1939.

KÖRTE, ALFRED. "Der Demeter-Hymnos des Philkos," *Hermes,* LXVI (1931), 442–54.

KÖVENDI, D. In: *Sziget.* Edited by Károly Kerényi. (Kétnyelyü klasszikusok.) Budapest, 1939. 3 vols.

KRETSCHMER, PAUL. "Dyaus, Ζεύς, Diespiter und die Abstrakta im Indogermanischen," *Glotta* (Göttingen), XIII (1924), 101–14.

———. "Zur Geschichte der griechischen Dialekte: 1. Ionier und Achäer, 2. Die Apokope in den griechischen Dialekten," ibid., I (1909), 9–59.

KROHN, KAARLE. *Kalevalastudien,* VI: *Kullervo.* (Folklore Fellows. FF Communications, 76.) Helsinki, 1928.

KURUNIOTIS, K. "Das eleusinische Heiligtum von den Anfängen bis zur vorperikleischen Zeit," *ArchRW* XXXII (1935), 52–78.

LAIDLAW, WILLIAM ALLISON. *A History of Delos.* Oxford, 1933.

Lalita-Vistara, or, *Memoirs of the Early Life of Sākya Siñha.* Translated from the original Sanskrit by Rājendralāla Mitra. (Bibliotheca Indica. Sanskrit series, fasc. 1–3.) Calcutta, 1881–96.

LAWRENCE, D. H. "Fidelity." In: *Pansies.* [London?, 1929.]

———. "Purple Anemones." In: *The Collected Poems of D. H. Lawrence.* London, 1928. 2 vols. (Vol. II, pp. 163–65.)

LEISEGANG, HANS. *Die Gnosis.* Leipzig, 1924.

LENORMANT, F. "Ceres, Δημήτηρ." In: CHARLES DAREMBERG and EDMOND SAGLIO. *Dictionnaire des antiquités grecques et romaines.* Paris, 1877–1919. 5 vols. in 10. (Vol. I, pp. 1021–78.)

LOBECK, CHRISTIAN AUGUST. *Aglaophamus; sive, de theologiae mysticae Graecorum causis libri tres . . . idemque Poetarum Orphicorum dispersas reliquias collegit.* Regiomontii Prussorum (Königsberg = Kaliningrad), 1829. 2 vols.

LUMHOLTZ, CARL. *Unknown Mexico: A Record of Five Years' Exploration among the Tribes of the Western Sierra Madre in the 'tierra caliente' of Tepic and Jalisco and among the Tarascos of Michoacan.* New York, 1903.

MAEDER, A. "Essai d'interprétation de quelques rêves," *Archives de psychologie* (Geneva), VI (1907), 354–75.

―――. "Die Symbolik in den Legenden, Marchen, Gebrauchen, und Traumen," *Psychologisch-neurologische Wochenschrift* (Halle), X (1908–9), 45–55.

Mahabharata of Krishna-dwaipayana Vyasa, The. Translated into English prose from the original Sanskrit text by Pratap Chandra Roy. Edited by Hiralal Haldar. 2nd edn. Calcutta, 1955. 6 vols. (Vol. III, pp. 382–505.)

MALINOWSKI, BRONISLAW. *Myth in Primitive Psychology.* New York (The New Science Series, I) and London (Psyche Miniatures, General Series, 6), 1926.

MALTEN, L. "Altorphische Demetersage," *ArchRW*, XII (1909), 417–46.

MANGETUS, JOANNES JACOBUS (ed.). *Bibliotheca Chemica Curiosa, seu Rerum ad alchemiam pertinentium thesaurus instructissmus. . . .* Coloniae Allobrogum [Geneva], 1702. 2 vols. (Vol: I: i, Hermes Trismegistus: "Tractatus aureus de lapidis physici secreto" [pp. 400–45]; ii, Morienus: "Liber de compositione alchemiae" [pp. 509–19].)

MANN, THOMAS. "Freud and the Future." In: *Essays of Three Decades.* Translated from the German by H. T. Lowe-Porter. New York, 1947. (Original: *Freud und die Zukunft.* Vienna, 1936.)

MECHTHILD, SAINT. *The Revelations of Mechthild of Magdeburg (1210–1297), or The Flowing Light of the Godhead.* Translated by Lucy Menzies. London, 1953.

MEULI, KARL. "Scythia," *Hermes,* LXX (1935), 121–76.

MIGNE, JACQUES PAUL (ed.). *Patrologiae cursus completus.* Greek series, Paris, 1857–66. 166 vols. (Referred to in the text as "MIGNE, *P. G.*")

MOOR, EDWARD. *The Hindu Pantheon.* London, 1810.

MÜLLER, WERNER. *Kreis und Kreuz.* Berlin, 1938.

MUNKÁCSI, BERNÁT. *Vogul népköltési gyüjtemény.* Budapest, 1892–1952. 2 vols. in 5. (especialy Vol. II, pts. 1, 2.)

MURR, I. *Die Pflanzenwelt in der griechischen Mythologie.* Innsbruck, 1890.

MYLIUS, JOHANN DANIEL. *Philosophia reformata.* Frankfurt a. M., 1622.

NELKEN, JAN. "Analytische Beobachtungen über Phantasien eines

Schizophrenen," *Jahrbuch für psychoanalytische und psychopathologische Forschungen* (Leipzig), IV (1912), 504ff.

NEUMANN, ERICH. *The Great Mother.* Translated by Ralph Manheim. New York (BS XLVII) and London, 1955.

NILSSON, MARTIN P. "Die eleusinischen Gottheiten," *Archrw,* XXXII (1935), 79–141.

———. *Griechische Feste von religiöser Bedeutung mit Ausschluss der Attischen.* Leipzig, 1906.

———. *The Minoan-Mycenaean Religion and its Survival in Greek Religion.* (Skrifter utgivna av Kungl. Humanistiska vetenskapssamfundet i Lund, IX.) Lund, 1927; 2nd rev. edn., Lund, 1950.

OHASAMA, SCHÛEI (trans.). *Zen: der lebendige Buddhismus in Japan.* Edited by August Faust. Gotha, 1925.

OKEN, LORENZ. "Entstehung des ersten Menschen," *Isis [von Oken]* (Jena), 1819, cols. 1117–23.

OLDENBERG, HERMANN (trans.). *Reden des Buddha: Lehre, Verse, Erzählungen.* Munich, 1922.

ORIGEN. *In Jeremiam homiliae.* In MIGNE, *P. G.,* vol. 13, cols. 255–544.

Orphicorum fragmenta. Edited by Otto Kern. Berlin, 1922.

OTTO, WALTER F. *Dionysos: Mythos und Kultus.* (Frankfurter Studien zur Religion und Kultur der Antike, IV.) 2nd edn., Frankfurt a. M., 1933.

———. *Der europäische Geist und die Weisheit des Ostens: Gedanken über das Erbe Homers.* Frankfurt a. M., 1931.

———. *The Homeric Gods: the Spiritual Significance of Greek Religion.* Translated by Moses Hadas. New York, 1954; London, 1955.

———. *Die Manen, oder Von den Urformen des Totenglaubens.* Berlin, 1923.

———. "The Meaning of the Eleusinian Mysteries." In: *The Mysteries.* (Papers from the Eranos Yearbooks, 2.) Translated by Ralph Manheim. (BS XXX 2.) New York, 1955.

PALLAT, LUDWIG. *De fabula Ariadnea.* Berlin, 1891.

PAULY, AUGUST, and GEORG WISSOWA (eds.). *Real-Encyclopädie der classischen Altertumswissenschaft.* Stuttgart, 1898ff.

PERSSON, AXEL W. "Der Ursprung der eleusinischen Mysterien," *ArchRW,* XXI (1922), 287–309.

PHILALETHES, EIRENAEUS. *Ripley Reviv'd: or, An Exposition upon Sir George Ripley's Hermetico-Poetical Works.* London, 1678.

PHILIPPSON, PAULA. *Griechische Gottheiten in ihren Landschaften.* (*Symbolae Osloenses,* suppl., fasc. IX.) Oslo, 1939.

———. *Thessalische Mythologie.* Zurich, 1944.

PICARD, CHARLES. "Die Grosse Mutter von Kreta bis Eleusis," *Eranos Jahrbuch 1938* (Zurich, 1939), 91–119.

PINDAR. *Pindari Carmina cum fragmentis.* Edited by C. M. Bowra. Oxford, 1935. 2nd edn., Oxford, 1947.

PRELLER, LUDWIG. *Griechische Mythologie.* Edited by Carl Robert. 4th edn., Berlin, 1887–1926. 2 vols. in 6 parts.

PREUSS, KONRAD THEODOR. *Der religiöse Gehalt der Mythen.* Tübingen, 1933.

PRINGSHEIM, HEINZ GERHARD. *Archäologische Beiträge zur Geschichte des eleusinischen Kulte.* Munich, 1905.

QUAGLIATI, Q. "Rilievi votivi arcaici in terracotta di Lokroi Epizephyroi," *Ausonia* (Rome), III (1908), 136–234.

RADLOFF, W. *Proben der Volksliteratur der türkischen Stämme Süd-sibiriens.* St. Petersburg, 1866–1907. 10 vols. in 13.

RADERMACHER, LUDWIG. *Der homerische Hermeshymnus* (Akademie der Wissenschaften in Wien, Phil.-hist. Classe. Sitzungsberichte, CCXIII: 1.) Vienna and Leipzig, 1931.

RANK, OTTO. *The Myth of the Birth of the Hero.* Translated by F. Robbins and Smith Ely Jelliffe. New York, 1952.

REITZENSTEIN, RICHARD, and H. H. SCHÄDER. *Studien zum antiken Synkretismus aus Iran und Griechenland.* (Studien der [Kulturwissenschaftliche] Bibliothek Warburg, [Hamburg].) Leipzig and Berlin, 1926.

Rig-Veda. See: *Hindu Scriptures.* Edited by Nicol MacNicol. (Everyman's Library.) London and New York, 1938.

RIKLIN, F. "Über Gefängnispsychosen," *Psychologisch-neurologische Wochenschrift* (Halle), IX (1907), 269–72.

———. *Wishfulfilment and Symbolism in Fairy Tales.* Translated by William A. White. (Nervous and Mental Disease Monograph Series, 21.) New York, 1915.

RIZZO, G. E. "Il Sarcofago di Torre Nova," *Römische Mitteilungen* (*Mitteilungen des . . . Deutschen archäologischen Instituts,* Römische Abteilung; Rome), XXV (1910), 89–167.

ROBERT, CARL. *Die griechische Heldensage.* Berlin, 1920–26. 3 parts. (In: LUDWIG PRELLER. *Griechische Mythologie,* q.v., II.)

ROUSSEL, PIERRE. *Les Cultes égyptiens à Delos du IIIe au Ier siècle avant J.-C.* Paris, 1916.

SALOMON, RICHARD. *Opicinus de Canistris*. (Studies of the Warburg Institute, I a and b.) London, 1936. 2 parts.

SCHELLING, FRIEDRICH WILHELM JOSEPH VON. *Philosophie der Mythologie* (2 vols.). In: *Sämmtliche Werke*. Stuttgart and Augsburg, 1856–61. 14 vols. (Abt. II, bd. 2, 1857; sometimes described as Vols. XI, XII.)

SCHILLER, FRIEDRICH. *Die Piccolomini*. In: *Schillers Werke*. Edited by Paul Brandt. Leipzig, [1923]. 5 vols. (Vol. III, pp. 59–174.)

SCHNEIDER, OTTO (ed.) *Callimachea*. Leipzig, 1870–73. 2 vols.

SCHREBER, DANIEL PAUL. *Memoirs of My Nervous Illness*. Translated by Ida Macalpine and Richard A. Hunter. London, 1955.

Shrī-chakra-sambhara Tantra. See AVALON.

SLOANE, WILLIAM M. *To Walk the Night*. New York, 1937.

SPAMER, ADOLF (ed.). *Texte aus der deutschen Mystik des 14. und 15. Jahrhunderts*. Jena, 1912.

STASOV, V. "Proischozdenie russkich bylin," *Věstnik Evropy* (St. Petersburg), V (1868), 702–34.

SZABÓ, Á. "Roma Quadrata," *Rheinisches Museum für Philologie* (Frankfurt a. M.), LXXXVII (1938), 160–69.

Theatrum Chemicum, praecipuos selectorum auctorum tractatus . . . continens. Ursellis [Ursel] and Argentorati [Strasbourg], 1602–61. 6 vols. (Vol. I: i, Dorn: "Speculativae philosophiae, gradus septem vel decem continens" [pp. 255–310].)

Tibetan Book of the Dead, or, The After-Death Experiences on the 'Bardo' Plane. Edited by W. Y. Evans-Wentz, with a Psychological Commentary by C. G. Jung. Oxford, 1927; 3rd edn., enl., London, New York and Toronto, 1957.

TOLNAY, C. DE. "The Music of the Universe: Notes on a Painting by Bicci di Lorenzo," *Journal of the Walters Art Gallery* (Baltimore, Md.), VI (1943), 83–104.

USENER, HERMANN. *Kleine Schriften*. Leipzig, 1912–13. 4 vols.

———. *Die Sintflutsagen*. Bonn, 1899.

———. *Vorträge und Aufsätze*. Leipzig, 1914.

———. *Das Weihnachtsfest*. 2nd edn., Bonn, 1911.

WARBURG, ABY MORITZ. *Die Erneuerung der heidnischen Antike: Kulturwissenschaftliche Beiträge zur Geschichte der europäischen Renaissance*. Leipzig, 1932. 2 vols. in 4.

WEEGE, FRITZ. *Der Tanz in der Antike*. Halle, 1926.

WEISWEILER, JOSEF. "Seele und See: ein etymologische Versuch,"

Indogermanische Forschungen: Zeitschrift für indogermanische Sprach- und Altertumskunde (Strasbourg), LVII (1939), 25–55.

WELCKER, FRIEDRICH GOTTLIEB. *Griechische Götterlehre.* Göttingen, 1857–62. 3 vols.

WILAMOWITZ-MOELLENDORF, ULRICH VON. *Der Glaube der Hellenen.* Berlin, 1931–32. 2 vols.

————. *Hellenistische Dichtung in der Zeit des Kallimachos.* Berlin, 1924. 2 vols.

WILHELM, RICHARD, and JUNG, CARL GUSTAV. *The Secret of the Golden Flower.* Translated by Cary F. Baynes. London and New York, 1931; 2nd edn., 1962.

WILHELM II, Kaiser. See HOHENZOLLERN.

WINTHUIS, JOSEF. *Einführung in die Vorstellungswelt primitiver Völker.* Stuttgart, 1931.

————. *Mythos und Kult der Steinzeit: Versuch einer Lösung uralter Mythos-Rätsel und Kultgeheimnisse.* Stuttgart, 1935.

————. *Die Wahrheit über das Zweigeschlechterwesen durch die Gegner bestätigt.* Leipzig, 1930.

————. *Das Zweigeschlechterwesen bei den Zentralaustraliern und andern Volkern.* Leipzig, 1928.

WOLLNER, WILHELM ANTON. *Untersuchungen über die Volksepik der Grossrussen.* Leipzig, 1879.

WUNDT, WILHELM. *Völkpsychologie.* Leipzig, 1911–20. 10 vols.

ZIMMER, HEINRICH. *Kunstform und Yoga im indischen Kultbild.* Berlin, 1926.

————. *Maya: der indische Mythos.* Stuttgart, 1936.

INDEX

active imagination, 74n, 164, 167

Aeschylus, 107, 143, 180

aetiological myth, 4–6

Agrai, 139f, 145, 152

alchemy, 90, 95

Alföldi, A., 138n

allegory, 45, 73

Altheim, Franz, 10, 11, 63n, 124n, 127n, 134n, 148n

Anadyomene, 102f, 151

Anaximander, 46, 48

anima/animus, 94, 96, 157, 171, 173ff

Antigone, 129

Anytos, 180

Apelles, 151

Aphrodite, 54ff, 102f, 128, 134, 140, 150

Apollo, 25f, 46ff, 51–2, 57, 69, 104, 105, 135

Arcadia, 121f, 143, 179

archetypes, 72ff, 79ff; purpose of, 80

ἀρχή, ἀρχαί, 7–11, 17

Areion, 123, 147

Ariadne, 134

Arion, 50

Artemis, 52, 105, 107f, 111, 128, 130, 136, 143, 145, 150, 169, 180

Asklepios, 105

Athenaeus, 50n, 149n, 151n

Athene, 106ff, 128, 179

Avalokiteshvara, 31

Bacon, Josephine D., 159n

Bastian, Adolf, 70

Baubo, 130, 159, 160

bear-goddess, 169f

bees, 159n

Benoît, Pierre, 174

biography, and mythology, 25–7, 45

birth, 144ff; miraculous, 85

Boibeis, Lake, 143

Botticelli, 102f

Brimo/Brimos, 142ff, 147, 148

Buddha/Buddhism, 12–13, 15, 31, 151ff, 155

Callimachus, 69n, 107, 110n, 143

Carus, C. G., 71

Cassian, 95

Cellini, Benvenuto, 158n

Ceram, 130f

Cicero, 28n, 117n, 143n, 144

Circe, 128

city founding, 10ff, 17–18

Clement, 2nd Epistle of, 95

Clement of Alexandria, 95, 118n, 128n, 141, 142n, 143n

Cnidos, 113

Colonna, F., 160

coniunctio, 94f, 165

Cora Indians, 116

Corfu, 128

Crete, 60ff

Creuzer, F., 48n

Cybele, 136, 139

Cypria, 122

dance, 133f, 141, 149

Dea Artio, 169

Delos, 28, 49, 134, 181

Delphi, 51, 56

Demeter, 19, 107ff, 113ff, 136ff, 157ff, 177, 178ff

Demophoön, 115, 116

Despoina, 180

Deubner, L., 111n, 139n, 140n

Diana, 112, 169

Diels, H., 120n, 134n, 139n

Dionysius of Halicarnassus, 11

Dionysus, 25f, 27, 39, 66ff, 104, 105, 127, 139, 148, 182

dog, 130

Dölger, F. J., 46n, 65n, 151n

dolphin, 50, 55, 119, 166

Dorn, Gerard, 167f